Kenneth Light

THE SAVING
OF AN EMPIRE:

The Journey of Portugal's
Court and Capital
to Brazil, 1808

Published by

MELROSE
BOOKS

An Imprint of Melrose Press Limited
St Thomas Place, Ely
Cambridgeshire
CB7 4GG, UK
www.melrosebooks.com

FIRST EDITION

Copyright © Kenneth Light 2009

The Author asserts his moral right to
be identified as the author of this work

Cover designed by Geoff Hunt RSMA

ISBN 978 1 906561 79 6

Printed and bound in Great Britain by:
CPI Antony Rowe. Chippenham, Wiltshire

FSC
Mixed Sources
Product group from well-managed
forests and other controlled sources

Cert no. SGS-COC-2953
www.fsc.org
© 1996 Forest Stewardship Council

Index

Preface

The importance of the voyage to Brazil undertaken, in 1807, by the Portuguese royal family, most of the Court and a great many citizens – in all, some 12,000 men, women and children – derives from the consequences this action had on history.

The man directly responsible for the decision that led to this audacious journey was the Prince Regent D. João.[1] Two incidents had profoundly altered his life. The first, in 1788, was the death of his elder brother D. José[2] who until then was being groomed to one day become king. The second occurred in 1792 when, at the age of 25, he took over the administration of his country, replacing his mother, D. Maria I,[3] who had become insane. Both happenings could never have been foreseen and consequently D. João was ill-prepared for these sad and dramatic episodes.

As often happens, the passing of time helps to illuminate and explain. Early critics, perhaps because they were too close to events, interpreted them in a negative way: they could not see the greatness and the courage of the decision taken by D. João, as proved by subsequent events.

Oliveira Martins wrote:

> "Everything was silent shame, passive ineptness, confessed weakness. The Prince had decided that the embarkation should take place at night, conscious of his shameful flight."[4]

Lieutenant Captain Lucas Boiteaux was even more emphatic:

> "On seeing the enemy forces devastating their native country, the legendary Lusitanian patriotism did not explode, as in the heroic times of Nun' Alves; but, paralysed by a lethal and criminal indifference, degenerated into shameful terror. The Royal Family, sharing in this weakness, was the first to set the example, leaving for Brazil on the 27th of November in the greatest desperation and confusion, taking in its wake an army of cowards, vain noblemen and parasites of every cast; degenerate offspring of a heroic past…"[5]

In the same line of aggressive criticism, Tobias Monteiro concluded:

"Preferring to abandon Europe, D. João acted knowing well his limitations. A strong king would have found out in time the weaknesses of Junot's forces and organised the resistance. If this failed, then that would have been the moment to depart for Brazil or even one of the nearer Atlantic isles, with all the Royal Family and, embracing openly the long-standing alliance with Britain, seek refuge on board his fleet, united to that of his ally and, await the day when he could return to his country and reconquer the land of his ancestors – as his subjects would be forced to do, but without his leadership. Recognising his ineptitude for heroics, he preferred the pacific solution of leading the migration, seeking in the contagious lethargy of the tropics the tranquility or idleness for which he had been born."[6]

Others believed that D. João's action, discussed by previous monarchs as an alternative strategy since the discovery of Brazil, was in fact a brilliant move. Oliveira Lima wrote:

"Withdrawing to America the Prince Regent without, in the end, losing more than he had in Europe, escaped from all the humiliations suffered by his Castilian relations deposed by force; moreover, with every probability of increasing his overseas territory at the cost of his French and Spanish enemies, he maintained the plenitude of his rights, ambitions and hopes. In reality, it was a live and constant threat to the Napoleonic system; advantage would be taken of the slightest carelessness or internal strife. For this reason, it is much fairer to consider the transfer of the court to Rio de Janeiro as an intelligent and successful political move rather than as a cowardly desertion."[7]

Afonso Zuquete also approved D. João's strategy.

" ...The move to Brazil that has been argued with total incompetence was in fact a brilliant decision that saved the monarchy and guaranteed the independence of Portugal ..."[8]

Of the four countries involved – Portugal, Brazil, Britain and France – only the latter was to regret the event.

Unlike other countries invaded by Bonaparte, the essence of the Portuguese nation and her royal family and Court survived unscathed, maintained its kingdom and even prospered in her rich colony. The presence of the monarchy in Brazil accelerated development of the country with the opening of the ports in 1808 and, with the creation of the United Kingdom of Portugal and Brazil in 1815, independence would become inevitable.

The longstanding amicable relationship with Britain, dating back to the fourteenth century, produced a Convention that would guarantee the safety of the journey. On landing her troops in Portugal, Britain would open the first front on the continent against Napoleon. Here began the fight that was to defeat Napoleon on the ground, even though it would take several years. Historians record that Bonaparte, whilst in exile, declared that the start of his downfall began when he invaded Portugal and tried to end the dynasty of the Braganças.

The journey undertaken by the Portuguese royal family 200 years ago has heretofore been but sketchily described by historians; principally, I believe, due to the lack of original documents from which the day-to-day events could be reconstructed and described. The inevitable confusion on arrival of the ships; and the tropical climate, one of paper's worst enemies, will not have helped in the conservation of these documents.

His Majesty's ships blockading the Tagus, and those detailed to escort the Portuguese fleet to Brazil, were on normal duty for a line-of-battle ship of that time. Logbooks were kept by the captain, the sailing master and by the deck. On return to base, perhaps after several years away at sea, these logs were sent to the Admiralty. These are important records of voyages – serving for audits, as evidence for court martials, and other purposes. The originals are kept at the Public Records Office in England.[9]

The work recently undertaken so as to make readable the 'discovered' logbooks of these ships, as well as the reports from their captains,[10] has enabled us to develop an accurate account of what was happening day by day, even hour by hour. The account is, however, the restricted viewpoint of that one particular ship. In order to broaden this viewpoint, several logs recording the same event have been taken as complementary to one another. Descriptions occurring in letters and reports have also been taken into account. Even then, the contents of these logbooks are inevitably slanted towards events closely tied to the British ships. They are, however, the main surviving sources of detailed information about the journey.

In addition to the logs and the reports from the captains, extensive extracts from the writings of two eyewitnesses – Count Thomas O'Neil and Luiz Gonçalves dos Santos – have been here reproduced. Their contribution conveys to us a colourful picture of the feelings, whether anxiety, danger, relief or exhilaration, existing at the moment in which they occurred.

Most readers will most probably be unfamiliar with the workings of a sailing ship of war of the beginning of the nineteenth century, whether British or Portuguese. Nor is it possible to obtain this knowledge in a practical way. To compare cruising in a modern warship to that of a warship of the nineteenth century is to compare a journey in a motor car with that in a tilbury! In order to better understand and appreciate the daily routine, dangers, hardships and privations suffered by the Portuguese passengers on board their ships, I have included detailed explanations, mainly of before the commencement of the voyage.

The lives of those individuals who participated in this critical period of Portuguese history would merit a book of their own. In appendix A I have included short biographical sketches of the most important personalities.

The ships of these two nations, in November 1807, already had a history of many victories. Their captains were in many cases national heroes: they had participated in battles that brought them this glory. The principal details of the ships, as well as their routes to Brazil, can be found in appendix B.

For a better understanding of the political/institutional events of that time, the main decrees and proclamations have been included under appendix C.

As far as possible, events follow a chronological order. The main sources of information of events at sea, as previously mentioned, are the logs maintained by the captains: individual pages written up for each day, ruled and noted, with a line for each of the twenty-four hours.

The number of individuals that came out from Lisbon, and their impact on the city of Rio de Janeiro, is a subject that has in the past been debated by countless historians. Some facts, I believe, have an important bearing on this debate. In the first place, I calculate that the crews of the war and merchant ships, even allowing for the fact that not infrequently they were undermanned, totalled some 7,000 to 7,500 men. The *Príncipe Real*, for example, carried a crew of 950 men. Fearing desertions, crews were maintained on board their ships. Secondly, the arrival of the ships at Rio de Janeiro occurred during a period of nearly two months. Thirdly, many passengers brought with them a large retinue. Lastly, many merchant ships belonged to other ports, so never went to Rio de Janeiro.

Surprisingly, a voyage of such importance has been largely ignored by artists. This and the detailed knowledge – gained through research – were the reasons that led me to commission the well-known artist, Geoff Hunt RSMA, to paint the scene of the arrival at Rio de Janeiro, on 7 March 1808, which I have used as the cover for this book.

In the centre of the painting the ship of the line, *Príncipe Real,* has just anchored. The queen's personal ensign can be seen on the mainmast. When D. João announced that he would only be disembarking on the following day, nobles and dignitaries waiting on shore took to small boats to go on board to greet him.

On the right the *Afonso de Albuquerque* and the *Medusa* prepare to come into the wind to moor. HMS *Marlborough* (on the left) and all the ships that were already in harbour, as well as the forts, fire a welcoming salute.

In the background the landmark of Rio's harbour, the Sugar Loaf, stands out.

I am particularly grateful to all those who offered suggestions and revised the text, and especially to Graham Salt for his diligent work at the National Maritime Museum and at the Public Records Office.

Although the events described appear, after 200 years, to be almost unreal, we must remember that if one were to take the generally accepted rule of thumb that a generation can be calculated as thirty years, then someone who knew his great-grandfather and knows his great-grandson, spans seven generations!

Kenneth Light 2009.

Chapter I

Bonaparte's total success was only checked by Russia and Britain. At Trafalgar, in 1805, England consolidated her control of the seas and so averted invasion. The Treaty of Tilsit enabled Bonaparte to turn his attention to the Iberian Peninsular. Portugal, under pressure to join the Continental System, tried to maintain her neutrality, even at a high cost. As time passed, the situation gradually deteriorated. At the beginning of October 1807 the French and Spanish representatives departed.

The peace treaty of Amiens, signed by Britain and France on 27 March 1802, effectively brought the European war to a close. However, its duration was limited, for a year later, on 16 May 1803, Britain declared a war that was to involve the whole of Europe and last for twelve years.

The rapid changes that were affecting the rest of Europe since the revolution that had erupted in France, had had as yet little effect on Portugal. The fact that she was located at the extremity of Europe and ruled by an absolute monarch, contributed to making these changes slow in reaching her: revolutionary ideas were only just beginning to be heard. Manners and customs were still those of another century. Portugal had been left behind, because of the physical distance that separated her from the changing world.

In spite of the reforms introduced by Pombal,[1] the Church was still the major influence on the monarchy, nobility and the masses. Marcus Cheke wrote:

> Out of a total population of about three million, three hundred thousand were either in holy orders or indirectly connected with monastic establishments. In Lisbon alone there were no less than a hundred and eighty monasteries…[2]

Its members, with few exceptions, were no more enlightened then those who relied on them for leadership.

> The science of medicine was almost unknown. If Saint Braz or Saint Marcos failed to respond to a votive offering, application was made to remedies

worthy of witch-doctors. Crushed snails were put to poultice open sores, and elderly invalids were nourished on viper broth.

The monarchy and nobles, also, were no better prepared. The same author continues:

> Though Queen Maria the First's reign was marked by the foundation of a Royal Academy of Sciences, and though the operatic performances of the countless musicians and singers maintained by the Royal Chapel were unexcelled in Europe, the education of the average Portuguese nobleman was confined to a smattering of fanatical doctrine. Having succeeded in his life object of securing a court pension, he passed his days in indolent vacuity...
>
> Queen Maria the First's consort D. Pedro[3] was commonly supposed to have been unable to read and write. His Minister of Marine could add and subtract, but had never mastered multiplication and division...

In spite of this, during this period several competent hands held the helm of the State. The credit must go to the prince regent, solely responsible for the appointment of ministers as well as their dismissal, and for leading them.

Superficially, during the period that preceded the final crisis of November 1807, Portugal appeared to be consumed by indecisiveness. The State Council was divided, with the majority in favour of neutrality; but if a choice had to be made between the warring nations, the same majority would prefer to side with France. This choice came from the conviction held by the influential councillor, D. Antônio de Araújo de Azevedo[4] – minister responsible for foreign and home affairs and war – that France's attitude towards Portugal was due to her own aggressiveness and, at the same time, her frustration in not being able to invade England in 1805; for Portugal was her oldest ally. So, if matters were to come to a head, France could be persuaded not to invade Portugal.

Maria Graham, the widow of a naval captain who had served in Chile and who later, whilst living in Brazil, became the governess of D. Maria da Glória, future Queen of Portugal, wrote in her precise and objective style:

> The Count of Barca, then prime minister, was certainly aware of the preparations of the French government. But with the obstinate blindness which sometimes seems to possess men like a fate, he persisted in regarding them only as measures to intimidate and harass England. This nobleman had been ambassador at the court of St. Petersburg, and, on his recall to lead the cabinet in Lisbon, he was ordered to go by sea to London, and thence

to Portugal; but he chose to make the journey by way of Paris, where he saw and conversed both with Napoleon[5] and Talleyrand.[6] There cannot be the least doubt that he was duped by these able men. Many considered him a traitor. But the vanity of the Count, who always said that he preferred to judge these men by his own eyes; even though this makes him weaker it makes him less wicked, and was, perhaps, the true intention of his actions.[7]

The safeguarding of her colonies was, for Portugal, another source of worry – in particular Brazil, being the principal source of continuous wealth and, even, of the nation's financial survival. On 19 March 1804 the negotiations to ensure neutrality resulted in a 'Neutrality Convention between the prince regent and the Republic of France', signed by the Portuguese Minister Plenipotentiary at Stockholm, José Manuel Pinto de Sousa, and by the Minister Plenipotentiary General Jean, on behalf of France. It stipulated the payment of a price to maintain peace, equivalent to 40,000 pounds per month.[8]

This analysis of events taking place in Portugal, that led up to the crisis of November 1807, presupposed a prince regent with his group of closest advisers that were far removed from reality, that staggered from one crisis to another without a clear notion of where their actions would take them. A naive, unintelligent and inefficient management of a delicate, difficult and potentially dangerous situation that would result in a cowardly flight and abandonment of a nation, with the undeniably successful outcome attributed to luck or fate.

A deeper and more thorough analysis however, would indicate that a parallel plan was in place and operational during this very same period. Well developed and administered, it was to prove successful politically and in managing the resources. Led by the prince regent, D. Araújo would certainly have participated, and perhaps others, such as members of the State Council and trustworthy men close to the prince.[9] According to Angelo Pereira this group would include José Egídio Alvares de Almeida, in charge of his cabinet; João Diogo de Barros, Secretary to the Infantado; Thomaz Antônio Villa Nova Portugal, revenue inspector; Manoel Vieira da Silva, his doctor; and the two gentlemen of the bedchamber: Francisco José de Souza Lobáto and Mathias Antônio de Souza Lobato.

There is ample evidence that D. Araújo was an extremely active, resourceful and intelligent man: as a lifelong bachelor he had few distractions from his work. Many years had been spent in preparation for this responsible post. During that time he had served as a diplomat at various courts, daily mingling with leaders of the country in which he was serving, and with ambassadors from other nations. In 1804 he had been recalled and appointed a member of the State Council. Although exhausted from the many daily tasks he undertook, and in poor health, he found time to pack and ship his immense library, which later he would donate to the National Library in Rio de Janeiro. His versatility, another sign of intelligence, shows itself when out of office, shortly after his arrival in Rio de Janeiro. He developed, in his garden, a scientific collection of 1,500 species of fruit trees and spices, which served to season food dishes – some native, others brought from Portugal's Far Eastern possessions – to be acclimatised. Later this collection would become the nucleus of the botanical garden, founded by D. João, also in Rio de Janeiro. Yet another facet of his character shows itself when, in 1816, the decree proposed by him, founding the Academy of Arts, was approved.

Portugal, well informed, for she had ambassadors and spies at all the major courts, was under no delusion as to her ability to defend either her land or sea frontiers. The preparations to transfer the royal family and Court to Brazil, as will be seen, began well before the French and Spanish representatives to the Portuguese Court made known their countries' ultimatums. The plan would have followed several stages: recall the fleet from its normal duties back to its home base in Lisbon, to be fitted out for the long journey; suspension of the transfer of goods and wealth from Brazil; gathering together of everything portable that could be taken, including the state archives. Last but not least, ensure a journey as far as possible safe from her enemies and from natural peril, by having an escort provided by the nation that dominated the seas.

The most difficult and delicate part of the plan was to carry out these practical and necessary arrangements without raising undue suspicion at the French and Spanish courts, as well as from the ordinary man in the street in Lisbon and elsewhere in Portugal, until reasonable acceptance could be guaranteed. History shows that these men were successful in carrying out their plans.

Lord Strangford,[10] Interim Minister to the Court at Lisbon, a friend and admirer of D. Araújo, many months before the event took place conferred and confirmed with him as to the real intentions of the prince regent. The preparations that were taking place could not be totally disguised.

No formal records have survived, if they ever existed, of such a plan. From close observation of the many decisions taken at this time there cannot be any doubt as to its existence; this alternate strategy was in place, as insurance should it be needed. In addition, at an early stage of the developments, D. Domingos,[11] in London, was authorised to negotiate a Convention that would provide the escort needed by the royal family for their journey to Brazil. Finally, following the decision taken at the historic meeting of the State Council, on the night of 24 November 1807, the plan was unveiled. By then it was too late for Bonaparte to take action to thwart it.

~ 1802

Looking back to the time of the signing of the Treaty of Amiens, Portugal, on the fringes of the Great War that was to consume Europe, was continuously forced to play a well-orchestrated political game in order to keep France at bay and at the same time maintain good relations with her traditional ally, Britain.

In April 1802 there arrived in Lisbon the newly-appointed French representative to the Portuguese Court, the Minister Plenipotentiary General Jean Lannes.[12] It was not long before his tempestuous nature was clashing with D. João de Almeida de Melo e Castro,[13] then Minister for Foreign Affairs and War, an Anglophile who was determined to hinder Lannes's attempts to impose Bonaparte's policies on Portugal.

The head of the police, Pina Manique,[14] also stood up to him.

> Lannes found only one Portuguese able to face him – Pina Manique. Nobody could intimidate him. His nobleness of character and dedication rose up against the complete contempt held by Lannes for the ceremonial of the court and respect for the royal family. He continuously requested audiences with the Prince Regent without applying through the right minister, and treated him as an equal. Lannes and all the members of the legation smuggled openly. Not only did the French Minister negotiate with merchandise coming from his own country, which was free of taxes, but also all his entourage participated in this lucrative business…[15]

His threat to ask for his passport was taken up by D. João de Almeida, who promptly sent it to him. On 25 August 1802 Lannes left Portugal without giving notice to his government. This action displeased Bonaparte, who ordered his immediate return, but not before demanding that the prince regent change his foreign minister. This duly took place a year later, when D. João de Almeida was sent to Austria as Ambassador. Lannes returned by sea in February 1803. Another victim of the pressure from France was Pina Manique: D. João was forced to dismiss him.

Another version claims that Lannes's return to Paris was due to his continuous conflict with Pina Manique:

> By the middle of 1802 the poor relationship between General Lannes and Pina Manique had reached its lowest level. The chief of police continued to curb, with all the means available to him, the smuggling openly carried out by the French Minister, and was not afraid of ordering the arrest of the assistant to the future Duke of Montebello. Diplomatic notes rained down on the Foreign Ministry. The least that Lannes demanded was the dismissal of Pina Manique. He threatened the Portuguese Government that if his demands were not met with he would leave, in this way breaking off diplomatic relations. Violent in his nature, he moved from threat to execution and left for Paris leaving the Prince Regent and the ministers extremely worried; the English community in Lisbon, on the other hand, who were accompanying these developments, was pleased.

The first consul did not approve of the attitude or of the action taken by Lannes; the French Foreign Minister – the celebrated Talleyrand – tried to obtain his dismissal, but the corporate spirit of the generals, the unwelcome presence of this comrade who had fought at Marengo, and the latent hostile attitude towards Great Britain made the future emperor take the decision, with the excuse that Pina Manique had not been dismissed, to send him back to the court in Lisbon. To this arrogant demand our government ceded, on the advice of the Portuguese ministers accredited in Paris and London and, of those foreign ministers resident in our country. Honourable, proud, upright and noble, only the chief of police remained.[16]

Subsequently, the prince regent was to develop excellent relations with the general, in spite of his involvement in the scandal of the contraband. It was common talk in Lisbon that, as godparents to his first child, the prince regent and D. Carlota Joaquina had, at the baptism, given Lannes several uncut diamonds. It was rumoured, at the time, that Lannes was desperate for money as he needed 300,000 francs to settle a debt with General Augereau.[17]

～ *1803*

Portugal's policy of buying her neutrality continued, but the price was high. On 7 May 1803 D. João agreed to a further demand from General Lannes: one million pounds, in instalments of forty thousand pounds per month. By June he was, in addition, demanding two hundred thousand cruzados for himself.[18] The demands escalated beyond any hope of payment. Councillor D. Rodrigo de Souza Coutinho[19] wrote to the prince regent on 20 June of that same year:

> Obeying with due respect the orders of your Royal Highness and, only mindful of the weakness of my abilities, and the lack of time with which to reply on such an important subject and, facing the difficulty of not fulfilling your Royal Highness's command; it is my opinion, expressed succinctly, that the demands from France are totally unacceptable for, in the first place, no country is in a position to pay 36 million pounds without obtaining a loan; secondly, even if a loan were to be obtained, all moneys in circulation would be used up; thirdly, it would be best if these 36 million pounds were to be added to the ordinary revenue and a major effort made to successfully put up a defence; in this way maintaining independence rather than be subjected to a system of perennial slavery, which your Royal Highness would be, as a vassal of the French Government.[20]

Whilst Portugal was thus being bled, French policy was to leave her colonies well alone. This was much easier than to invade and have to maintain them under possession.

By a rigorously imposed policy Portugal had always insisted that all trade with Brazil had to pass exclusively through her ports and transported aboard her ships. Foreign ships, except in an emergency, were discouraged even from putting in to Brazilian ports.[21] Even the presence of foreigners was not encouraged.

> Brazil was so monopolised that no foreigner was allowed to travel inland; strict orders existed to expel them, even to arrest them, as happened to the distinguished Baron Humbolt, as can be seen from the following document.[22]

More recently this policy had been, to a certain extent, relaxed. Although still closed to foreign traders, men-of-war and such merchant ships as could find no other port to refit in could, in the future, freely use Brazilian ports.[23] This happened, for instance, to a fleet under Sir Home Popham on Sir David Baird's expedition to the Cape of Good Hope in 1805, and to that of the French Admiral Guillaumez in 1806.

～ 1804

General Lannes's term of office came to an end in 1804. Bonaparte, crowning himself Emperor on 2 December of that year, now needed him in Paris. To take his place he nominated Jean Andoche Junot,[24] but it was not until April 1805 that he took office, and then not for long. As the war resumed almost immediately, before the end of the year Bonaparte, as promised, recalled him. He left in October of that year, to be replaced by François Gérard,[25] chargé d'affaires.

Meanwhile in France, as success after success crowned Bonaparte's ambitions, it became increasingly clear to him that the fulfillment of his desire to dominate the whole of Europe had become a distinct possibility.

～ 1805

In the year 1805 it would appear that only two nations, Russia and Britain, could present serious resistance to Napoleon's plans. Russia, with her immense population, was able to raise a considerable fighting force, however badly equipped and trained; and a substantial navy, operating in the Black Sea and the Baltic: the latter sea, because of ice, only open for part of the year. These same harsh weather conditions were her ally, as the long communication lines needed by the enemy became unmanageable under winter conditions.

Britain's strengths were her navy and her geographical position as an island. The latter was the main reason why in the last twenty centuries she had only three times been successfully invaded; by the Romans in the year 43, the Danes (Vikings) and by the Normans in 1066.

It was evident to Bonaparte that to dominate Russia he needed to raise a sizeable army in France and in the conquered countries, and carry out his campaign from spring to autumn.

Britain, on the other hand, presented quite a different problem: he must invade the island and, with forces superior in number and experience, destroy the enemy. For this purpose he built, on the northern coasts of France, Belgium and Holland, a flotilla of 2,000 vessels to transport his army of 150,000 men and 10,000 horses across the thirty-mile English Channel.[26]

It was also clear to him that to get across this quite narrow channel he had to be in complete control of the seas. The vessels to be used were defenceless: easy targets for any man-of-war. Even though France could count on the Spanish navy as allies, she had experienced considerable difficulty in getting the two navies to join and take the initiative as a fighting force. Britain, on the other hand, was anxious for a confrontation: she was confident of her abilities at sea and would like to remove the threat of invasion once and for all. This same problem faced Hitler a century and half later, the main difference being that he needed to dominate the air rather than the seas.

The opportunity finally came on 21 October 1805 at Trafalgar (near Cádiz, in southern Spain), after a frustrated chase from the Mediterranean to the West Indies and back. On that date the combined Franco-Spanish fleet of thirty-three ships of the line faced Britain's twenty-seven ships. This, one of the most famous of sea battles ever fought, brought about a decisive result. The French and Spanish ships that were not captured, destroyed by gunfire, blown up or shipwrecked on the coast – ten in all – ran for cover in Cádiz, there remaining whilst the port was under blockade. Although many of the British line-of-battle ships were severely damaged, not a single one was lost.

~ 1806

Following this defeat, Bonaparte developed new tactics. He knew that Britain must trade with other nations and her colonies in order to retain economic health and, for example, maintain her navy. Even to avoid serious supply problems, as she did not produce sufficient food for her needs. Based on this judgment, he decided to close all ports on the continent to British shipping and trade.

On 21 November 1806, following his annihilation of the Prussian army, Bonaparte issued the Berlin Decree: no British vessel, goods or even citizens were to be allowed into any part of the French Empire or to any territory governed by or allied to France. The Continental System had been instituted.

During the next few years this land blockade was to have serious negative effects on British trade.

Britain, now completely dominating the seas, retaliated by blockading ports that held war vessels, stopping and capturing all enemy ships, and even boarding neutrals that might be supplying France.

Meanwhile, Portugal continued to hope and believe that France's attitude towards her was but a menace, and that she had no intention of carrying out her threats. This was not the view held by Charles Fox,[27] then Foreign Minister in London.

Britain's watchfulness over Portugal arose from the importance of maintaining her (i.e. Portugal) neutral or, in the event that France invaded Spain, as a point from whence to attack the enemy. As a precaution a strong squadron was always kept off the coast, partly to watch the proceedings on shore, and partly to prevent Portuguese vessels from coming out of port and joining the French and Spaniards.[28]

The threats made by Talleyrand to Lord Landerdale, on the invasion and breaking up of Portugal, were carefully weighed by the Court in London.[29]

> In 1806 the demonstrations of hostilities against Portugal on the part of France were so evident that Lord Rosslyn was dispatched thither on a special mission, in which Lord St. Vincent and General Simcoe were joined with him. His instructions were to lay before the ministry of Lisbon, the imminent danger which threatened the country, and to offer assistance in men, money and stores from England, to put Portugal in a state of defence, in case the government should decide on a vigorous and effective resistance. If, on the other hand, Portugal should think itself too weak to contend with France, the idea of immigrating to Brazil and there establishing the capital of the empire was to be revived and promises made of assistance and protection for that purpose. If, however, Portugal insisted on rejecting assistance in either case, the troops under general Simcoe were to be landed, the strong forts on the Tagus occupied by them, and the fleet was to enter the river and secure the Portuguese ships and vessels, taking care to impress the government and people with the feeling that this was done out of regard for the nation, and by no means for the sake of selfish aggrandizement on the part of England. It appears, however, that the French preparations for invasion were not at that time so far advanced as had been imagined, and at the earnest entreaty of the court of Lisbon the troops and fleet were withdrawn from the Tagus.[30]

Portugal's preoccupation in maintaining her neutrality was evident. On this occasion she was able to show that the rumours of an army 30,000 strong that had assembled in Bayonne ready to cross Spain to invade her were but rumours; in fact, it was a small detachment of 1,700 Italians.[31]

The Portuguese Ambassador to the French Court, D. Lourenço de Lima,[32] also did not believe that Bonaparte's intentions towards Portugal could lead to hostilities. On

2 September 1806 he wrote to the prince regent a detailed report of his audience with Bonaparte. After complaining that Portugal had allowed a squadron under Lord St Vincent, carrying troops, to enter the Tagus, and being assured that the number of vessels was within the established treaties, Bonaparte stated that Portugal had nothing to fear provided that she continued neutral. Talleyrand shared this same opinion.[33]

In Portugal, towards the end of 1805 and at the beginning of 1806, D. João became seriously ill with depression and remained in his palace at Mafra. In his absence his wife, D. Carlota Joaquina,[34] planned to take over control of the state by inventing a story that, like his mother, he had lost his mind and could no longer reign. Her plans, according to historian Octávio Tarquíno de Sousa,[35] were supported by the marquises of Alorna[36] and of Ponte do Lima,[37] and the counts of Sarzedas[38] and of Sabugal.[39] Her attempts to induce her father, D. Carlos IV of Spain,[40] to take up arms against Portugal so as to enforce her rights, went unheeded.

The discovery of the plot served to put an end to any hope of improving their relations. D. Carlota expressed her dissent with her sharp tongue, D. João in silence, retiring to seclusion in Mafra.[41]

The marriage of D. João to D. Carlota Joaquina had taken place strictly for state reasons; to help weld the relationship between Portugal and Spain. It was but one of many marriages arranged between the infantes of the two nations. The marriage took place on 8 March 1785, when D. João was 18 and D. Carlota Joaquina was 10. However, they only started living together when she reached the age of 16.

~ 1807

The Franco-Russian War, fought towards the end of 1806, had been indecisive. Now, as the spring of 1807 approached, there was great expectation as to how the new campaign would develop. By the middle of June it had become clear that, once again, Bonaparte had been victorious.

> Good sense prevailed and the decision to converse met with the approval of those exhausted troops. As protocol required that the meeting had to be on neutral ground, the middle of the River Niemen was chosen, on a purpose built raft. Subsequent to this first meeting, it was decided that discussions should take place in a more comfortable location, the town of Tilsit.
>
> The treaty agreed upon left both sides satisfied. Russian possessions would remain intact, but no longer would she collaborate with England but join France in maintaining peace on the Continent. Russia would try and negotiate a peace between France and England and, in case she was not successful, would join up with France. A 'secret' treaty allowed Russia to take Finland (that belonged to Sweden), whilst Bonaparte would seize Portugal.[42]

The treaty was signed on 25 June 1807.

Spain, like Portugal, was also going through difficult times. Her weak king, D. Carlos IV, who had been crowned at the age of forty in 1788 had, by 1807, handed over power to D. Maria Luisa, his wife, and her lover D. Manuel de Godoy.[43] Godoy had been raised from the rank of officer in the Royal Guard to Captain-General of the Army and Grand Admiral of Spain and the Indies. His ambition was to rule a territory of his own in the future and, hoping to achieve this objective, he actively sought Bonaparte's aid. The Treaty of Fontainebleau,[44] signed by General Miguel Duroc on behalf of France, and D. Eugenio Isquierdo de Ribeira e Lezaun on behalf of Spain, was in consonance with his ideas. Napoleon ratified it on 29 October 1807.

The treaty provided for the invasion of Portugal and its division into three parts: Entre-Douro and Minho to be given to the Queen of Etruria in exchange for Tuscany; Alentejo and Algarves to belong to Godoy; and Beira, Traz os Montes and Estremadura to be kept for the Braganças if certain conditions were met (including the highly unlikely return of Gibraltar to Spain). The Portuguese colonies were to be divided between France and Spain.

It was the instrument necessary for the approval of the passing of a French army, now gathered in Bayonne, through Spain. The march overland, albeit harder and time consuming, was necessary as there was no possibility of transporting the army by sea without risk of losing it to the superior British navy. Spain would provide 8,000 men and 3,000 cavalry to join them and, in addition, would invade Entre-Douro with a force of 10,000 and take Oporto. Another force, 6,000 strong, would take Alentejo and Algarves.

In spite of this treaty Bonaparte was not above double dealing;[45] during the next two months, whilst in Italy, he repeatedly offered the kingdom of Portugal to his brother Lucien.[46] None of Napoleon's brothers were interested in Portugal, as Brazil was not included in the offer.

As time passed the Berlin Decree was gradually imposed or accepted, until eventually only Denmark and Portugal remained outside the System.

Peace with Russia now established, Bonaparte turned first to Denmark, to force her to adhere to the Continental System. The response from Britain was immediate and in great strength. Many historians believe that Britain's reaction was premature and that she was too harsh on Denmark. A squadron under Admiral Gambier, with 27,000 troops, sailed into Danish waters on 26 July 1807 and issued an ultimatum to the crown prince: Denmark must ally herself with Britain and put its navy at her disposal. On the prince's refusal, Copenhagen was bombarded from both land and sea, but not for long. On the fifth day she surrendered her fleet.[47] A total of eighteen ships of the line, ten frigates and forty-two smaller vessels were taken. Inevitably Denmark then joined the Continental System.

Bonaparte wasted no time; he immediately turned his attention to Portugal.

Portugal's position was, to say the least, very delicate: allying herself, whether with Britain or France, would bring about immediate consequences. Her long coast-line, impossible to defend with the troops available, made invasion by sea a practicable proposition. French troops brought in to defend her from an attack from the sea might well make Portugal a battleground, with inevitable bloodshed, including that of the civil population. With Britain dominating the seas she would lose her colonies; their wealth diverted to Britain to make up for the loss brought about by the Continental System. As had occurred elsewhere, Bonaparte would require Portugal to cede troops, to be used in other parts of Europe in accordance with his ambitious campaigns.

On the other hand, if she sided with Britain, Bonaparte's army would in no time be at her frontiers and her countryside made a battlefield. In addition, Portugal feared, almost as much, the new philosophy introduced by the Revolution. National policy was to make every effort to prevent the French revolutionary ideas from reaching Portugal. The man primarily responsible for implementing this policy of censorship was the head of the police, Pina Manique: books and pamphlets had been seized, and meetings, particularly of the freemasons, banned.

D. João's policy since Spain's invasion of Portuguese territory in 1801, with the much felt loss of Olivença, had been to play for time. It was his hope that the powers that were making war might come to terms. Even, in some miraculous way, the scenario might change so that the pressure on Portugal would end and with it the gradual depletion of the Treasury – the cost of maintaining her neutrality. If all else failed, and as a last resort, he could transfer the essence of his kingdom to Brazil.

This idea had matured over the centuries, always at times when extreme crisis, usually brought about by Spain, affected Portugal. This discussion had taken place at the time of the Prior do Crato, who was unsuccessful in defending Portugal against an army led by the Duke of Alba in 1580, which resulted in Portugal becoming a province of Spain during the next sixty years. D. João IV, the first of the Bragança kings, follow-ing an uprising in 1640, led Portugal to independence.[48]

Brazil, the source of much of Portugal's wealth, was now much more than that: it was a place to safely ride out the storms of Europe, until peace returned.

More recently D. Pedro, Marquis of Alorna, had written to the prince regent in May 1801:

In any case, what is needed is that your Royal Highness should continue to reign and that your crown should not suffer the same as happened to Sardinia and to Naples, and which may well be within the plans of the major powers, to be applied to the weaker crowns in Europe. Your Royal Highness has an important empire in Brazil and the same enemy that now attacks with advantage may perhaps tremble and change its plans, should your Royal Highness threaten to go and be Emperor in those extensive lands, from where you can easily conquer the Spanish colonies and, in a

short time, take over those belonging to the powers in Europe. It is necessary therefore that your Royal Highness give orders to prepare all your war
and transport ships that are in Lisbon.[49]

That same year, D. Rodrigo de Souza Coutinho had also written to the prince regent:

The treaty recently signed with France, only missing the secret articles that
you did not trust me with, although for a State Secretary of Finance they
might well have contained essential information on how to meet the harsh
monetary conditions that you are about to approve. Unfortunately, that part
that you permitted me to see is enough to persuade me, that the downfall
of your Royal Highness's throne is inevitable and that, delivered into and
abandoned in the arms of your enemies, you will also be torn apart by your
allies. As your Royal Highness is not prepared to defend yourself even in
these extreme circumstances; even to transfer the capital of the empire (if
need be) to Brazil, before accepting these harsh and odious conditions.[50]

In 1803 he again promoted the same idea:

When you consider that the Portugal that can be defended is not the best
and the most essential part of the monarchy; that after it has been devas-
tated, by a long and bloody war, there yet remains for its king and its people the possibility of removing themselves to the empire of Brazil, there
to conquer that which has been lost in Europe, and there also to continue a
never-ending war against the savage enemy who refuses to recognise the
neutrality of a Country that shows that she wishes to keep it. Whatever the
dangers that come with such a noble and courageous decision, they are
surely less than the result of an invasion of the ports by the French, which
would either bring about the abdication by your Royal Highness of your
Royal Crown, the abolition of the monarchy, or a fatal persecution.[51]

~ July–August 1807

As early as 25 July Lord Strangford was informing London that there were strong
rumours coming from Spain that M. de Beauharnais, the French Ambassador, was
negotiating for French troops to pass through on their way to Portugal; also, that the
closure of ports to British shipping might well be within Bonaparte's plan.[52]

On 29 July, two days after Bonaparte had returned to Paris from Tilsit, D. Lourenço
de Lima was called by Hauterive – who had replaced Talleyrand as Interim Minister
for Foreign Affairs – and informed of France's demands. This information was
transmitted to the Lisbon Court on 10 August.[53] A similar note was received by the

Court from the Count of Ega, Ambassador to Spain.[54]

The French and Spanish[55] representatives to the Court in Lisbon must have been instructed simultaneously as, on 12 August, a note signed by both of them was handed to D. Antônio de Araújo.

Even before France had declared her intentions, orders were given to the arsenal in Lisbon to start preparing those ships already in the river, for a possible journey. They included the line-of-battle ships *Afonso de Albuquerque, Medusa and Conde D. Henrique,* the frigates *Minerva, Princesa and Carlota,* and a number of smaller vessels.[56]

France in her note demanded that Portugal join the Continental System, in accordance with the Berlin Decree. She should, therefore, close her ports to British shipping; expel the British Minister from Lisbon; recall the Portuguese Minister to the Court of St James; declare war; imprison British subjects and confiscate their property and join her navy with that of France and Spain.[57] In addition, Portugal should provide an unspecified amount of money to help pay for the war, as well as 4,000 men. These measures were to be adopted by 1 September. Failure to comply with them would result in France declaring war.[58]

One of the first reactions, on receipt of this ultimatum, was to advise the British government. D. Antônio de Araújo wrote in a dispatch to José Egídio Álvares de Almeida,[59] the prince regent's secretary:

It is my duty to inform the Prince Regent, My Lord, that yesterday I had lengthy discussions with the Spanish ambassador and with the representative from France on the subject of this important business... I have the pleasure of adding that Strangford is well in our favour... It would be highly convenient to send word to England to maintain this minister here for, should they send Lord FitzGerald, it would be terrible.[60]

Lord Robert FitzGerald, officially the Minister Plenipotentiary was, during this crucial period, absent from Portugal.

The Portuguese Ambassador in London had, by then, received this same news. It had come from Paris, via Holland, through the secret agent M. de Brito, resident in that town.[61] This agent would be used, during August, to distribute a large quantity of diamonds in Paris to certain individuals with influence.[62] However, this was to no avail.

A matter of such national importance required discussion and decisions of the State Council, and for this purpose a meeting was called for 19 August.

The Council, created when Portugal was governed by the Cardinal Infante D. Henrique, tutor to the young king, D. Sebastão, had been in existence since 1562. The Council was presided over by the prince regent and included D. José Xavier de Noronha Camões de Albuquerque de Sousa Moniz;[63] D. Henrique José de Carvalho e Mello;[64]

D. José Luis de Vasconcelos e Sousa, Justice Administrator for the Kingdom;[65] D. João Rodrigues de Sá e Melo, State Secretary of the Admiralty and Overseas Possessions;[66] D. Rodrigo Domingos de Sousa Coutinho; D. João de Almeida de Melo e Castro; D. Antônio de Araújo de Azevedo; and D. Fernando José de Portugal e Castro, president of the Overseas Council.[67]

During this time, the prince regent, indisposed, was residing at the baroque Mafra Palace, some fifty kilometres northwest of Lisbon.

From the lengthy opinion written by D. João de Almeida,[68] we learn that the Council on 19 August agreed that letters should be sent to Paris and Madrid rejecting their notes. Britain was to be officially informed and instructions sent to the "… Minister accredited to his Britannic Majesty… authorising him to handle the important mission that your Royal Highness has entrusted him …"[69] These, most probably, were the instructions to open negotiations which resulted in the Convention between Portugal and Britain, signed on 22 October.[70]

D. João de Almeida suggested that in order to appease Bonaparte, and with prior agreement from Britain, the ports should be closed.[71] He reminded the prince regent that this ruse had been used before, but proved very costly to the nation:

> During less dangerous times, although still very difficult (1797), agreement was sought with the court in London for your Royal Highness to close the ports to British ships, both naval and mercantile, and make peace with France, even though this would be breaking the Treaties that existed between Portugal and Great Britain. Your Royal Highness entrusted me with this unseemly mission in the year 1801, the last one spent in London and, in the august hands of your Royal Highness, you will find the original of the letter written by the hand of Lord Hankesburgh, then Foreign Secretary… But it would be sufficient, august Sir, the terrible blows that would be given to our commerce on closing the ports, the shortage of essential goods, the delay with the correspondence to our colonies, the loss in value of our paper-money with its inevitable consequences, even though the war with England is make-believe, august Sir, these and others that for the sake of brevity and because they are obvious I do not mention, are really necessary in order to satisfy the ambition and animosity of France?[72]

The event referred to took place in 1801, when Spain invaded Portugal:

> The Spaniard's arms were antiquated and their generals incompetent, but the Portuguese had no equipment and no generals at all. A German princeling, the Duke of Waldeck, was hastily summoned to command the Prince Regent's troops. On arrival in Lisbon he caught cold and expired. His place

was taken by the eighty-year-old Duke of Lafôes, a fantastic figure in black velvet boots, his cheeks covered in rouge and patches. This commander did not even acquire the distinction of leading the retreat. A few weeks after war had been declared the futile campaign petered out, and peace was signed at Badajoz.[73]

The conditions for establishing this imposed peace were the closure of the ports and the payment of a considerable ransom. The cost of this action was very high: "… the depleted Treasury could not face the bleeding that this agreement required…"[74]

There were rumours that an ambassador extraordinary would be sent to London, to negotiate this apparent warlike strategy on the part of Portugal, in exchange for commercial advantages when peace returned.[75] Subsequently it was agreed that D. Domingos de Sousa Coutinho was quite capable of undertaking this negotiation.[76] Lord Strangford wrote:

> All we require, said M. d'Araújo in our last conference, is that England shall not destroy our Colonies and Commerce. It is in her interest that we should be independent of France, even at the expense of some temporary sacrifices. She has nothing to dread from the mock warfare we may be compelled to engage in.[77]

In principle the State Council agreed that Portugal should close her ports to Britain and join the Continental System, but did not accept the confiscation of property or the imprisonment of British subjects. D. Rodrigo de Sousa Coutinho cast the one dissenting vote. In his opinion, Portugal should gather an army of seventy thousand men and forty million cruzados and declare war against France and Spain. In the event that she was unsuccessful in defending herself the royal family should transfer to Brazil.[78]

Other measures agreed included strengthening the defences of the port of Lisbon, advising the colonies and recalling the squadron patrolling the Straits of Gibraltar, on the lookout for pirates.[79] On 3 October the *Rainha de Portugal* left for Lisbon (from Gibraltar) with the line-of-battleship *Vasco da Gama*, the frigate *Golfinho* and the brig *Vingança.* They anchored in the Tagus on 8 October 1807.

As the end of August approached the French and Spanish representatives threatened to break off diplomatic relations and leave Portugal.

From Belém, D. Araújo wrote to the prince regent's secretary, José Egídio:

> I am writing from the residence of the Viscount of Anadia… Today, after sending their notes, the ambassador and Rayneval came to speak to me; I told them that by leaving they would be making a mistake, that Bonaparte would most probably agree to the proposals made by His Royal Highness,

that I would answer their notes after I had received orders from my master. However, if they really had made up their minds to go, His Royal Highness would not withhold their passports.[80]

At the State Council meeting of 26 August, held at the Mafra Palace, the sending of D. Pedro[81] to Brazil was debated and approved, with once more, the dissenting vote of D. Rodrigo. It was decided that one of the infantas, D. Maria Benedita,[82] sister to the queen, should accompany the young prince. She was the widow of her nephew and heir to the throne of Portugal, Prince of Beira D. José: D. João's brother and eldest son of D. Maria I.

Letters informing the Portuguese representatives of this decision would be sent to the Paris, Madrid and London[83] courts. The replies to the demanding notes, received from France and Spain, were read and approved.

Thomáz Antônio de Villa Nova Portugal, although not a member of the Council, was one of the few whose opinion was heard by D. João. He recommended "...the Prince of Beira, with the title of Lord High Constable, should leave at once for Brazil with troops; accompanied by the infantas and by two generals, and take up residence in São Paulo..."[84]

~ *September 1807*

On 1 September the deadline stipulated passed, without any reply to the notes. On 4 September Rayneval asked for his passport.[85] As Rayneval and Campo-Alange were aware that letters had been sent to their respective governments and as yet no reply had been received, D. Araújo was able to persuade them to withdraw their requests. On their own account they decided to postpone the deadline to 1 October. This was a victory for D. Araújo, who was responsible for administering the policy of stalling.

It would appear improbable that the plan to send D. Pedro to Brazil would be carried out, in view of the affection that D. João had for his family. Because of this D. Araújo, who had had a similar idea, had hesitated in presenting it to the prince regent. The plan, however, was useful to D. João: the preparation of four line-of-battle ships for the voyage, the remainder made ready to defend the port, could be carried out with haste but without undue adverse comment. They would serve just as well to carry the Prince of Beira as to transport the whole of the royal family.

D. Araújo was of the opinion that Bonaparte's demands, if not attended to, would not lead to an invasion of Portugal; that the most likely and immediate danger of an attack came from Britain, apprehensive of seeing the Portuguese naval and merchant fleets, voluntarily or otherwise, join those of France and Spain. Nevertheless, D. Araújo supported the fall-back strategy of sending the Prince of Beira to Brazil: he knew that the prince regent was unlikely to let his son go without following him shortly afterwards. The next State Council meeting, on 2 September, discussed whether the Infante

D. Miguel[86] should go instead of D. Pedro, the heir apparent. The Council confirmed the Prince of Beira. At this meeting a proposition was presented by D. Araújo: that the prince should receive the title of Lord High Constable of Brazil and that the colony should be administered by a council, presided over by the prince and consisting of the Viceroy and one or more generals. This was rejected in favour of continuing with the present system of administration. The meeting also agreed to reject any offer that might be made of receiving French or Spanish troops into Portuguese territory, for whatever reason.

During the month of September there must have been a change of mind over the title to be given to D. Pedro, as 'High Constable' is mentioned in the proclamation to the general public. The proclamation was, in due course, printed, but not distributed.

Lord Strangford wrote that at this meeting: "…It has been resolved in the Council, that should the Enemy enter Portugal, His Royal Highness, accompanied by His Family & Court, should retire to the Fortress of Peniche, a place not very far from Lisbon, which is almost inaccessible except by sea…"[87]

The situation had now deteriorated to such a point that on 7 September *Gavião*, a 22-gun brig with a complement of 118 men commanded by First Lieutenant Desidério Manuel da Costa, was sent to Rio de Janeiro with orders to the Viceroy to suspend, until further notice, the sailing of all merchant ships. He was warned that there existed the possibility that part or the whole of the royal family might, in the near future, be going out to Brazil.[88]

During the month of September the awaited replies from Paris, Madrid and London arrived. Bonaparte continued in his demands, at the same time making it clear that he would not tolerate, for much longer, Portugal's indecisiveness. From Madrid the Prince of Peace replied that Portugal should unite with France and Spain and on no account consider transferring the Court to Brazil. He had a high regard for Portugal, otherwise during the war of 1801, he would have invaded her and taken her over. This answer from Spain reflected the apprehension felt regarding her American colonies. If the Court were to transfer to Brazil, an invasion of Portugal by Spain would be met with a similar action by Portugal, in Spain's Rio de la Plata.[89]

George III wrote that he was grateful for the consideration with which his subjects had always been treated, and urgently recommended D. João transfer his Court to Brazil, offering to provide, if necessary, an escort.[90] George III was the reigning monarch at this time, the Duke of Portland his Prime Minister, and Lord Mulgrave the First Lord of the Admiralty.

The Marquis of Angeja, knowing well the feelings of the prince regent for his son, persuaded the Marquis of Belas and the Marquis of Aguiar to change their vote. At the next meeting, held on 23 September, the eight councillors that were present were evenly divided on whether the Prince of Beira should or should not be sent to Brazil.[91] The fourth vote was probably that of D. Rodrigo, who from the beginning, had been in favour of declaring war against France and Spain and, if necessary, for the royal family to go to Brazil. At this same meeting it was further decided that D. Araújo should continue trying to negotiate with France.

Lord Strangford realised that the most influential member of the Council was D. Araújo and, even though Councillor D. Rodrigo was known to be an Anglophile and perhaps his main source of confidential information, he informed the Court that D. Rodrigo had passed detailed information on Council matters to his brother, D. Domingos in London, and had accused D. Araújo of being a Francophile.[92] The prince regent's reaction was to exclude D. Rodrigo from any further Council meetings. Lord Strangford now had confirmed that, which he had long suspected, the strategy enacted by the Council had, as its main objective, the transfer of the royal family to Brazil. He discussed this with D. Araújo, who concurred that this was also his point of view. It was believed that Rayneval and Campo-Alange, even though they had their informers, having being told so categorically that there were no travel plans for the royal family, firmly believed that the prince regent would not, under any circumstances, leave the country.[93] On 20 September and again on the 24th, Rayneval expressed his concern that the royal family were planning to leave Portugal. D. Araújo insisted that the preparations were for the voyage of the Prince of Beira, about which he had already written to the courts of London, Paris and Madrid. The danger and discomfort that such a journey would entail added to the reasoning that it would not take place.

At the end of the month of September and with the approach of the deadline, it became increasingly clear that the policy of negotiating for time was about to suffer a setback. The representatives of both France and Spain stated that since the actions demanded against Britain had not taken place, they would break off diplomatic relations and leave the country.

At Mafra, still recovering from his illness, D. João was being advised, especially by Thomáz Antônio de Villa Nova Portugal, to return to Lisbon, to show his people that he was active in safeguarding their interests and to receive in audience the representatives of France and Spain before they left the country.

The next State Council meeting, that of 30 September, agreed to close Portuguese ports to British ships, but went no further in ceding to Bonaparte's demands. One of the reasons given for not taking measures against British citizens and property in Portugal was the fear of retaliation against Portuguese property and citizens living in Britain.

D. Araújo judged that half measures would, in fact, displease Bonaparte. In addition the demands against British citizens, a carefully kept secret, would now become public knowledge. On the other hand Britain could well construe the closing of the doors as adherence to the Continental System and abandonment of the idea of transferring the heir and Court to Brazil, with two immediate consequences: the seizure of any naval ships still cruising against Barbary pirates in the Straits of Gibraltar, and the invasion of the port of Lisbon to apprehend or destroy the naval and merchant fleets. The example of what had happened at Copenhagen had not been forgotten.

D. João de Almeida de Melo de Castro was also fearful that on the one hand Bonaparte would not be satisfied with the reply; on the other neither would Britain, so that Portugal ran the risk of being at war with two enemies at the same time. In addition her colonies would, under the influence of Britain, within a short period of time become independent and so open for trade. He argued that preparation should be made, with all haste, to transfer the Court and all those that wished to follow, to Brazil. In addition, public and private property should be prepared for shipment.[94]

In fact the prince regent had already made a number of decisions, as reported by Lord Strangford. On 25 September he had gone to Mafra to deliver the reply that had arrived from His Majesty George III. The prince regent gave him a long interview:

> The Prince, in reply, said that every feeling of religion and duty forbade him abandoning his People until the last moment, and until some efforts should have been made to save them, & to justify Himself to God and the World; that in case of extremity he had made up His Mind to retreat to His Transatlantic Dominions.[95]

Lord Strangford tried to persuade the prince to adopt the strategy suggested by Britain:

> During an Interview of nearly an Hour and a Half, I employed every argument in my power to induce His Royal Highness to consent to the only measure which now affords him a Chance to continue to exist as an Independent Sovereign.[96]

He was to argue later, when under criticism, that his actions had been decisive in persuading the prince regent to leave for Brazil.

The French chargé d'affaires had, on the previous day, delivered the reply from Bonaparte, but was received for only a few moments "…in consequence of the timidity and difficulty experienced by the prince when obliged to express Himself in any language except his own…"[97]

By September it had become clear to D. Carlota Joaquina that her husband was planning to transfer the Court to Brazil. Her relationship with her husband seemed to follow the same pattern as that existing between their two countries. As Spain now prepared to wage war against Portugal, their relationship deteriorated still further. The last thing she wished was to be taken away to another continent, where the influence of her mother country would be virtually non-existent. Desperately, she wrote numerous letters to her parents beseeching them to invent any excuse and call her to Madrid.[98]

On 29 September the Viscount of Anadia reported to the prince regent that the line-of-battle ships *Afonso de Albuquerque* and the *D. João de Castro*, as well as the frigate *Urania* and the brigantine *Voador*, were ready and would sail just as soon as he gave the order.[99]

Foreseeing that matters were coming to a head the prince regent, on 30 September, moved to the Palace of Nª. Sª. da Ajuda, in Lisbon.[100]

On 1 October the French chargé d'affaires, François Maximilien Gerárd, Count of Rayneval; and the Spanish Ambassador D. Manuel José Antônio Hilário, 2nd Count of Campo-Alange, on receiving their passports, left Portugal.

Chapter II

The situation in Portugal becomes more critical as tension builds. Bonaparte's continued insistence forces the State Council to take the measures demanded against Britain; if only to postpone the inevitable invasion. The situation becomes untenable when Junot finally invades Portugal and, at the same time, Sidney Smith blockades the port of Lisbon. Time runs out and makes D. João decide to lead the court and make the journey to Brazil. Final preparations and embarkation.

~ October 1807

The departure of the French and Spanish representatives had the effect of making public that which previously had been kept secret: the seriousness of the situation.

The people were now beginning to show signs of despair at the prospects that lay ahead:

> There was a procession on Sunday to avert the dangers impending over Portugal and, I am told that many ladies of rank walked barefoot in it – what can be expected from a people who resort to such actions at such a moment.[1]

The state councillors were to meet on 12 October, at the residence of D. Araújo in Belém, and again, on 14 October; on both occasions without the presence of the Prince Regent. The decision to send D. Pedro was once more discussed and agreed, with the contrary vote of the Marquis of Belas. His opinion was that this decision only served to hasten a French invasion. The gradual disclosure to the general public of the journey of the young prince may well have been a way of getting the country used to the idea of the royal family leaving Portugal.[2]

British merchants in Portugal, expecting the worst, also reacted to the news:

> English merchants now started to leave; the people of Lisbon saw this with a feeling of sorrow; this was the first general manifestation of hate against French injustice and high praise for the Monarch who, in spite of personal danger, had not violated the rights of these visitors.[3]

In *História do Império*, Tobias Monteiro describes the situation:

> In an attempt to find the way around the situation but, at the same time leaving clear to the Englishmen the inconsistency of his guarantees, the Prince Regent placed four ships at the disposal of those who wished to abandon Portugal taking their assets with them.[4]

Monteiro wrote that the United States Minister calculated that 2,000 Englishmen accepted the transport. The embarkation was planned for the 12th and departure definitely for the 15th or 17th. A few Irishmen remained behind. The value of the property taken was immense. The Danish Consul reported that the convoy finally left on the 20th, and that it was composed of some thirty English and American ships.

On Saturday, 17 October, a convoy of sixty-four sail, escorted by HM frigate *Lively*, left for England.[5]

Preparations continued to go ahead for the journey, with the nomination of those that would accompany the young prince. The principal Lord- and Lady-in-Waiting would be the Count and Countess of Belmonte.[6] It was decided that troops would not be sent – a Brigade of Marines would be sufficient – and that Rio de Janeiro rather than São Paulo would be his home.[7] Orders were given to the Count of Redondo[8] to embark the victuals necessary for the journey.[9]

According to a Mr H Chamberlain, writing from Lisbon on 20 October, the Portuguese vessels, as yet with incomplete crews, were now ready to sail.[10]

The Viscount of Anadia, as State Secretary of the Admiralty, was responsible for the preparations. Daily he visited the dockyard at Ribeira to ensure that his orders were being carried out. The line-of-battle ship *Afonso de Albuquerque* was being prepared to carry the Prince of Beira. During the month of October the Prince Regent was to pay her a visit to see the accommodations which, by then, were ready.[11]

When, on 22 October, the Prince Regent signed the decree which had been approved by the State Council on 30 September, closing all the ports to British shipping,[12] it became unlikely that Britain would let Portuguese ships go unobstructed. Some prior arrangement would have to be made or the journey of the heir was no longer a viable proposition.

Precautions were also being taken over the island of Madeira. The closure of ports was not to apply to Madeira. British troops would be allowed to land there provided that, on the reopening of the mainland ports, they would depart. In addition, private and public property, religious cult and civil and ecclesiastic authority should be respected.[13]

The repercussions of these actions, taken in Lisbon, were far and wide. A brig, which had left Lisbon on 1 November, carried a copy of the proclamation closing the ports to British ships. From Funchal a Mr Hartford Jones wrote to the Rt Hon Robert

Dundas with this news, adding that he would communicate it to the governors at Cape of Good Hope and at Bombay.[14]

Communications were relatively slow at the beginning of the nineteenth century. The Commissioners of the Affairs of India only reacted to the news on 10 December, when a dispatch was sent to the Governor-General in Council in Bengal through the Secret Committee. Orders were given to seize Portuguese settlements and possessions in India, preferably through prior arrangements with the Captain-General in Goa; however, should it prove necessary, by the use of force.[15]

Macao was politically more delicate. No steps should be taken without first consulting the Select Committee in Canton. It was important that the Chinese government should be in total agreement with any action taken.[16]

These orders were countermanded on 21 December, on receipt of the news that the Prince Regent had departed for Brazil with an escort of British men-of-war. The Foreign Office sent orders to the Governor in Council at Bombay, to cancel previous instructions relative to Portuguese possessions in Goa and Macao.[17]

In Lisbon, the apprehension felt that Britain might mount an attack was evident, as can be seen from the note from D. Araújo to the secretary to the Prince Regent: "… All haste in the preparation of the port defences is not enough, I fear Collingwood's squadron in the vicinity…"[18] Following the death of Lord Nelson at Trafalgar, Lord Collingwood had taken over command of the Mediterranean fleet. On the 18th the Prince Regent again requested the attendance of Lord Strangford at the Ajuda Palace. On receiving him, he showed much apprehension at the news, received from England by the recently arrived packet, that an expedition had sailed from England destined to seize the port of Lisbon and the Portuguese ships of war. Arguing that he needed the ships to remove his family and treasures to Brazil, he suggested that England should blockade the port:

> Thus, England will effectively hinder our Navy from falling into the hands of France; the mode which she will employ for that purpose will be just and honourable, whereas a forcible attempt to seize our fleet, would certainly tarnish the unsullied reputation that England has hitherto enjoyed amongst nations.[19]

Whilst worrying, on the one hand, over a possible invasion by France and on the other, with the reply from England, the Prince Regent asked for England's intervention in obtaining the return of Olivença, taken by Spain in 1801, if a general peace were to be negotiated. The preoccupation with loss of territory was to manifest itself again much later, when the Prince Regent, by then D. João VI, would insist on maintaining during his life the title of Titular Emperor of Brazil, when independence for that country was finally agreed in 1825. In effect, Brazil has had three individuals with the title of Emperor (D. João, D. Pedro I and D. Pedro II), and four with the title of Empress (D. Carlota Joaquina, D. Maria Leopoldina, D. Amélia and D. Teresa Cristina).

D. Araújo continued to worry over the reactions provoked by the decisions taken by the State Council. A week later, on the 27th, he was again writing: "…it is necessary, very necessary, to hasten the port defences, for there is news from England that a squadron is on its way…"[20]

In spite of the greatly reduced likelihood of conveying the Prince of Beira to Brazil the Portuguese fleet, moored in the Tagus and being made ready, continued to increase in numbers, causing an increase in the unease felt by Britain at the possibility that this fleet might join that of France.

Further evidence of the preparation is the note: "…The proclamation has been printed, and I am sending you a case with the leaflets, for the Viscount; it is necessary that he gives the orders for their distribution…"[21] Tobias Monteiro wrote that the notice referred to the journey of the royal family. More probably is that it referred to the voyage of the heir, D. Pedro,[22] destined not to take place.

One of the problems arising from the departure of the French and Spanish representatives was the interruption of communications, inevitably made worse by the expulsion which would follow, of the Portuguese representatives to those countries.

Meanwhile, at Fontainebleau on 15 October, Bonaparte at a diplomatic gathering and within hearing of D. Lourenço de Lima had said: "…If Portugal does not carry out my wishes, the House of Bragança, in two months time, will no longer be reigning…"[23]

D. Lourenço reported this conversation in a note written on the 17th and, without consulting his government, immediately left for Lisbon to personally relate what was happening. The means of overland travel at that time was by private carriage accompanied by servants and personal guards. D. Lourenço chose the regular stagecoach.[24] He took some fifteen days, arriving on 1 November.

On 22 October the Portuguese diplomat Fernando José Antônio Alvares, left in charge of the embassy in the absence of D. Lourenço, received the following letter:[25]

Fontainebleau 22 October 1807

Monsieur: La Légation Françoise n'est plus à Lisbonne. Le Régent Votre Souverain a mieux aimé la lassier partir que d'adhérer aux justes propositions que lui faisait l'Empereur e Roi. Ainsi il a rompu toutes ses relations avec l'Empereur, et les liens de Paix qui l'unissaient à la France: ainsi il se met en guerre avec l'Empereur. Sa Majesté n'a pu voir qu'avec regret cette détermination qu'elle a cherché à prévenir; mais elle n'est point accountumée à se laisser braver impunément. Le Portugal veut la guerre: Le Portugal aura la guerre. L'Empereur la lui déclare dans ce moment, et m'ordonne de vous faire connaître que son intention est que vous et toute la Légation Portugaise, quittiez Paris dans les vingt quatre heures, et la France dans les quinze jours, qui suirvront la date de la Lettre et des Passeports que j'ai l'honneur de vous adresser.

M. Le Chevalier Alvares.
Champagny[26]

Fontainebleau, 22 October

Sir, The French Legation is no longer in Lisbon. The Regent, your Monarch, preferred to see the Legation leave rather than accept the just proposals made by the Emperor and King. By so doing, he broke off all relations with the Emperor and the peace treaties that united him to France; consequently, he declared war on the Emperor. His Majesty sees, with sadness, this decision that he tried to avoid; however, he is not used to leaving insults without an answer. Portugal wants war: Portugal shall have her war. The Emperor, at this moment, declares it and orders me to communicate that you and the Portuguese Legation shall leave Paris within the next twenty-four hours, and France within the next fifteen days as from the date of this letter and that of the passports that I have the honour to send you.

M. Le Chevalier Álvares
Champagny

Two days later Fernando José left Paris, heading for Bayonne near the Spanish frontier, where he would receive his passport.[27]

The Count of Ega now also arrived in Lisbon:

At this time the Count of Ega, Portuguese ambassador to the court in Madrid, also arrived unexpectedly. He came, as did D. Lourenço, without being called and without permission from his government. He made the most forceful requests and supplications and used every possible means of persuasion that on no account should the journey to Brazil be undertaken. He had the assurance from the Prince of Peace and the word of General Bournouville (French ambassador): he used relations and friends, made promises and threats, but all to no avail; nothing would change the decisions already made.

Portuguese diplomats only had eyes for the court where they were accredited; they looked after their interests (courts) even before those of their own (country). Napoleon's prestige could seduce the reason and endanger the loyalty of these men, it would be better to attribute it to this reason rather than more heinous crimes.[28]

Even now, the Council did not know that the Portuguese legation had been expelled from France and war declared. "...From Paris by ordinary mail or perhaps by the express that arrived from Madrid came news that D. Lourenço had left; the reason, generally believed, was to escape from his creditors..."[29]

The next meeting of the Council, which took place on 30 October at the residence of the Viscount of Anadia, decided that in view of the disquieting news in the note of the 17th from D. Lourenço, received in Lisbon on the 27th, it was important for the Prince Regent to reopen the channel of negotiation with France.

An ambassador extraordinary: the Master of the Horse, Marquis of Marialva,[30] was chosen to go to Paris. His appointment was predated, so as not to offend D. Lourenço. "... If D. Lourenço comes, your Royal Highness can tell him that this ambassador to the Emperor was appointed in addition to him and not to succeed him, D. Lourenço..."[31]

～ *November 1807*

The Marquis of Marialva, one of the richest men in Portugal, duly left for Paris on 16 November, with an untold quantity of diamonds and a sword made of gold encrusted with diamonds.[32] This treasure was, according to the American Minister, worth a million dollars.[33] In addition, D. João gave him instructions to negotiate the marriage of D. Pedro, when of age, with Bonaparte's niece, daughter of his sister Carolina with General Murat.[34] His mission was to inform Bonaparte that the demands he had made had been met with, and that therefore there was no reason to take action against Portugal.

The Marquis de Marialva was a singular figure within the Court. His coat of arms was quartered twice with the arms of the royal family, which showed his proximity to the throne. William Beckford, who had been befriended by the Marialva family when he visited Portugal in 1787, wrote:

> Crown favours have rained on him during the present and in previous reigns – a chain of prosperity, not even interrupted when Pombal was all powerful! *Do as you think best with the rest of my nobles* – D. José, then king, used to say to his much feared minister – *but leave the marquis of Marialva alone.*[35]

The Marquis had a frustrating journey. His first stop, on the 21st, was at Elvas, some ten miles from Badajoz but still in Portugal. From there he wrote to D. Araújo:

I arrived at this place yesterday afternoon and immediately asked the Interim Governor to write to the Governor of Badajoz to enquire from him whether the passport which had been requested for me was with him.

His intention, if he was not allowed to go to Paris, was at least to inform the French government of the steps taken by Portugal against Britain: "...Today at midday I am planning to be in Badajoz, and as soon as I arrive I shall post the letters to M. Champagny, Beauharnois, Strognoff[36] & c ..." The reply from Spain was not encouraging: "...Colleague and friend. No Passport has arrived for your Excellency, however you can continue your journey as a private individual to the court of the king, my master..."[37] He accepted this advice, as he was accredited to the Paris Court, but was unsuccessful in his mission as he got no further than Madrid.

Preparations for a possible invasion and an eventual voyage continued. D. Araújo wrote:

The prior of the Benedictines spoke to me saying that it did not make sense to send the silver to Coimbra, and as the Benedictines have many abbeys on the river Minho, they would be grateful if it (silver) could be deposited in Oporto, a more convenient place where it can also be sent abroad; not so from Coimbra.[38]

Although policies and decisions were being concentrated and coordinated by D. Araújo, in practice the Prince Regent was the sole administrator of his kingdom. His return to the Palace of Mafra, because of ill health, created a communication problem for D. Araújo and delayed important decisions; as he wrote to the Prince Regent:

I would be very grateful, on all accounts, to find your Royal Highness feeling better, one of the reasons is that you are able to return to Ajuda because at every moment orders have to be received for a thousand different matters; the situation requires it and I cannot think of more dangerous times than those in which we find ourselves – if the French do not invade our frontier, or the English enter the Tagus – any of these things can happen in a short space of time. At a less critical moment the Marquis of Pombal left for Salvaterra to convince the King, D. José, the need for his return to Lisbon.[39]

One of the strangest episodes that occurred during this turbulent period was the arrival in the Tagus, between 10 and 12 November, of several Russian warships under the command of Admiral Siniavim. This squadron had been ordered to sail from Corfu (off the Greek coast) back to its home base in the Baltic. The westerly gales, fatal for ships sailing up the coast close to land, had forced the squadron to enter the Tagus, the only shelter on the coast. Admiral Siniavim chose to ignore the treaties that limited to six the number of foreign warships that were allowed to enter the port at any one time. In addition he did not land his gunpowder. In spite of this, the Prince Regent received him in audience. The prince realised, as a result of the Treaty of Tilsit, that the Russians could not be considered friendly. On the other hand, he had too many problems with Britain and France to want to start yet another front.

Sir Sidney Smith, when he arrived off the bar of the Tagus a few days later, was to find the situation equally confusing.[40]

Amongst the various lines of action under development, as already mentioned, was a Convention with Britain. There is no specific mention in the minutes of the State Council meetings of instructing D. Domingos to negotiate on behalf of his country. Although D. Domingos appears not to have returned to Portugal during the 1807 crisis, the Convention that would directly and indirectly regulate the relationship between the two powers, during and subsequent to the 1807–08 crisis, was presented to D. João, who signed it on 8 November with certain restrictions:[41]

> With reference to that which came from Domingos, it should be kept totally secret, for if anything were to be divulged it would be disastrous… a reply to that which came from England also is urgent, for D. Domingos will not come without it.[42]

The news brought by D. Lourenço, that he had been told by Talleyrand that Bonaparte did not have malicious intentions towards Portugal and that within three days retaliations would be suspended, was not accepted in Lisbon, especially as D. Lourenço had not brought anything in writing. The army of 25,000 men under the command of Junot, known as the 'Armée du Portugal', gathered in Bayonne; and the presence of Spanish troops in Badajoz, were clear indications of Bonaparte's intentions.[43]

Government circles in Lisbon believed that the reason that Junot had been put in command was not because he knew Portugal (he had been there before as Ambassador), but because he had become involved in an affair with General Murat's wife during his absence from Paris. On his return Murat had demanded from Bonaparte the imprisonment or banishment of Junot.[44]

At the end of October news was received in Lisbon that the Spanish army had left the frontier and had returned to Madrid. For a moment, D. Araújo believed that the measures taken by the State Council had been effective in averting the invasion; all in vain, for within a few days both the French and Spanish armies were marching to the frontier.[45]

On 1 November the disquieting news was received that in Spain the heir apparent, D. Ferdinando, Prince of Astúrias,[46] had been jailed by order of Godoy – who, together with the queen, his lover, effectively ruled the country – on the discovery of a plot. The origin of this conspiracy was because of the prince's fear that Godoy would not allow him to succeed his weak father. This fact may explain why the troops had temporarily returned to Madrid.

The Prince Regent's next step was to ask each of his councillors to prepare a written opinion on what should be done, particularly in view of the latest developments. Enéas Martins Filho transcribes these notes.[47] They agreed, without exception, that in spite of having done everything possible to reconcile the demands of France with the minimum of aggression towards Britain, Bonaparte had shown that he was not prepared to accept less than his original demands. The disastrous consequences to the people that would result from a French invasion had to be weighed before any negative trading effects that might be suffered by Britain. This being the case, they should cede to Bonaparte's demands, but treating Britain in the least offensive way possible. The Marquis of Belas wrote:

> Order the confiscation and detention of individuals with the least possible offence, for this purpose choose the most prudent officials, give them private instructions, so that they may not offend, as far as possible, the Englishmen's interests…

In total agreement, D. Fernando José de Portugal wrote:

> This violent measure, but necessary at this moment, I do not believe so damaging to England, if it should have been taken at the beginning; the richest English merchants have already left, after settling their accounts and assets.

In his opinion, the British representative, Lord Strangford, should leave Portugal at once: his presence was embarrassing and might give France a false impression of friendship with Britain. On 30 October D. Araújo wrote: "…Today the English representative took down the coat of arms …"[48]

On learning of the closure of the ports Lord Strangford, on 4 November, wrote to D. Araújo demanding to know what other measures were being planned, threatening that Britain would take strong action should any of her subjects be harmed.[49] D. Araújo wrote to the prince's secretary:

> At last the note from Lord Strangford, which is so important, has been received; its contents as I had expected. I will show it to the Councillors, but today I do not have time, so will only show it to the Marquis of Belas; let him confirm afterwards whether he still intends to vote as previously, as

yesterday he did not seem to believe that the English would enter the Tagus to burn and capture the squadron. What a blow that would be.[50]

On 5 November, the Prince Regent signed the decree that completed Bonaparte's demands against Britain.

On the 9th the State Council, presided by the Prince Regent, met at the Palace of N[a]. S[a]. da Ajuda. The minutes show that the official declarations of war, from both France and Spain, were formally registered. In spite of them, the Council approved the immediate return of D. Lourenço to Paris,[51] in addition to the sending of the Marquis of Marialva. It was decided that the fleet should be made ready should it be necessary to transport the royal family to Brazil. In the meantime troops should be sent to guard the country's frontiers. The British representative should be asked to leave "…by every polite means the representative of England should be persuaded to leave this capital, his continued presence here implicates us with France…"[52]

In Lisbon, on the night of the 17th, Lord Strangford received a letter from D. Araújo urging him to leave Lisbon at any cost "…by land or sea…" Sir Sidney Smith later wrote that in his opinion the letter was "…a distinct avow, on the part of the Portuguese government, of the relinquishment of neutrality …" It was the second important communication that Lord Strangford had received that day for, earlier on, dispatches from England and from Sir Sidney Smith, a few leagues off the Tagus bar, had arrived with Sir Sidney's secretary. He had had an eventful journey, first transferring from the flagship HMS *London* to the *Active* – a brig sailing under a letter of marque,[53] that took him to the bar; and then to a Portuguese fishing boat. Lord Strangford decided to follow D. Araújo's advice and next morning, accompanied by his staff and taking the legation archives, left Lisbon by the same route followed by Sir Sidney's secretary the day before, and at approximately 5.30 p.m. was received on board the *London*.[54]

The march of the French army across Spain, and the massing of the Spanish army in preparation to cross the Portuguese frontier, was closely followed in Lisbon.[55] The only doubt remaining was as to whether the Prince Regent had full access to this information. The French headquarters would be in Alcântara, so wrote on 11 September M. Hermann, the ex-French Consul in Lisbon. During the occupation he was named Commissioner of France, attached to the Regency Council and General Administrator of Finance.

Throughout September and October French armed forces had been collecting in Bayonne. This news had been received intermittently in Lisbon. Spanish troop movements, across the border in Badajoz, were also reported. Between 19 October and 3 November[56] French troops passed through Irun and entered Spain. The long march to the Portuguese frontier had begun. The account of the crossing into Portugal and the subsequent progress towards Lisbon is taken from an anonymous report written by one of Junot's officers.[57]

The march across Spain to Alcântara was uneventful except that, as little warning had been given to the Spanish government, supplies with which to feed the troops were scarce. On 14 November the first detachment of 8,000 men reached Alcântara, the remainder arriving over the next few days.[58]

At the beginning of November the Marquis of Alorna, Governor of the Alentejo, received orders to keep Junot's troops, who were bivouacked in Alcântara, under observation.

The invasion of Portugal was scheduled for the night of 20 November. The Tagus and its tributary, the Erges, marked the frontier nearest to Alcântara. The initial plan was to avoid any existing bridges which, it was imagined – incorrectly – would be heavily guarded. The River Erges, beside Salvaterra, was chosen but as it turned out, a combination of a river greatly swollen from the recent heavy rains and the lack of materials with which to build a bridge soon made the reconnoitering party give up. The existing bridge in Segura would be used instead. Although many of the small villages – Penamacor, Rosmaninhal and Monsanto – had defences, none were used against the French.

In Lisbon the imminent invasion by the French forces made the Marquis of Angeja recommend to the Prince Regent that he should send an emissary to enquire from Junot as to his intentions. Oliveira Barreto[59] was chosen. On 1 November D. Araújo wrote:

I will carry out, as I must, the orders of your Royal Highness sending Barreto, perhaps leaving tomorrow afternoon. What I would wish is that your Royal Highness tell him, or anyone else, that it is your firm determination to go to Brazil, and would only not do so if troops were not to invade.

Barreto left on the 22nd.

D. Araújo considered sending D. Lourenço to confer with François Hermann, in Alcântara. The lack of transport was the excuse D. Lourenço gave not to travel.[60]

The bad weather and the extreme poverty of the sparsely-populated region, with almost total lack of food, made the next stage of the march, to Castelo Branco, difficult to accomplish. However, the region was well supplied with wine. Drunkenness and disorder became rife, obliging Junot to carry out severe punishments in order to maintain discipline.[61]

Divided into small detachments, the armed forces made their way slowly to Abrantes. Fortified positions, in São Domingos and Mação, could easily have halted them – in the opinion of the French officer writing the report. Beyond Abrantes, their next obstacle was the River Zêzere, flowing at great speed and with an increased volume of water. The troops had little respect for sacred buildings. The Parish Church of Sta. Maria do Castelo and, in Abrantes, the Church of St Anthony and the convent of the Capuchins suffered much damage.

A bridge made up of boats was constructed and the baggage was taken across the water, helped by the local population. Tomar, Santarém and Vila França, the next towns on their route, were better provided with food, making their journey easier.

Barreto wrote that he hoped to meet Junot on the night of the 26th, either in Punhete or in Tancos. Surprisingly, Junot was badly informed:

> I can already assure your Excellency, that the General was ignorant of the fact that the English had left Portugal and that the ports are closed to them; they are also unaware that a Russian squadron had entered the Tagus.[62]

He goes on to comment on the state of the troops:

> I can also tell your Excellency, that the troops come in a miserable state, lacking in even the basics: they do not create disturbances other than to plunder for their necessities, which have run short; very few shoes, which they also require, have been obtained.

Tobias Monteiro[63] confirms the poor condition that the French fighting forces found themselves in after a month's forced march under adverse weather conditions and with little food:

> Bare-footed and without ammunition, the soldiers gathered together all the shoes that they could find, turned the paper archives in Alcântara into wadding then took the gun powder they found there and made for Abrantes. The Spanish troops were of little help – of a low quality – and, for this reason, sent back. Of the 23,000 men that set off from Bayonne only 15,000, much weakened, managed to arrive there; the remainder had been left or deserted on the way. Quickly repairing those arms which were of use and choosing the best men, after crossing the River Beira, Junot continued on his way to Lisbon; even then he was to be delayed a further two days, the 26th and 27th, as the Zêzere was in flood, and there was no means of crossing.

Meanwhile at sea, HMS *Plantagenet* and HM sloop *Confiance*, which had left Plymouth on 15 November and had brought dispatches for Lord Strangford and Sir Sidney Smith, almost certainly brought out the copy of the French newspaper, *Le Moniteur*, published on 11 November. It carried an article that left no doubts as to France's intentions:

> The Prince Regent of Portugal loses his throne; he loses it because of the intrigues of the English... What does England, this powerful ally, do? Looks on with indifference as to what is happening in Portugal. What will she do when Portugal is taken? Will she go and take possession of Brazil?

… The fall of the House of Bragança is but another proof of the loss which is suffered by all those united with the English.[64]

On 24 November HM sloop *Confiance* sailed for Lisbon under a flag of truce, taking dispatches from England and letters from Sir Sidney Smith and Lord Strangford. It is probable that the *Le Moniteur* was amongst the papers being taken. *Confiance* moored opposite Belém tower, at 7 p.m. The officer in charge of the correspondence was rowed ashore.

The news received the day before – that French troops were inside Portuguese territory, making all haste to reach Lisbon – added to the information carried by *Le Moniteur* as to the destiny that Bonaparte had in store for Portugal and her royal family, closed off any options she might have had.

On 24 November, at the Palace of Nª. Sª. da Ajuda, the last meeting of the State Council, prior to embarkation, took place.

The Council recognised that the situation was such that all possible alternatives were exhausted and, that being the case, the royal family should leave for Brazil at once. The port would be reopened to British ships, both naval and merchant. Troops guarding the river front would be moved elsewhere. A note received from Sir Sidney was answered and the request from Lord Strangford for a meeting with the Prince Regent granted. It was further decided that in the absence of the Prince Regent whilst in Brazil, a Regency Council[65] would be instituted, with powers to be delegated by him.

This Regency Council was to be created with the following members: D. Pedro de Lancastre da Silveira Castelo Branco Sá e Meneses, 1763–1828, 5th Marquis d'Abrantes; the lieutenant generals D. Francisco Xavier de Noronha and Francisco da Cunha Meneses; D. Francisco Rafael de Castro, Head of the Patriarchal Church; Pedro de Melo Breyner; and D. Manuel Antônio de Sampaio Melo e Castro Muniz e Torres Lusignano, Count of Sampaio. Substitutes were D. Miguel Forjaz; and D. Francisco de Melo da Cunha Mendonça e Meneses, 1761–1821, 1st Count of Castro Marim and 1st Marquis of Olhão.

In the early afternoon of 27 November, as described by the Viscount of Rio Seco,[66] the royal family went on board the ships that would take them on the long voyage. The scene recorded by L'Evêque, an Italian engraver who had worked in England before moving to Portugal, and later reproduced by Bartollozi, a painter and engraver of the Swiss school; in contrast to the reality of the occasion, evoked organisation and tranquility.[67]

In 1821 the Viscount of Rio Seco wrote his memoirs[68] and as he took an active part in the arrangements for the embarkation, they are a valuable record of these last few hectic days before departure:

On November 25, at about midnight, orders were received to go and speak to the King… at Ajuda. Without wasting one moment I left accompanied by the bearer of the order... there the Viscount of Rio Seco was given his orders directly by His Majesty as to arrangements for the embarkation which had to take place, without fail, on the afternoon of the 27th... he immediately took action, making his way to the office of the Gentleman of the Bedchamber, the Marquis of Vagos,[69] so that he should summon the Count of Redondo, Administrator of the Royal Stores and Manoel da Cunha, Admiral of the Squadron; together they would decide on the action to be taken, each within his own sphere. In the meantime he made his way to the Palace of Necessidades to begin the embarkation of those effects which were to be found there and, to arrange with Father José Eloi, the removal of all the belongings of the Holy Patriarchal Church... he went on to Belém, to establish his office at the wharf, and from there to distribute the families amongst the various ships, in accordance with the space available, and also to send (on board) all the baggage arriving from the Treasury: he continued until three o'clock of the afternoon of the 27th, when His Majesty arrived at the wharf to embark, followed by all the other members of the royal family... when nearly all the baggage and families were organised, he set about making arrangements for himself, his wife and children, to follow the same path as those that had already embarked. On the night of the 27th, at 9 p.m., he was called by the government that His Majesty during his absence had left behind to rule, and informed that he had been made responsible for the quarters (Lisbon) to be occupied by Junot. This measure upset his own plans...

After a day of many adventures the Viscount of Rio Seco, in return for sending some cattle on board the frigate *Urânia*, which had on the 27th moved her berth to a position in front of Belém castle at the request of D. João de Almeida, managed to get his family and himself on board the *Principe do Brasil*. "It was between nine and ten o'clock in the morning when a search carried out by an official of the Treasury located a boat to ferry him to the ship, leaving behind, in his office, some money, a hat and papers."[70]

In addition to the royal family, members of the Court and their families that made the voyage included the dukes of Cadaval; the marquises of Alegrete, Angeja, Belas, Lavradio, Pombal, Torres Novas and Vagos; the Marchioness of St Miguel and Lumiares; the counts of Belmonte, Caparica, Cavaleiros, Pombeiro and Redondo; the Viscount of Anadia; D. Antônio de Araújo de Azevedo; D. Fernando José de Portugal; D. João de Almeida; D. Rodrigo de Sousa Coutinho; Chief Justice Tomás Antônio de Vila Nova Portugal and many others.

Preparations for such a journey were not made from one moment to another, as Oliveira Lima pointed out:

Following the news of the invasion of the national teritory by French troops, to embark in a squadron of eight line-of-battle ships, four frigates, three brigs, a schooner and a number of merchantmen, a complete court, with its furniture, household wares, paintings, books and jewellery… even with today's facilities, this cannot be done from one moment to another.[71]

A certain Christiano Muller, that some months before had been put in charge of making an inventory of the papers, books, maps, and prints belonging to D. Antônio de Araújo, wrote from Lisbon to D. Domingos Coutinho in London, that on the night of the 25th of November, he was woken up and ordered to pack all the belongings of the Secretary of State, which he did, sending on the following day 37 large boxes on board the *Medusa*, under heavy rain.[72]

There was no longer any point, and nor was it feasible, to maintain the departure secret. It came as no surprise, therefore, when the formal public proclamation was issued by the Prince Regent, on 28 November, when already on board.[73]

As soon as he heard of the intended departure of the royal family, the Apostolic Nuncio, Monsignor Caleppi,[74] prepared himself for the journey. On the 26th, in an interview with the Prince Regent, he reminded him that he should try and take with him the gold, silver and jewels from the Patriarchal Church and royal chapels, so as to save them from the pillage habitually practised by the French. The prince, pleased with the desire of the Nuncio to follow him in spite of his age and of the fact that at that moment he found himself infirm, told him to make his arrangements with the Viscount of Anadia. However, in spite of all the efforts of this minister and, even after contacting the captains of both the *Medusa* and the *Martim de Freitas*, it became clear that there was not enough room to convey all those who wanted to accompany the royal family. Camilo Luis de Rossi writes:[75]

In fact the disorder and confusion during those few days were such that, not even the bishop of Rio de Janeiro,[76] even though required by the responsibilities of his office and bearing express orders from the Prince Regent to be received on board the Portuguese squadron, not even he was able to find a place, and so was forced to remain in Lisbon. D. Pedro de Sousa Holstein,[77] in spite of his prestige – he was a Captain in the Royal Guard – also was unable to find room on board a ship. The same thing happened to various cases containing silver and valuable sacred vessels, already packed; as also several coaches belonging to the court. In addition many valuables not yet packed remained forgotten and abandoned on land and not embarked.

The confusion at this last moment was such that orders from the Prince Regent dated 28 November on board the *Principe Real* authorising the necessary expenditure on water, firewood and other necessities, only reached the Viscount of Anadia a year later, on 11 December 1808![78]

Various accounts exist of the embarkation, all of which describe, to a varying degree, the utter confusion. This is not hard to understand. On the one hand there was a multitude of civilians, most of whom had never been on board a ship, having to close up and leave their homes, and with a foreign army invading their town at any moment, having to put their persons and belongings on board ships anchored in the middle of the River Tagus on those rainy, windy, cold winter days. On the other hand, all this was happening whilst surrounded by relations, friends and strangers, who would be staying behind to face the unknown consequences under an army of occupation. The Viscount of Rio Seco wrote in his memoirs:

> The noble and always loyal citizens of Lisbon, could not get used to the idea of the departure of the King for his overseas possessions… Wandering aimlessly in the squares and roads in disbelief of what they were seeing, they found relief in tears, cursing the hardship that pressed on their breast, their hearts painful from their sighs; everything was horror, everything sorrow, yearning, and that noble suffering character, that has always sustained the people, nearly sank into despair![79]

Eusébio Gomes, storekeeper of the Mafra Palace, wrote in his diary:

> It is impossible to describe what happened at the Belém quayside on the occasion of the embarkation of the royal family that had left Mafra with all haste when it was learnt that the French were about to arrive in Lisbon. What confusion then ensued! Everyone wanting to embark, the quay covered with boxes, chests, trunks, cases, and one thousand and one items; many were to remain behind as their owners embarked; some were embarked even though their owners could not follow. What disorder and what confusion: the Queen not wanting to embark at any cost, the Prince worried for this reason!!! It was Laranja (Francisco Laranja, frigate captain and head of the royal galliots) who persuaded the Queen to embark. Then all present kissed the Prince's hand and, between tears and sighs, they started to board; it is not possible to describe what happened here.[80]

Marcus Cheke, although not identifying his sources, wrote of this utter confusion:

> Meanwhile, Lisbon was in a state of pandemonium unparalleled since the great earthquake. The priests of San Roque hurried to conceal their far-famed relics. They bricked up the skull of St. Crysanthus of Basle, the

thigh-bone of St. Procopius, the arm of St. Josippa, the authenticated skulls of several of the eleven-thousand virgins and (O wonder!) the complete head of St. Gregory Thaumaturgus… the Lisbon quays, blocked with carriages, and piled with furniture, treasure and trunks, presented a scene of indescribable confusion. The books and manuscripts of the royal libraries, the archives of the Foreign Office, the silver plate from the Ajuda Palace and the fabulous accoutrements of the Patriarchate, lay sprawling under torrents of rain.[81]

The consequences of the approaching army under Junot now began to be felt. Lieutenant Count Thomas O'Neil, a marine officer on board HMS *London*, describes in detail, including dialogue, a meeting that supposedly took place, on the 28th, on board the *Príncipe Real*, between the Prince Regent and Junot.[82]

Junot's arrival in Lisbon, in the early hours of the 30th, is so well documented that we can discard O'Neil's version of the event. On the date in question O'Neil was far away in the open sea. However, it is possible that he heard rumours that a meeting had taken place with an important Frenchman, whom he presumed to be Junot. Camilo Luis de Rossi, secretary to the Nuncio Apostólico, wrote that the Nuncio, on returning home after giving up all hope of embarking, found a message from M. Hermann asking him to meet him at a private residence where he was staying. From Santarém, accompanied by José de Oliveira Barreto, he had come down the Tagus to Lisbon[83] and now, having arrived secretly, he was very uneasy to learn that the royal family had embarked. The Nuncio, foreseeing that his intention was to try and forestall the sailing, went to meet him and recommended that he try and obtain permission to go on board from the Chief of Police, Lucas de Seabra.[84] Immediately after this conversation had taken place the Nuncio made his way to the Chief of Police's residence and, rousing him from his bed, warned him of M. Hermann's intention. M. Hermann's visit to Lucas de Seabra was frustrated, as the latter told him that he did not have authority to issue a permit to go on board the Prince Regent's ship.[85]

Historian Luz Soriano[86] claimed that M. Hermann managed to see the Prince Regent that night. Even so, it would appear improbable. The most appropriate person to be contacted by a diplomat, to obtain the required permission, would have been D. Araújo:[87] he was State Secretary for Foreign Affairs and, by then, on board the *Medusa*. When writing to the Prince Regent that night about the visit of Lord Strangford, he would certainly have mentioned meeting M. Hermann, had he received him on board. As will be seen, later that very same night Lord Strangford went on board the *Medusa* to arrange with D. Araújo the time of his appointment next day with the Prince Regent.

The royal family and Court on board their ships waited for final preparations to be completed and, most importantly, for the westerly wind to swing round to the east. Without it the ships remained prisoners in the Tagus, powerless, expecting at any moment the arrival of the French troops.

Chapter III

Portugal and Britain negotiate a Convention. A British squadron, under Sir William Sidney Smith, puts to sea and sails for Lisbon. The weather continues both cold and windy. Sir Sidney experiences considerable difficulty in maintaining the squadron off the Portuguese coast. Events lead him to institute a blockade of the port.

The signing of the Convention on 22 October[1] made the British Cabinet ponder on the principal objectives which, it was hoped, could be achieved within the worsening situation and within the political and commercial longstanding relationship with Portugal.

In the first place, and above anything else, on no account should the Portuguese fleet be allowed to fall into the hands of France. Although not large if compared to that of Britain, France or Spain, it nevertheless was substantial: eight line-of-battle ships, four frigates and a dozen corvettes, brigantines and schooners[2] – a useful increase to the enemy fleet. Portuguese officers were an additional asset as far as Britain was concerned for, during the period 1750–1800, a large contingent of British naval officers had been recruited to serve in the Portuguese navy.[3] During the two decades before 1807 at least thirty-five officers had served in the Portuguese navy. Several of them: Philip Hancorn, Thomas Stone and Donald Campbell reaching a rank equivalent to that of Admiral. As a result, the two services had a certain uniformity in their training, discipline and seamanship.

Commercial interests were at stake, as Portugal was an important trading partner; more so now, since the introduction by Bonaparte of the Continental System. By the autumn of 1807, following the capitulation of Denmark, trading by Britain with Europe had, with the exception of Portugal, virtually been brought to a standstill. Some goods got through by being landed in Gibraltar and then transferred to neutral ships.[4] If Portugal was, as appeared likely in the near future, to be part of the Continental System, then Britain had to look elsewhere to substitute this loss. Nothing could be more natural then than to replace this shortfall with trade with Portugal's colony, Brazil.

The opportunity to force a change to this, one of the pillars of Portuguese commercial policy was, for Britain, an important moment. The very substantial help that Britain could offer through its domination of the seas would give the Portuguese monarchy a lifeline to survival and, in its overseas colony, even to prosperity. In exchange for the safe conduct of the royal family to Brazil and then guarding the newly-formed nation from an attack from the sea, Portugal agreed to open at least one of its Brazilian ports, possibly that of Santa Catarina, to Britain. This change of policy was not difficult to rationalise.[5] In fact, with the monarchy firmly established in Brazil, with Portugal occupied by France, with whom would Brazil trade if not with Britain and other friendly and neutral nations?

By offering help at this, Portugal's hour of need, Britain would in the future establish and maintain a base from which a bridgehead could be built, in due course, allowing forces to be garrisoned and trained to fight against Bonaparte. The troops, whilst on Portuguese territory, would be greeted with friendship and co-operation – a material asset to any occupying force. Wellington[6] was to raise a substantial number of Portuguese troops to fight alongside his own. Once fully trained, under Marshal Viscount Beresford,[7] he considered them second to none.[8]

Portugal, in the weaker bargaining position, was fighting for her very survival as a nation. By the terms of the Convention, in exchange for protection during the journey to Brazil and subsequently whilst establishing herself, she had to hand over to Britain, in trust until peace returned, any ships that for whatever reason could not embark on the voyage or, in the event that the voyage did not take place, her military and merchant fleets. Also, Portugl was to hand over the island of Madeira, on deposit until peace was restored. The island was an important staging point, both to garrison troops and as a supply and watering base on the route to South America or South Africa. Portugal stipulated that Britain, with the void left in Portugal in the absence of the monarchy, would not, in the future, recognise any other prince as having the right to that crown. D. João feared the imposition of Bonaparte's relations, or the breakup of his kingdom, as had occurred elsewhere. In this he was right, as the Treaty of Fontainebleau, signed subsequently to this Convention, was to show.

The Convention – agreed by D. Domingos Antônio de Souza Coutinho, Plenipotentiary Minister, on behalf of the Prince Regent; and the Rt Hon George Canning,[9] Principal Secretary of State for Foreign Affairs, on behalf of the king – had a rough passage before final consensus was reached. On 22 October D. Domingos, on signing, stated that he had not been instructed on the two additional articles, and that therefore they were outside his powers.[10] The Prince Regent ratified the Convention subject to changes in the preamble, the first and second articles, and in the first of the additional articles,[11] also excluded by D. Domingos. The Rt Hon George Canning disagreed with the changes and suspended the signing of the Convention.[12] Final ratification by Britain only took place on 4 January 1808. By then Portugal's action showed that she meant to observe the Convention.

Time was running out both for Portugal and for Britain, if they were to take steps to safeguard the Portuguese fleet from falling to France. The Convention, which required

Britain to provide vessels and forces, was the instrument that set the Rt Hon George Canning at the Foreign Office, and the lords of the Admiralty, into activity.

To mount a squadron at short notice was a monumental task. Ships had to be chosen and made ready for sea, perhaps to spend several months without entering a port, and several years without returning to Britain.

Victualling was highly organised and less of a problem than providing a full complement of crew: 600 or more men for a typical 74-line-of-battle ship. Difficulties with manning were such that a homecoming vessel might well transfer part of her crew before docking, to another setting out on a voyage so as avoid losing any of the trained men. On occasions ships did not come alongside a dock in port. It was said that the Admiralty did not encourage the art of swimming, to prevent men quitting their ship whilst it was tied to a buoy. Even merchant ships were in danger, for they were habitually stopped on the high seas and, subject to certain regulations, could lose part of their crew to a fighting ship.

The commander chosen to lead this mission was Rear Admiral Sir William Sidney Smith,[13] recently returned from a successful action against the Turks.

Britain had a number of naval bases, of which the most important were Chatham and Portsmouth. Plymouth, however, was chosen as being the natural departure point for a squadron whose destination was Lisbon. Although at a greater distance from Whitehall, where the Admiralty was located, orders could be sent in a very short space of time by telegraph: a wooden frame with movable shutters. In the case of Plymouth, it involved twenty-eight stations along a line that had been inaugurated the year before. Bonfires could be lit so that the line, if necessary, could operate at night. Mists and fog, however, made the system unreliable.

Orders of a more complex nature or those that had to be kept secret, as was this case, had to be taken by hand. So at 3 p.m. on Saturday, 7 November, messenger George Lilburne set off from the Admiralty at Whitehall with Sir Sidney Smith's secret orders and, travelling non-stop via Bath, reached Plymouth at 5 a.m. on the 9th.[14]

~ Monday, 9 November

The orders from the Admiralty to Sir Sidney Smith were concise and clear. Take command of HM ships *London, Elizabeth, Marlborough, Monarch and Bedford* and HM frigate *Solebay*; proceed at once to sea and remain off the Tagus until further orders. On arrival establish communications with Lord Strangford or, in his absence, with Lt Gen Sir John Moore, with whom the fullest co-operation is expected.[15]

The ships at anchor at Cawsand Bay, Plymouth, were preparing to put to sea. The movement in the harbour was intense, with the coming and going of lighters and the arrival of further vessels. HM ships *Foudroyant* and *Plantagenet*, destined to join the squadron later, came in on the 8th. Likewise, HM frigate *Solebay* anchored on the evening of the 9th. Supplies taken on board included water and beer, dry provisions, boatswains and carpenters' stores and gunpowder. The *London* recorded receiving two thousand seven hundred and thirty seven pounds of fresh beef, part of it destined for the Ferrol blockading squadron, which they would meet en route. In preparation for sailing the rigging had to be set up. This involved raising the various masts and spars, checking that all the cables were in position and that all the sails, including spares and sail cloth, were on board.

Sir Sidney Smith wrote that the *London* was not fitted to be used as a flagship.[16] The second rate 98-gun three-decker had been launched at Chatham in 1766, so she was by then forty-one years old, nearing the end of her useful life.[17] He had hoped to be able to sail in the much larger *Hibernia*, a first rate of 110 guns, built in Plymouth and launched in 1804. Compared to the *London* she was some twenty-five feet longer and 700 tons heavier. HMS *Hibernia*[18] was nearby, in Torbay, and on 7 November put to sea to join the squadron in Cawsand Bay.[19] From the force and direction of the wind, it was improbable that she would arrive before the squadron sailed. Foreseeing this, *Marlborough* took on board her purser's stores.

Ships of the line were classified according to the number of guns with which they were armed. A first rate carried over 100 guns, a second rate 90 to 98 guns, a third rate 64 to 80 guns, a fourth rate 50 to 60 guns, a fifth rate 30 to 44 guns and a sixth rate 20 to 30 guns. For the purpose of classification the carronade, with its short barrel and heavy shot, very effective at close range, did not count as a gun. The weight of shot that her broadside could throw was the determining factor in deciding whether a ship was of sufficient size to go into the line and face the enemy. In practice, third rate ships were the smallest size employed in a line. From the numbers built, third rates were a popular size: in 1807 there were 145, as compared to 8 first rates, 15 second rates and 20 fourth rates.[20] Within that class, the 74-gun line-of-battle ship was by far the most numerous – the result of many decades of experience. In 1807 the British navy comprised 850 ships and 120,000 men.

In a fighting ship her sailing qualities and the size and location of her guns were of paramount importance. Conflicting requirements had to be managed. Placed too low down, near the waterline, her gun ports could not be opened in rough seas or when sailing with a strong wind producing a list. Their range was limited. Placed too high, they required heavily-reinforced decks built from much more expensive timber, and raised the centre of gravity – an important consideration regarding the ship's safety when sailing in gale force winds and heavy seas. In order to build such a ship 2,000 oak trees were needed, occupying fifty-seven acres of forest. Design of a '74' had evolved to a vessel some 175 feet long by 50 wide and 20 deep, with three covered decks: the orlop, the lower or gun deck and the upper; and also the quarter deck, open to the sky in the centre part, and closed at the stern (the poop) as well as at the bow (the forecastle).[21] The lower and upper decks were the main gun platforms, but lighter guns were placed on the poop, and bow chasers could be mounted on the forecastle, so as to be able to fire forward.

Space on board a fighting ship was extremely tight. A 74, for instance, had to carry guns, powder and shot, a crew of 600 men as well as 150 marines, provision for several months, and water: in the case of *Bedford,* some 224 tons. In addition, these ships carried five boats, each of between twenty-five and thirty feet in length, half a dozen anchors, sails for all types of weather, cables, arms and stores for the marines, spare masts and spars, sail cloth, stoves, hammocks and untold amounts of other essential equipment.

Ballast, in the form of pig iron, lined the bottom of the hold. Then came water casks and dried provisions in different-sized containers. Dry bread, or biscuit, as it was generally known, was kept in a separate room, as were spirits. Gunpowder was also kept in the hold, with a small room beside it known as the 'light room' to provide illumination, but at the same time avoid the risk of contact and explosion. Spirits and gunpowder were kept under permanent guard.

The orlop deck contained cabins for the surgeon and junior officers; stores of lighter materials, such as clothes; and a central area where the main cable was stowed. It was here that during battle space would be made available for use as a temporary hospital.

The gun decks were the sleeping quarters for the crew. This is where they slung their hammocks and bedding. The area available, divided by the size of the crew, only permitted a width of fourteen inches per man. In practice, at sea this would be greater, as part of the crew was always busy on watch. The head room between gun decks was five feet, the orlop somewhat less. Officers had cubicles made from removable partitions on the upper decks. The captain occupied the stern of the quarter deck, a relatively large area with windows; suitably divided for daytime duties, eating and sleeping.

At 10.30 a.m. on the same day as he had received his orders, Sir Sidney Smith and his staff went on board HMS *London*. Capt Thomas Western fired the regulation 13-gun salute in honour of Admiral Bertie Young,[22] the Commander-in-Chief of the Plymouth base. A similar number of guns returned the salute from shore. The salute formally recognised that the command of the ship was being transferred from one admiral to another. The Rear Admiral's blue ensign was hoisted on the third or mizzen mast. Watchers on nearby ships had no doubts as to what was happening; their only doubts lay with the destination which, for security reasons, would only be revealed to their captains when they were at sea. The squadron was going to the United States, speculated the press in England.[23]

The upper hierarchy of the Admiralty was made up of officers of flag rank: those officers who were entitled to have their distinctive flag flown when on board their ship. This ship, from which all orders then originated, was known as the flagship.

The rank structure in the navy had, at its apex, the Admiral of the Fleet. Under him came admirals, vice-admirals and rear admirals, divided in order of seniority, into red, white and blue. An admiral was entitled to fly his ensign on the mainmast, similarly a vice-admiral on the foremast and rear admiral on the mizzen mast.

The squadron was now in perfect readiness but a southwesterly wind, with a great deal of sea in the offing,[24] made it impracticable to leave harbour, so reported Sir Sidney Smith[25] to the Secretary to the Admiralty, the Rt Hon William Wellesley-Pole.[26] The same wind kept the *Hibernia* from joining them at Cawsand Bay.

~ Tuesday, 10 November

The wind, still blowing from the southwest, freshened to a full gale with a heavy swell. The ships put out their largest anchor, the best bower, hung from the bows on the starboard side (her twin, the small bower, hung on the port side) and plenty of cable. *Marlborough* put out 900 feet, to help take up the strain. Most ships put out a second anchor to be on the safe side. Topgallant, topmasts and their yards were taken down, to reduce the drag from the gale force winds, and the remaining yards pointed into the wind. Under such conditions there was nothing that could be done; even Admiralty orders could not be obeyed.

~ Wednesday, 11 November

The wind began to abate and swung round to the northeast; masts and yards were raised again into position. At 2 p.m. Sir Sidney Smith returned to his flagship. She unmoored by bringing in one of her anchors and hove short on her second anchor, the best bower. *Marlborough* took a pilot on board and the various ships of the squadron began to weigh anchor, ready to depart. It was *Marlborough*'s maiden voyage, as she had only been launched on 22 June of that year.

The process of weighing required a great deal of brute force. The main weight was not of the anchor (three and half tons) or of the waterlogged cable – 25 inches in circumference and 300 yards in length – but to haul the ship, weighing perhaps 2,000 tons, to a position immediately above the anchor. Only then could she be released from the seabed. A capstan was used to bring in the cable. Slots on the upper part enabled bars to be inserted, which could then be turned by teams of ninety sailors and marines, producing a great deal of force. The cable, as it was brought in, was stowed by another team in the lowest deck, the orlop. The anchor, carefully raised so as not to damage the hull, was firmly lashed to the ship, preventing movement even in the roughest seas. This laborious process occupied, in a large vessel, over 350 men.

On being released from the seabed a vessel needed to have some sails already in position, so as to maintain control. The need for men to carry out this task was simultaneous with that of raising the anchor. This was one of the reasons why a ship carried such a numerous crew.

By the end of the afternoon of the 11th, the squadron was under sail. After rounding Penlee Point the pilot was discharged. As night descended the Eddystone Lighthouse was passed, its light shining some five or six miles away. The wind, although squally, returned to gale force. The squadron steered southwest under courses and reefed topsails, moving away from the land.

Before midnight, storm damage, very much part of shipboard life and usually quickly repaired by the carpenters and other specialists, had begun to take its toll. The *London* lost overboard her studding sail boom. After the two-day delay, Sir Sidney Smith would be pressing hard to reach the Tagus.

∼ *Thursday, 12 November*

Daybreak saw the squadron still moving at a fast pace. If the wind held and did not change direction, the squadron would make a very fast crossing of the Bay of Biscay.

Weather permitting, the latitude was checked at noon every day by measuring the angle between the sun and the horizon. Longitude, the other important coordinate, was more difficult to measure. Traditionally it was calculated by measuring the height of the moon and of a star and of the angle between them. The result could then be checked against the almanac.

Even after the introduction of an accurate clock, the chronometer, the older method continued in use.[27] The chronometer, a clock that could maintain accuracy even under the most adverse conditions, was accepted by the navy in 1774 when its inventor, John Harrison (1693–1776) was awarded the greater part of a £20,000 prize by the Board of Longitude. If bad weather prevented the carrying out of these procedures, then the only alternative was to collect the information obtained during the day from the log and course steered and, after allowing for the effects of wind and tide, plot on the chart the position by dead reckoning.

Life on board the ships had begun to settle down. On board HMS *Elizabeth*, after a short service, the body of one Benjamin Gallop, who had died the day before, was committed to the deep. Caulkers were at work caulking the lower deck. A cask of water and five of beer were opened, as well as one of butter and two of cheese.

The staple food on board consisted of bread, salted beef and pork, dried peas, oatmeal, sugar, butter and cheese. Bullocks, pigs and chickens were sometimes kept live on deck, and consumed as the voyage progressed. In port fresh beef, fruit and vegetables would be brought on board daily. In addition to water, each crew member was entitled to a daily ration of alcoholic drink: beer when available was issued at a rate of one gallon per man, or else a pint of wine or half a pint of rum, watered down by two parts to one.

In the early evening a strange sail was sighted on the starboard bow. Standing orders required that every vessel be intercepted and identified. The *London* changed her course so as to intercept the stranger and at 8.30 p.m. fired a loaded gun. The other vessel immediately responded by showing her private signal, identifying herself as HMS *Niobe*.

Flags flown by ships did not necessarily imply that they were of that nationality: every ship carried a supply of enemy and neutral flags. There was even a signal, no.

130, which read: "Hoist foreign colours the national jack to be shown at the time". The private signal, followed by her number, identified ships of HM Navy. If a conflict was about to take place, honour required that the true colours be shown, even if only at the last minute, just before giving the order to open fire. Whilst the flag was flying, fighting would continue. In the event that it became clear that defeat was inevitable, honour permitted that the colours be lowered, as a sign of surrender and to prevent unnecessary carnage. As a precaution against losing, during battle, the yard on which the flags were being flown, several might be hoisted on different yards and broken out as needed. In the British navy, if a ship was lost, for whatsoever reason, her captain was automatically court martialled.

~ Friday, 13 November

Next day, the fresh gales and squally weather continued unabated. Sailing close together under royals and, whenever conditions permitted, studding sails on both sides, their hulls raced through the turbulent seas. Only the *Monarch* sailed alone, for at daybreak she had received a signal to take up station far to the southwest, in order to extend the range of vision of the squadron; from this direction Sir Sidney expected to sight the Ferrol squadron or even the coast. The logs showed that the squadron was averaging seven and eight knots per hour.

Speed was measured by the log – a piece of wood known as a log ship fastened to a line on which knots had been tied at regular intervals. When tossed overboard and once past the turbulence caused by the ship's wake, it was allowed to drift for seven or fourteen seconds, as measured by the small sandglass. The length of line that had drifted out with the log enabled the speed of the ship to be calculated.

In the meantime HM frigate *Solebay*, which had left Cawsand Bay with the squadron, was sailing alone, nearly twenty-four hours behind. Nevertheless she was fully occupied. At 2.30 p.m. she hauled up and went in chase of a brig, but it was nearly 5 p.m before she was close enough to fire a six-pounder to bring her to. Her documents showed her to be a merchant from Amsterdam bound for Oporto. At 9.45 p.m. another vessel was sighted, this time clearly a warship. The crew sprang into activity with the order to beat to quarters and clear the ship for action. A further two hours passed before the *Niobe* was close enough for her identification signal to be recognised. The ships exchanged news and sailed on together until 3 a.m., when the *Niobe* parted company in chase of a sail bearing north.

The beating of drums, usually playing the tune 'Hearts of Oak', summoned the gun crews to their stations. In order to prepare for battle the gun decks had to be cleared of all obstructions. These included partitions forming the cabins, chairs, personal belongings, hammocks and so on. It was not unknown, if the battle was about to take place, to clear the decks by throwing everything overboard, rather than stowing below as was more usual. Guns would be untied and got ready, powder and shot brought up, and fires lit beside each gun. The gun crews, trained from regular practice, would take up their stations and prepare for aiming and firing. Supremacy in a battle was decided, just as often, by the speed with which broadsides could be delivered as the accuracy of the firing.

Still the officers and crews of the squadron did not officially know their destinations. But now, far from their port of departure, the risk of information leakage had disappeared. In the early afternoon the flagship signalled no. 151: 'Open sealed orders no. 1'.

~ *Saturday, 14 November*

At first light of dawn, signal no. 161: 'The Admiral has discovered land' was hoisted on the flagship. The lookout had spotted Cape Belém, one of the many capes on the northwestern coast of Spain. The crossing of the Bay of Biscay, renowned for its bad weather, was over.

At 10 a.m., after the exchange of private signals to identify each other, part of the squadron blockading the port of Ferrol joined company.

Blockading an enemy port was a duty requiring great skill, because of the weather, but at the same time boring, as attempts to draw the enemy out of port were nearly always frustrated. Every three or four months a blockading ship had to be relieved so that she could replenish her water and provisions. The Ferrol squadron, comprising HM ships *Achilles*, *Audacious* and *Theseus* and HM frigates *Amazon*, *Iris* and *Penelope*, was no exception.

The meeting of the two squadrons did not last long. HMS *London* received on board Capt Sir Richard King[28] of HMS *Achilles* for a briefing. Then, after transferring five hundred and twenty-seven pounds of fresh beef and vegetables brought out from Plymouth, the squadron continued on its way.

Fame and honour had come to Captain King at Trafalgar when, as part of British Lee Column and in command of this same *Achilles*, he had entered battle, chasing the Spanish 74 *Montañes*, under Captain Francisco Alced, who moved out of range, refusing to fight. Then, in sailing to the aid of the 74 *Belleisle*, under Captain William Hargood, which, under attack from three enemy ships was by then already without her masts, he intercepted the Spanish 74 *Argonauta* and after an hour-long exchange of broadsides, the Spanish vessel, after trying unsuccessfully to raise her mainsail and escape, appeared to be giving up as she withdrew her lower-level guns and closed their ports. As Captain King prepared to board, the French *Achille* passed by, forcing her to exchange broadsides and, at the same time, another French 74, the *Berwick*, under Captain Jean Camas, hove to between the *Achilles* and her prize. The French *Achille* moved off in the direction of the already outnumbered *Belleisle*, leaving the *Achilles* and the *Berwick* to fight alone. After another hour of broadsides, the *Berwick* struck her colours and was captured by the *Achilles*. Captain King reported only seventy-four casualties, a miraculously small number, as his ship had lost all three masts and her bowsprit, and her hull was badly holed. The French *Berwick*, previously a third rate, in a worse state, suffered 250 casualties, including her captain. The Spanish *Argonauta*, much damaged, lost 300 men, including her captain, Antônio Pareja. The French *Achille*, later in the battle, exploded and sank and, in spite of all efforts to reach survivours, lost over 500 men.[29]

After four days of incessant gales it was inevitable that dampness would invade every corner. The officers of different vessels tried to deal with the problem in several ways. *Elizabeth* lit Brodies stoves between decks, whilst *London* ordered the airing of bedding and the slinging of clean hammocks.

Another important face of shipboard life was discipline; strict but fair disciple on board a fighting ship was of paramount importance. The guidelines were laid down in the Articles of War, regularly read out to the crew; usually when mustered for divine service on Sundays. The penalty for violation of many of the articles of war was death. The more usual punishment, for lesser offences such as drunkenness, fighting, stealing and falling asleep whilst on duty, was flogging – carried out with the cat-o-nine-tails: nine pieces of rope, each with three knots tied at intervals. More serious offenders would be taken by boat from ship to ship and flogged before each ship's crew. Officers were not immune from punishment: Admiral John Byng, court-martialled for failing to prevent the French from taking Minorca in 1756, was shot on the quarterdeck of HMS *Monarch*, a previous namesake of the present ship.

∼ *Sunday, 15 November*

The gale finally moderated and the fresh breeze allowed for an increase in sail area. The reefs were taken out of the sails; and as a result the logs of *Elizabeth*, *Marlborough* and *Monarch* were able to record nine and ten knots. At such speeds some damage was inevitable. *London* lost the recall flag from her masthead, *Marlborough* sprung her main topsail yard and *Monarch* split a jib. The *Solebay*, then approaching Cape Finisterre, fared worse. In the early morning she lost her mizzen topgallant mast, but as her carpenters set to work at once, before midnight they had made another one, and soon it was back in place.

A three-masted ship would, weather permitting, carry sail on her fore, main and mizzen masts. The quadrilateral sails, carried on yards, were referred to by the mast, then by the position of sail on the mast, the lowest being the mainsail or course, then topsail, topgallant, royal and sky. A small sail was sometimes carried above the sky, without a yard, attached to the mast itself. The mizzen mast did not carry a mainsail. Instead a boom projecting back carried a spanker or driver. Studding sails were carried on yards that could be extended out from the fore and mainmast yards, so that they would hang over the sea. They took their name from the yard on which they were tied. Staysails, which were triangular or quadrilateral, hung between masts, also forward of the foremast, attached to the bowsprit. They were named after the mast where their heads were tied. A boom extending from the bowsprit carried the triangular flying outer and inner jibs. Sprit sails were carried from yards hung underneath the bowsprit.

The squadron, in two lines and keeping close order as signals nos. 72 and 56 demanded, swept down the Portuguese coast. Just after daybreak various landmarks came into sight, beginning with the high land above Oporto. At the end of the afternoon, on reaching the Burling rocks, near the fortified town of Peniche, the squadron hove to and the captains went on board the *London* for a meeting with their commander. The second rendezvous was communicated to all ships.

The need for a rendezvous was a precautionary measure so that should any ship, through weather or any other reason, lose sight of the remainder of the squadron, she had a position to head for. Occasionally a ship would be detached from the squadron to carry out special duties, after which she should rejoin the squadron. As the squadron had probably moved on, she needed one or more rendezvous so as to know where to rejoin.

∼ *Monday, 16 November*

At last the estuary of the Tagus had been reached. Sir Sidney Smith, in his dispatch to the Secretary to the Admiralty Board,[30] explains the difficulties in carrying out the next part of his orders: to establish contact, on shore, with Lord Strangford.

As the fresh breeze, sometimes reaching gale force, was blowing in a general westerly direction, that part of the coast of Portugal, including the bar of the Tagus, was impossible to approach with line-of-battle ships, whose manoeuverability in these circumstances was limited. The squadron did not have with it any smaller ships; nor were the Lisbon fishing boats that might be possible to hire, coming out so far.

A square-rigged ship was limited in her ability to sail close to the wind: her yard arms had to be braced round as far as possible, and the shrouds that supported her masts would normally limit them from going any further. In this position, and after allowing for the sideways movement of her hull sliding through the water, she could sail at best some fifty-seven degrees from the wind. In order to stop, or heave to, she would have to arrange her sails in exact balance so that some would be pushing her forward whilst others would be pulling her back. She would change direction when sailing into the wind, by tacking. But if short of forward speed, she would wear, by coming round stern first into the wind in order to get to her new tack.

Sir Sidney goes on to compare, unfavourably, the present situation with that of the blockade of Cádiz, where ships have the recourse of passing through the straits of Gibraltar should a westerly gale blow; or Brest, which has the Channel; and at Ferrol, where the bay is open if southwesterly winds have to be faced, and ships can drift along the coast southward with a northeasterly. At normal times, when a westerly gale blows, ships can sail straight into the Tagus for shelter within the high river banks, but under the present circumstances this was not possible.

The Tagus, which runs across Portugal, rises in the Sierra de Albarracin, beyond and to the east of Madrid. As it approaches Lisbon it runs northeast to southwest but, as it reaches Lisbon, it widens and turns sharply to run east to west all the way to the Atlantic. Its entrance, although wide, is deceptive in appearance, as the greatest part is very shallow. The deep water channel, no more than 2,000 yards wide, makes it almost impossible for a ship to enter undamaged from the cannons of the forts guarding the bar: the island fort of Buggio and, on the mainland, St Julião. Once the bar has been crossed, the approach to Lisbon is well protected by the Arieiro, Maias, Giribita, St Bruno and Belém forts that line the river bank. On the coast the St Antônio da Barra, Sta. Maria[31] and St Braz[32] complete the fortifications.

At dawn the *Marlborough* had set out in chase of a strange sail. At 2 p.m., after exchange of signals, HMS *Hibernia* identified herself. She had arrived in Cawsand Bay too late to join Sir Sidney's squadron but, without wasting time, had sailed straight on and was now doing her best to join the squadron. It would be another two days, however, before she succeeded in doing so.

∼ *Tuesday, 17 November*

The problem of finding a small vessel, so as to be able to sail in close to shore and take a message to Lord Strangford, was solved next morning. At daybreak the flagship signalled *Bedford* to examine a sail in the southeast quarter. At 8.10 a.m., on reaching her, she fired a shot across her bows as a signal to halt. She proved to be the *Active* privateer – an armed brig bearing a letter of marque from London. That same afternoon the *Active* set off for Lisbon.[33]

Privateers were ships owned by merchants, who armed them and paid for their upkeep. Once they had obtained a letter of marque, from the lords of the Admiralty, they were free to attack and capture enemy vessels. If successful, the captured vessel would be sold and the proceeds distributed to the owners and crew.

The squadron persevered in keeping its station, about seven or eight leagues off Cape Raso. The southwesterly winds continued but were more moderate, now accompanied by heavy showers. All merchant ships sighted were chased and stopped. The *Monarch* brought to an American brig, from Dublin bound for Lisbon; the *Marlborough* a Portuguese schooner, from Lisbon going to Figueiras.

∼ *Wednesday, 18 November*

In the early morning the *Active* started her journey back to the squadron, carrying the members of the British Legation. At 5.30 p.m. Lord Strangford was received by Sir Sidney on board the *London*.[34]

Lord Strangford's news on arrival was, to say the least, extremely disquieting. He related that following a meeting of the State Council on 20 October, the decision had been taken to embargo British war and merchant ships and on 5 November the order had been given to detain British subjects and confiscate their property. As a result three merchant ships and a number of subjects remained imprisoned. HM Consul General, Mr Gambier, had stayed behind to urge their release. Further, he had placed the *Active* at the bar of the Tagus, to warn off any British ships approaching Lisbon.[35] Both France and Spain had declared war on Portugal, on or about 24 October, and the Portuguese Legation had left Paris on the 25th. Furthermore a French army, comprising three divisions of 3,000 men each, under Generals Junot, Laborde and Kellerman were, since the 11th of that month, in Salamanca, less than 150 miles from the Portuguese border. Lord Strangford's information was, with some discrepancy as to dates, largely correct.

Another disquieting information, for which precise instructions were required, was the presence in the Tagus of a Russian squadron, arrived between the 8th and 12th, showing every intention of wintering in the port. It was composed of nine line-of-battle ships and two frigates. A further three vessels: a Turkish eighty-gun (a prize), a frigate and a sloop were expected at any time, coming through the Straits of Gibraltar. With Russia again siding with France following the Treaty of Tilsit, signed in July 1807,[36] Sir Sidney feared that these ships might join with those of Portugal against Britain.[37]

Lord Strangford and Sir Sidney Smith now decided that, in view of the unequivocal evidence of hostilities, a blockade should be declared, albeit imperfect, as Lord Strangford later wrote to the Rt Hon George Canning.[38]

Chapter IV

The Squadron increases in size, as the true extent of the problems faced are revealed. Considerations on taking the port of Lisbon. Both Sir Sidney Smith and Lord Strangford are concerned with the need to persuade HRH to leave for Brazil or place his fleet on deposit with Britain. On 29 November 1807 HRH finally leaves Lisbon with the Portuguese military and merchant fleets.

~ Thursday, 19 November

In London a decision to add to the squadron had been taken. HM ships *Plantagenet* and *Conqueror*[1] and HM sloop *Confiance,* which had left Plymouth on the 15th, were now approaching Cape Finisterre. HMS *Foudroyant*, another line-of-battle ship, had weighed and set sail from England that very morning. A smaller vessel, HM sloop *Redwing,* attending a requisition made by Lord Strangford to Rear Admiral Purvis, the commander of the squadron blockading Cádiz, for transport to take him and Mr Gambier to England[2], was rounding Cape St Vincent in the south. HM frigate *Solebay*, which had left with Sir Sidney, was now in the vicinity.

Sir Sidney was glad to see the *Hibernia* approaching for, as he wrote to the Admiralty,[3] he feared that the enemy squadrons from Rochefort, Ferrol or Cádiz might slip past the blockades and, before reinforcements could arrive, make their appearance. It would not surprise him if the squadron sheltering in Cádiz was to come out should the blockading ships move from their station in order to oppose the Russians as they came past the Straits of Gibraltar.

The weather continued very squally, which tended to cause more damage than a steady stronger-blowing wind. Just after midnight the *Elizabeth* was caught in a sudden squall that carried away her main topmast, mizzen topgallant mast, fore topgallant yard and studding sail boom. She later reported that in clearing away the wreck she found the royal and the main topgallant studding sails gone, as well as a great deal of the remaining rigging. The other ships did not go untouched: the *Foudroyant* split her fore topmast staysail and *Bedford* sprung her fore topmast. The squadron was beginning to feel the need for additional masts and spars so, before the end of the month, Sir Sidney wrote to the Admiralty asking for replacements.[4]

The bad weather did not prevent an increase in activity, now that the blockade had been decided on. When at last the *Hibernia* came up to the *London,* her pinnace was lowered and Captain John Conn went on board. In the afternoon the *Marlborough* boarded another privateer. She was the schooner *Trafalgar*, of Gibraltar, coming from Lisbon with dispatches for the first British man-of-war that she could find. The *Solebay*, still some twenty leagues away, boarded yet another privateer, this time a cutter.

~ *Friday, 20 November*

Early in the morning, the *Hibernia* and the *London* hoisted their boats out; stores belonging to Sir Sidney and Lord Strangford were transferred. At 1 p.m. Sir Sidney left the *London* and raised his flag on the *Hibernia*. An hour later he was followed by Lord Strangford. Both were entitled to a 13-gun salute, from the ship they were leaving and from the ship that was receiving them.

By the evening, HM ships *Plantagenet* and *Conqueror* and HM sloop *Confiance* had sailed past the estuary of the Douro and were closing with the Burlings', on the lookout for Sir Sidney's squadron.

Since early afternoon, *London* had been lying to. Now she set her foresail in chase of a brig. At 11 p.m. she caught up with her. She proved to be American, bound for Lisbon.

~ *Saturday, 21 November*

Another busy day for the squadron. The strong gales of the day before had abated, but a fresh breeze, with the occasional squall, continued to blow. It was cloudy and rainy. At daybreak several strangers, which during the night had come up over the horizon, were now in sight. The squadron set out to investigate and identify. *Foudroyant* approached two men-of-war, who identified themselves as HM ships *Revolution* and *Rose.* In the early afternoon *Bedford* boarded an American brig from Copenhagen bound for Rhode Island. The *London*, after a chase, intercepted with a gun, an American brig in ballast bound for Lisbon.

The *Solebay*, newly arrived from the south, after a chase, boarded a sail and left an officer and men on board, then continued to chase another ship, which proved to be the *Monarch.* Her captain went on board to receive the squadron's orders. After recovering the officer and men from the ship boarded earlier that day, the *Solebay* spoke to the *Hibernia* and at 5 p.m. Capt Sproule went on board to report to his commander, Sir Sidney Smith.

As so many British ships were now off the Tagus, there was no longer any need for the *Active* to remain at the bar. As she could not now go back to Lisbon, together with the *Trafalgar*, she joined the squadron.

The sloop *Confiance* – the ex-French privateer *La Confidence* of Bordeaux, taken in 1805 – sailing ahead of the *Plantagenet* and the *Conqueror* in the early morning, tacking occasionally for the wind was blowing from the northeast, worked her way up towards the Tagus. Ahead, moored in the river, she reported seeing several line-of-battle ships flying Russian colours. At 1 p.m., with all sails set, she tried to cross the bar but was fired on by the Portuguese batteries and immediately hove to. Undeterred, she moved out of range and went in chase of two vessels that had just come out of the Tagus. One proved to be a Venetian, the other a Portuguese brig with HM Consul General, Mr Gambier, and several English families on board.

Mr. Gambier, although not succeeding in freeing the prisoners had, after again applying insistently through Mr John Bell for their release, decided to leave. As from the 9th, the Prince Regent had confirmed Lord Strangford's nomination of John Bell, to perform the functions of "…agent for British prisoners of war …"[5]

Back in London, news of the embargo of British ships had reached the Rt Hon George Canning at the Foreign Office. On 11 November he wrote to the lords commissioners of the Admiralty with the orders that should be given to Sir Sidney Smith:[6]

On arrival off the Tagus to enquire from Lord Strangford or, if he had already left Lisbon, directly, whether the Portuguese Government had ratified the Convention signed on the 22nd of October. If so, to declare his readiness to co-operate. If not, or if ratified but preparations to carry out the terms of the Convention were not apparent then, steps should be taken to ensure that the military and merchant navy do not fall to France or Spain in the event of hostilities, either by conveying the Prince Regent to Brazil or else by joining the British fleet so as to be taken in trust by Britain. If that should be the case and, unless in his judgment there were reasons not to push matters to an extremity, then to institute a most rigorous blockade making it clear to the Portuguese Government that he had not the authority to lift it under any condition whatever other than that of the surrender of the Portuguese ships of war and the Brazil ships now lying in the Tagus. Should this be refused then to seize, capture or destroy every Portuguese ship in his path. In the event of its appearing practicable with the forces under his command, then to force his way into the Tagus and seize and bring away all the Portuguese shipping, or destroy such part of it that he may find it impossible to remove. Should it be inadvisable to undertake the operation with the forces under his command he should, after collecting information, inform the Admiralty of the force that would be required to undertake such an operation with a prospect of success. In the meantime, to maintain the blockade until further orders.

~ Sunday, 22 November

The Secretary to the Admiralty, the Rt Hon William Pole, issued the order the next day and sent it with the messenger Sylvester, as it was classified most secret, to Plymouth.[7] A copy, with Capt Bradley of the *Plantagenet*, was the first to arrive. On the morning of the 22nd at 6 a.m. she sighted the squadron and an hour later joined it. The messenger with the original was on board the *Confiance*; and after showing her identity number, she joined the squadron at 11 a.m.

It was quite usual to send several copies of an important dispatch, for practice had shown that the original could get delayed because of adverse weather conditions affecting a particular ship, or even enemy action. In an emergency, to avoid capture, important documents such as secret dispatches or signal codebooks would be thrown overboard in weighted bags.

The instructions from London, for a much stricter blockade than had been enforced up to now, were duly put into effect, both for the Tagus and for the nearby port of Setúbal.[8]

Amongst the officers and crews of the blockading squadron, this decision must have been met with satisfaction: now that the blockade was official, it was unlikely that there would be any discussion as to whether Portuguese ships taken should or not be classified as prizes.

At this time the wage received by sailors was £15 per annum before any discounts – a very low rate even for those days. Pay was, more often then not, in arrears of several months. The possibility, therefore, of sharing in a prize was an attractive one. In 1762, to mention an extreme example, sailors who had helped to capture the Spanish *Hermione* received thirty-six years' pay as prize money! Following a chase, the vessel would be boarded and taken; then a prize crew, consisting of an officer and a number of seamen, would be put on board. The prize would sail with the squadron until such time as she could be taken, with an escort to discourage the retaking of the vessel, to a home port. The prize court would then confirm the capture as a prize and decide who was entitled to a share. This followed a well-established set of rules. The final step was the selling and distribution of the proceeds. If the prize was a ship of war, the chances were that she would be purchased by the Admiralty and, after repair and being suitably renamed, would be integrated into the navy.

Sir Sidney Smith, in writing to the Secretary to the Admiralty, describes the difficulty of a close blockade on this coast:

> It blows so hard from the Westward, at present, that I am obliged to carry
> sail to keep the Ships off the land; as soon as it is more moderate, the
> blockade which I have instituted in consequence of Lord Strangford's

letters of this date, will be rendered more close by the Ships being able to keep nearer the shore; but for this purpose, I am in the most absolute want of more Frigates, which class can venture, and remain, near the bar without being committed, as Line of Battle ships would be, with the tide of flood when the wind sets strongly on it. At present the wind is dead on the shore and blowing strong, the sea so heavy that if it were to increase to the degree of putting us past carrying the sail we have at present, or if anything material were to fail in any ship, the lee way would of course be much more than two points, in which case I need not say that on such a straight coast as this there would be no clearing the land on either tack; I have reason to be glad that I took an early decision to get an offing.[9]

Pondering on the orders received from Whitehall, to attack and capture or destroy the Portuguese fleet, Sir Sidney was of the opinion that the squadron alone, however superior, could not successfully undertake this operation. The squadron might pass all the way up into the town, more or less disabled, under considerable crossfire from the forts at the entrance and from those lining the shore. Once inside the river, and unlike Copenhagen, where a similar expedition had successfully taken place a few months before, there was no clear anchorage out of gunfire. The passage out, with the captured ships, would again be under heavy fire.[10]

The employment, therefore, of a land force was an essential requisite. A detailed plan could only be worked out after further reconnoitering the coast. The risks of a lee shore to HM ships,[11] and the difficulty of maintaining a close blockade during the winter, made it imperative that the whole operation should take place as soon as possible. Sir Sidney felt that a British army, equal in numbers to the French but with superior discipline and prowess, drawing its resources from a navigable river, would more than counterbalance the present dominant influence of Bonaparte.

The same opinion was held by Mr Gambier, HM Consul General who, on 20 October, had prepared a detailed account of Portuguese military forces, which was by now with the Foreign Office.[12] Sir Sidney sent a copy of this same report to Lt Gen Sir John Moore who, at the head of a force, was expected to pass through the Straits of Gibraltar at any moment.[13]

Mr. Gambier's detailed account of the forces made it clear that an attack was expected from the sea, and not from the French and Spanish armies. A force of some six thousand troops under a lieutenant general had been ordered to be stationed on the coast north of Lisbon, at Ericeira, Mafra and Peniche. A second force, of equal size, was to occupy Almada, Setúbal, and Alcácer to the south. This force would come under the command of the Marquis of Alorna – although there was doubt as to his state of health and mind. The Lisbon garrison would be under the command of General Gomes Freire, an officer who had seen service in the Russian army.

Additional battalions were being recruited in the interior.[14] Moore's troops should be added to those expected shortly from England. Lord Strangford wrote that, in view of the danger to troop transport vessels resulting from the lack of shelter from a westerly wind on that coast, it was Sir Sidney's plan, on the arrival of the first force, to land them by seizing a position on the coast where they might remain in safety, until joined by the remainder. The Peniche, a small fortified peninsula north of Lisbon, opposite the Burlings', had been chosen.[15]

Additional frigates continued to be an urgent necessity. At that moment only the *Solebay* was attached to the squadron, and so could not be spared to be sent to England with dispatches. Instead, the privateer schooner *Trafalgar* would have to be used. The changing scenario required that the Foreign Office and the Admiralty be constantly supplied with up-to-date information and, as the scope for taking the initiative locally by Sir Sidney Smith or Lord Strangford was limited, new instructions and orders had to come from London.

On board the *Hibernia,* Sir Sidney and Lord Strangford discussed the situation as it developed, and were in total agreement.[16] Every decision taken was backed up by a letter of confirmation from Lord Strangford. Both wrote almost daily to their superiors – the Rt Hon George Canning at the Foreign Office in the case of Lord Strangford; and the lords of the Admiralty, in the case of Sir Sidney. However, these letters would, in actual fact, be sent all together. Notwithstanding, London continued to be ignorant of the developments that had taken place, as their orders had been issued on 11 November. The weather, wrote Sir Sidney on 22 November, had prevented the dispatches from being transferred to the schooner *Trafalgar*, hence the delay in sending her off on the journey to England.[17]

From their letters, it is possible to note that they both recognised the difficult position in which the Prince Regent had been placed, by circumstances entirely outside his control. "Fear in one party and corruption in another seem to have urged and forced the councils of the Prince Regent (most unwillingly on his part) to his present fatal line of Policy," wrote Sir Sidney.[18] "...a misguided and unfortunate Sovereign ..." wrote Lord Strangford.[19]

In their separate ways they attempted to force the prince's hand to take the difficult decision: leave his kingdom, in the face of the almost certain invasion, in order to save the institution of the monarchy and his person. Sir Sidney considered that as the Portuguese Cabinet had acted from fear of a land attack from the French army, then the greater apprehension of one from the opposite quarter might have the effect of producing a contrary decision and conduct.[20]

Under this supposition he wrote to D. Araújo, confirming that he had come as a friend, to co-operate in the execution of the articles of the Convention. But, finding that the agreement had not been put into effect, and that Lord Strangford had been obliged to quit Lisbon, he had had no alternative but to institute a rigorous blockade; and further, with no authority to lift it other than against the surrender of the Portuguese ships of war and Brazil ships now lying in the Tagus: these ships to be taken in deposit until a definite peace had been concluded between France and Great Britain. He continued, declaring that although it was not his intention to menace, it was obvious that the British fleet and army destined to counteract the operations of the enemy, when and wherever to be found, could not have been assembled for the mere purpose of demonstration or simple blockade. He cites the recent example of Copenhagen, where the alternative offered by HM Government was not accepted, and the resulting scenes of horror. He continued by calling on the Prince Regent to reconsider the line of policy that he had adopted, whilst there was yet time, and spare himself the regret now felt in Copenhagen that the offered alternative had not been accepted, since the result could not be any different. He ended by stating that Lord Strangford, having some important communications to make to the Portuguese government in consequence of recent instructions, offered to land under the protection of a flag of truce, and that he would send one in provided that His Excellency (D. Araújo) agreed that he would be admitted to an immediate audience with His Royal Highness the Prince Regent, and be allowed to leave and return to the squadron.[21]

Lord Strangford wrote that he was convinced that if only he could meet with the Prince Regent, he could persuade him to follow the best course for himself and his country: the transfer of his family and Court to Brazil, taking with him his military and merchant fleets; or the transfer of the fleets to Britain. He had lived long enough in Lisbon and, because of his position, maintained close contact and valuable relations with the prince, who had always showed him the highest consideration. He had also developed a close friendship with some of his ministers. He knew the prince's character, his strengths and weaknesses and the pressures to which he had been subjected. He knew of the ambitions and interests of each minister, and the effects of corruption and intrigue that many times affected the best interests of Portugal. Because of the structure of the Court, he also knew that the Prince Regent had to rely almost exclusively, for information and to a great extent for advice, on that offered by his State Council.[22] During the last month the appearance of two enemy forces to Portugal, on her land and sea frontiers, would have given the Prince Regent the power to take action that in normal circumstances would not have been possible: action that, under normal conditions, would not necessarily meet with approval or even be tolerated by the general public.

His reason for wishing to establish a personal dialogue with the prince was:

> To point out to Him, in the plain and simple language of Trust, the only means of Safety which he yet retains. I cannot but think that something is due to the peculiar circumstances in which the Prince Regent is placed;

that he has not been a free agent in the conduct which he has been advised to adopt.[23]

Lord Strangford argued, in his communication to the Rt Hon George Canning, that since Britain and Portugal were at war and, as he had been given his passport and left Portugal, any action taken by him now could not be construed as coming from an official representative of Britain. He was acting as a private individual. This separation of identities was important, lest it be seen that Britain was in some way weakening in her position, officially seeking a negotiation. A second danger, of his capture and detention, arising from the overwhelming French influence that must now exist in Lisbon, would be insured against by obtaining from the Prince Regent, before embarking, the most satisfactory assurances of protection and security. During his stay in Lisbon no cessation of hostilities would take place, the blockade continuing as before.[24]

The dispatches for Lord Strangford received from England on the 22nd and already referred to, included a letter from D. Domingos to the Prince Regent, in which that diplomat asks him "…to transmit in safety …" The fact that the dispatch was an official diplomatic communication between an ambassador and his sovereign did not deter Lord Strangford. He wrote:

I have thought it my Duty to learn the Contents of it; and it appears to me to be so calculated to operate strongly upon HRH's mind, that I am very desirous of being able to lay it before Him, as speedily as possible.[25]

This, most probably, was the copy of Le Moniteur of 11 November.

A notice of the blockade, signed by Sir Sidney Smith on 22 November, directed at the consuls of neutral nations, was made ready to be taken to Lisbon. It advised that the River Tagus had been declared to be in a state of blockade, and that at this time all measures authorised by the law of nations and the respective treaties between His Britannic Majesty and the different neutral powers would be adopted and executed with respect to any vessels which might attempt to violate the said blockade.[26]

Another letter, to John Bell, acting agent for British prisoners of war in Portugal, urged him to solicit the release of all civil persons, particularly women and children, since the detention of such persons was a gross violation of the principle of humanity: "…that the example of France should remain a single one, without imitation …"[27] With respect to the blockade, all ships were prohibited from entering the Tagus. As to departures, particularly of neutrals that may, with reason, wish to withdraw from a place that may soon become a theatre of warlike operations – similar to Copenhagen – they should apply to the commanding officer of the blockade, through their respective consuls, supported by authentic documents. It was not the intention to interfere with pilots that brought vessels out to sea; nor with fishermen in their lawful occupation on their usual ground – even though it may be occupied by the squadron – provided they were unarmed.

The wind, which the day before had been easterly, now turned westerly again, but more moderate. The squadron continued intercepting all vessels that came into sight.

Just after midnight *Solebay* sent her cutters, 'manned and armed', after four ships she had sighted close in shore. At daylight she reported seeing two ships towing her cutters. One of them was the *Redwing*, the other the *Alegro Constant*, a prize. At 2.30 p.m. fifteen prisoners came on board; the *Solebay* supplied the prize with 31½ gallons of spirits, 40 lb each of beef and pork, 30 lb of flour, 9 lb of suet, 7½ lb of cheese and 7½ lb of sugar, for her own people. Next morning, at 6.30 a.m., she wore and made sail after the prize. Shortly after, in trying to manoeuvre, the prize ran on board the *Solebay*, losing her bowsprit and fore topmast. The *Solebay* put carpenters and seamen on board to carry out repairs, and took her in tow.

That morning, 22 November, *Elizabeth* boarded the *Minerva* from London bound for Lisbon; *Bedford* stopped an American brig and spoke to her; *London* boarded an English brig from North Yarmouth bound for Gibraltar laden with herrings and, later, a galliot from Bremen bound for Lisbon. *Plantagenet* boarded an American from Baltimore going to Lisbon. Her master was taken to the Admiral, who warned him not to enter the port and endorsed his papers to that effect. The number of ships mentioned gives some idea of the intense sea traffic at the estuary of the Tagus. Many of the ships were American.

∼ *Monday, 23 November*

The squadron was now composed of eleven HM ships, two privateers and a prize, and although during the course of the day individual ships might be instructed to chase a strange sail, order still prevailed. On the morning of the 23rd, although a fresh gale was again blowing, *Bedford* reported receiving a signal to form the order of sail, in two columns. She tacked and then wore to take up her position.

During the day HM sloop *Electra*, escorting a convoy of merchantmen from Falmouth to Gibraltar, passed through the squadron sailing southwest. Several times she had to show her signal to different vessels that challenged her. *Marlborough*, after a chase, boarded and took as a prize the *Balsimas*, from Brazil, returning to Lisbon. She put on board two petty officers and twenty seamen and took off thirteen prisoners. In the afternoon *Redwing* boarded the *Mentoo*, from London, escorting merchantmen but having lost their company.

~ *Tuesday, 24 November*

When the day dawned, the weather had improved. The previous day's gale had moderated to a fresh breeze and the wind, which had for several days been blowing northwest to west-northwest, had by the afternoon swung round to the southwest. The *Confiance*, under Capt James Yeo,[28] set sail for Lisbon in the early morning, flying a flag of truce. On board, Lieutenant Smith,[29] accompanied by a Portuguese messenger, was taking dispatches from Sir Sidney to D. Araújo and John Bell, as well as the official notice of the blockade. Her log records: "… [24th] 6.30 Wore and made all sail for Lisbon. Squally with Rain hoisted a flag of truce…" Once again she was fired at by the batteries guarding the bar but, through a misunderstanding, they had not noticed her flag of truce. Undamaged, she was now allowed to slip into the river.

> 9 light airs anchored abreast of castle with the best bower in 15 fms. sent a flag of truce up the River… 3 Weighed and made sail up the Tagus ahd. The Russian fleet… 4 weigh and hove further up the harbour… 7 Anchored abreast of Belém Castle best bower in 10 fms.

Outside the bar, in the open sea, *Marlborough* was busy transferring provisions for the twenty men she had, on the previous day, put on board the prize *Balsimas*. *Bedford*, in answer to a signal, was unsuccessfully chasing a sail in the east-north-east. *Plantagenet* had better luck: after a short chase she brought to and boarded an English ship from Montevideo bound for Lisbon. She was then sent over to the Admiral for instructions. *Redwing*, the small brig sloop that had arrived from Gibraltar on the 22nd, obeyed signal no. 108: 'Close nearer the Admiral'. At 2.30 p.m. Captain Thomas Ulsher reported on board the flagship; he brought news that on leaving Gibraltar on the 18th, General Moore, coming from Sicily, had not yet arrived.[30]

The knowledge of the Foreign Office was also incomplete as, at the time of sending the last dispatch, only five Russian ships had arrived in the Tagus. The various changes would influence the British government, making it desirable to forward an early statement of the situation of affairs in Lisbon.[31]

~ *Wednesday, 25 November*

The day began with light winds and cloudy weather. As the day progressed the wind changed, returning to a more westerly direction and increasing in strength. By the evening a whole gale was blowing, forcing all vessels to furl their mizzen topsails and close reef their main and fore topsails.

In the morning *Elizabeth* boarded a schooner from St Johns bound for Lisbon, as well as the *Collins*, from the River Plate going to London. *Redwing* spoke to an American schooner from Lisbon going to England. *Bedford* kept watch over the prize captured by *Marlborough* the previous day. In the afternoon she fired several muskets to bring her to, in order to speak to her. HM brig *Rennywood*, which had joined the squadron, kept *Bedford* company.

Solebay and *Plantagenet* were sailing quite a distance from the squadron, so signals from the flagship had to be relayed by the *Monarch*. Her morning was spent chasing a lugger which, in trying to get away, lost her mainmast, which went over the side. She proved to be Spanish from Vigo, eight days at sea, but in that time had captured an English brig from London on her way to Providence. *Solebay* received thirty men on board, between prisoners and Englishmen. The prize was much battered and in distress so next day *Hibernia* sent on board a Lieutenant Killwick with twenty men to take charge of her; and material to carry out repairs: a mainsail and four spars. The prize, a privateer lugger, joined the squadron. Later in the day *Plantagenet* brought to a frigate flying Portuguese colours for *Solebay* to board; but as it was getting dark she lost her. A frigate again reappeared but after closing, found her to be the *Solebay*. Both ships then tacked, one to larboard and the other to starboard. Shortly afterwards the prize, *Conceição S. José Fama*, was captured by the *Solebay*.

In London, HM Government recognised the special and unusual circumstances that had forced Portugal to close her ports. The feeling towards Portugal, far from being belligerent, was understanding and condescending and as a result, the orders given at the first reaction of the news received from Portugal were cancelled. Ships and goods belonging to Portuguese merchants in Britain should now be released.[32]

Confiance, still moored in the Tagus, was now almost ready to return to the squadron. Whilst in the river she had made good use of the sheltered water between the high banks, to carry out various chores: cleaning and painting the ship, impossible to undertake in the open sea. She took on board 5 tons of water, to complete her carrying capacity of 42 tons, and 532 lb of fresh beef. Her captain, although junior compared to those of a ship of the line, as he had been promoted from the rank of commander that year, was active and resourceful and had perhaps one of the most responsible missions in the blockade. Sir Sidney certainly recognised this, as he wrote to the Admiralty, when sending him back with dispatches:

> This dispatch will be delivered by Captain Yeo, of his majesty's sloop *Confiance*, who has shown great address and zeal in opening the communications by flag of truce, which it was the interest of those in power, who were against the measure of emigration, to obstruct. Lord Strangford speaks of his conduct in warm approbation; on this ground I beg leave

to recommend him to their lordships, to whom his general merits as an officer are already well known. Having been in Lisbon without restraint, during the intercourse, he is qualified to answer any questions their lordships may wish to put to him.[33]

~ *Thursday, 26 November*

Confiance spent the morning waiting for a pilot; at regular intervals she fired a signal gun. At noon, at last, a pilot came on board; the *Confiance* weighed and moved down river in a fresh breeze, occasionally squally with rain. At the bar, the wind was variable and inclined to calm, making control of the sloop very difficult. On crossing it, *Confiance* was caught in a heavy cross sea which washed away the jollyboat from the quarter. In order to regain some degree of manageability, she put out the best bower and wore away from it to half a cable. The cross sea at the bar was so heavy that she could not weigh anchor. In spite of all her efforts, she was forced to cut the cable and so lost her best bower. She set off westward to rejoin the squadron.

The dispatch from Sir Sidney Smith to D. Araújo had been received by him and, as already stated, its contents recorded at the meeting of the State Council that took place, in the presence of the Prince Regent, at the Palace of Nª Sª da Ajuda on 24 November. Now, on her return, *Confiance* brought back the reply from D. Araújo.[34] On her arrival, both Sir Sidney and Lord Strangford would become aware that the decision to undertake the voyage had been taken: only the date remained open.

During the afternoon *Plantagenet*, sailing between the body of the squadron and the Tagus bar, boarded one of the Russian vessels that had been expected: the frigate *Frattog Geogin*, coming from Gibraltar. In the early evening she reported seeing a ship coming out of Lisbon. It was the *Confiance*, with all sails set, on her way back from the Tagus.

The presence of a Russian squadron in the Tagus was, to say the least, confusing. Sir Sidney's instructions from the Admiralty were not directed specifically at the Russian warships, except in so far as a 'strict blockade' also applied to them.[35]

The *Solebay*, after a four-hour chase, brought to a ship flying Portuguese colours, bound for Lisbon. The First Lieutenant sent an armed party, which took possession of the prize.

The hired schooner *Trafalgar* was now making final preparations for her journey to England, with dispatches. *Hibernia* sent over two bags of bread and thirty-five quarts of rum.

~ *Friday, 27 November*

All through the night, *Confiance*, now clear of the Tagus bar, slowly closed with the squadron, which at daybreak lay to the west and southward. Now all sails were set as she raced to intercept the flagship *Hibernia*. As she approached, at 8 a.m., she lowered one of her boats and took across the dispatches she had brought from Lisbon: the replies from the State Council to the note from Sir Sidney Smith and the request from Lord Strangford for an interview.

Another dispatch, brought by the *Confiance*, dated 25 November, was from John Bell. He reported that on the merchant ship *Diana*, Master John Tomkin, with some sixty English subjects on board waiting to be taken home, was still being detained. He had twice spoken to D. Araújo, who promised a decision for that day. Subsequently he had noticed that the ship had weighed and moved down to Belém, he presumed as a result of some order received. No further restraint had taken place with regard to those British subjects notified not to leave Portugal.

He further reported that the notification of the close blockade had been duly delivered to the Russian, Austrian, Swedish and American consuls, and that "…it had caused the greatest consternation in this City…" Replies from the Swedish and American consuls were forwarded with Captain Yeo.

The *Confiance* hove to, waiting for further orders, but not for long. At the signal to 'close nearer the Admiral' she brought up to the flagship. At 2 p.m. Lord Strangford went on board and, once more, she set sail for Lisbon. The squally weather continued, with occasional rain. The wind, blowing easterly, was favourable for leaving the Tagus but not for entering it. It would be a long journey.

Lord Strangford had no means of knowing that at that very moment the Prince Regent and the remainder of the royal family were already embarked, and were only waiting to complete preparations and for a favourable wind, to commence their voyage.

The original plan had been to send the *Confiance* back to England with dispatches just as soon as she came out of the Tagus, thus attending to Admiral Young's request of the 15th. However, the continuing lack of smaller vessels meant that her journey would have to wait.[36]

~ *Saturday, 28 November*

Other ships of the squadron were busy with their blockading duties. When dawn broke, *Hibernia* hoisted signal no. 120 to *Bedford*: 'Examine strange sail' followed by south-southeast. She immediately made sail and set off in that direction. She soon caught up with the chase and, after shortening sail and coming to, sent a boat across. She was another Russian, the twenty-gun frigate *Stigburg* which, from the direction that she had approached the squadron, was on her way up from Gibraltar. As she went by, *Hibernia* hoisted her colours.[37] In the afternoon *Bedford* again chased a sail, but this time a Portuguese schooner. After being boarded she was brought into the squadron as a prize.

Since early morning *Redwing* had been chasing a brig close in shore. At 10.30 she brought her to, after firing a gun, and sent across a boat 'manned and armed'.

She proved to be English from La Caudore – a disappointment, as there would not be any prize money.

In the afternoon the Portuguese vessel captured by the *Solebay* the previous evening signalled the *Hibernia* that she was in distress. A petty officer and eleven seamen from the *Solebay* – part of the crew that had been left on board the prize – brought over thirty prisoners; then returned to their prize.

During the night of the 27th the wind came round to the northwest, but more moderate. At dawn on the 28th *Confiance*, with all sails set, steered towards the bar of the Tagus. The westerly wind had almost died away, causing her to struggle against the tide in order to cross it. She reported: "…Moderate all sails set 10 a.m. light airs out sweepers swept the Ship…" At 1 am:

> Light breezes all hands employed sweeping the Ship into the Tagus 2.30 Obsd. The Ship could not stem the tide Anchored with the small Bower in 14 fms. veered to half a Cable sent a flag of truce on Shore with Lord Strangford etc. etc.

She would have been just inside the bar. The tide must have been pulling strongly, for she reports adding her stream and kedge anchors over the bower, to ensure that she would not drag and run aground. The *Confiance* will have moored opposite the town of Oieras, or perhaps Caxias. In order to reach the centre of Lisbon Lord Strangford would then have to make his way overland – some ten miles. Since it was already past 2.30 p.m. when he was rowed ashore, by the time he found a horse or carriage and covered the distance it would be early evening and he would arrive in the dark.

In the meantime, *Hibernia* was supplying the Russian frigate with coal, 3,300 lb of rice in 18 barrels, and 88 bags of bread. Obeying the strict instructions from the lords of the Admiralty, Sir Sidney warned the captain of the *Stigburg* against going into the Tagus.[38] Captain Thomas Western of the *London* was not taking any chances: as the Russian passed close by he hoisted out his boats in readiness to put them in the water, should it prove necessary.

The *Solebay* was busy, discharging amongst the various ships of the squadron all the prisoners that had come off the prize she had captured on the 22nd. *London, Elizabeth* and *Monarch* each took ten, *Conqueror* nine and the much smaller *Redwing*, five.

On arrival in Lisbon Lord Strangford was to find that the Prince Regent, with all his family and ministers, had embarked the day before.[39] He would have had to take a boat to go on board the *Medusa* to confer with D. Araújo. The latter wrote to the Prince Regent[40] that Lord Strangford had come on board, and that they had discussed and agreed on certain aspects of the Convention, but without going into details.[41]

D. Araújo refused, in spite of the declaration in the Convention, to hand over the forts for fear that the French, on arrival, would seek revenge against the artillery-men. Lord Strangford's request for an audience with the Prince Regent was confirmed for next morning, at 8 a.m. Lord Strangford, therefore, would not meet the Prince Regent before the *Príncipe Real* weighed, at first light next morning.

There are various versions of this conversation with D. Araújo, none of which are particularly convincing. An anonymous manuscript claims that Lord Strangford tried to impose conditions additional to the Convention, as a prerequisite for Sir Sidney Smith to lift the blockade to allow the ships to leave. D. Araújo is said to have energetically rejected this argument and obtained Lord Strangford's agreement that the clauses, agreed in good faith, should stand.[42] In another version Lord Strangford asked D. Araújo to inform the prince that Britain had declared war on Portugal and that the navy had been ordered to capture the Portuguese fleet, even if it sailed for Brazil. The only way to avoid this was for the two navies to join forces and fight the French troops. If successful then the prince could leave for Brazil.[43]

On the night of the 28th Lord Strangford wrote excitedly to Sir Sidney Smith, from Lisbon:

> I am to inform you that a great and rapid change has taken place in the Conduct of the Portuguese Government... The Prince Regent and all the royal family are embarked and propose to sail instantly, as a French Army is within 9 leagues of Lisbon... Time will not permit your entering into the Tagus for the purpose of co-operating... HRH does not acquiesce in the preliminary surrender of the Forts of St. Julien [sic] and the Buggio... Every vessel belonging to the Portuguese Marine, whether Royal or Commercial, is engaged and prepared to accompany HR Highness... It is utterly inexpedient to throw any unnecessary difficulties in the way of HRH's departure, or to raise any questions that might be avoided, for I am convinced that so great is the discontent of the People, and so strong the consequent alarm of HRH that all depends on the support which HRH may receive from us, and of which I have given him the most frank and unequivocal assurance.[44]

At 10 p.m. that night the wind moved round from northwest to southeast. It was now certain that the fleet, at daybreak, would try to leave the Tagus.

~ *Sunday, 29 November*

Lord Strangford returned to the *Confiance*, his arrival on board being recorded as 8 a.m. There is no record in the log of the *Confiance* as to when Lord Strangford next disembarked. This is unusual, for every movement of such an important personage is recorded, even in the log of the larger ships.

The *Confiance,* the only British ship of war in the Tagus on the morning of the 29th, reported that since daylight the Portuguese fleet had been weighing anchor and making preparation to depart. It was important that the news brought by Lord Strangford should, therefore, reach the Admiral as soon as possible. Captain Yeo sent an officer ahead in a fishing boat with this 'intelligence' to Sir Sidney.

The *Medusa* and the *Martim de Freitas* led the fleet out of the river, deliberately passing close to the Russian squadron anchored just inside the bar, to evaluate their intentions and watch for possible reactions. Next, it was the turn of those line-of-battle ships carrying members of the royal family to reach that stretch of the river. The *Martim de Freitas* carried a Lisbon pilot to guide her as far as the bar. As there was no means of returning, this pilot made the journey to Brazil!

If Admiral Siniavin had known that Russia, on 2 December, was to declare war against Britain, the departure of the Portuguese fleet might have had another outcome.[45]

Confiance suffered a short delay when she found that her main topgallant mast had cracked, and that her buoy and rope had gone. She then records: "…9.30 Weighed and made Sail…" The next entry in her log reads: "…Obsd. The Portuguese Men of War passed us sailing out of the Tagus…"

If Lord Strangford crossed the bar with the Prince Regent, as he later claimed, then this must have been the moment when he transferred from the *Confiance* to the *Príncipe Real.* An undated letter, from Lord Strangford to the Prince Regent asking for a position for a certain João Carlos de Azevedo, son of the 1st Baron of Rio Seco, ends by reminding the prince "…that he had the honour of accompanying His Royal Highness, when crossing the Lisbon bar, occasion when he nearly broke his best sword, as the Prince well knows …"[46]

The *Confiance,* on coming within sight of the squadron, sent her news to the *Hibernia* with her wooden telegraph, but took a further four hours to reach her.

By 9 a.m. it was apparent to Sir Sidney Smith's squadron, lying a fair way out at sea, that the Portuguese fleet was coming out of the Tagus. Signal halyards were kept busy first, advising of the appearance of the fleet and, next – from the flagship – commands from the Admiral.

Sir Sidney was not taking any chances, for he could not be totally certain that the Portuguese fleet now approaching was coming in peace. Portugal and Britain were, until very recently, at war. A further possibility was that the French army had reached Lisbon and was, even now, on board the ships in sight. In succession, the halyard of the *Hibernia* hoisted a signal saying they were friends,[47] then signal no. 2: 'Prepare for Battle', followed by no. 36: 'Engage the enemy on the starboard side if before the wind or to windward'.

All round the squadron, officers and crews sprang into action. *Bedford* recorded in her log receiving the signal: "…answered signal to prepare for action & formed line of battle ahead of the *Hibernia*…" *Elizabeth* noted: "…cleared Ship for action… answd. & made signal as pr. Log formed line & prepared for action… stove 10 empty barrels to clear the ship and cut up 6 D for shot & match tubs…" *Foudroyant*: "…answd. The Signal to prepare for Battle, beat to Quarters & Cleared Ship for Action…" *London*: "…Cleared Ship for Action pr. Signal…" *Marlborough*: "…answd. Signal to prepare for battle… ansd. signal N 9 (move ship closer to the Admiral)… " *Monarch*: "…answd gen. Sigl. N 13 (prepare for battle) …beat to quarters & cleared for action …" *Plantagenet*: "…Preparative n 21 (attack the enemy on the bearings indicated)… cleared Ship for Battle… Boxed up formed the Line of Battle…"

The squadron, a highly-trained and efficient fighting force, was now perfectly ready should there be any hostile intentions on the part of the fleet of approaching Portuguese warships.

Chapter V

The Prince Regent, accompanied by his family and ministers, leaves Portugal. The meeting with the British Squadron, under Sir Sidney Smith. The voyage starts as they sail towards Madeira. Separation of the fleet on 8 December. Junot enters Lisbon and commences to rule.

∼ *Sunday, 29 November*

Any doubts Sir Sidney Smith might have had about the intentions of the Portuguese fleet, which was crossing the Tagus bar, were soon dispelled from the 'intelligence' received from Captain Yeo, from the royal standard seen flying on the *Príncipe Real*, and from the large number of merchantmen crossing the bar in the wake of the naval fleet.

Thomas O'Neil wrote that the lack of time to complete preparations was evident as:

> The Portuguese men of war presented a wretched appearance, as they had only three days to prepare for their escape: scaffolds were still hanging by their sides, and in short, they rather resembled wrecks than vessels of war.[1]

In the early afternoon the *Hibernia* closed with the *Príncipe Real*. The Admiral's barge was lowered into the sea and Sir Sidney went on board.

Sir Sidney Smith wrote on that date:

> When I went on board the *Princepe Reale* [sic] to pay my visit of respect and congratulations to HRH the Prince of Brazil who was embarked in that Ship... After the Compliments natural in such an extraordinary situation of things had passed, between the Prince Regent and me on the poop of the ship bearing his standard (the only part of the Ship clear of lumber and crowd), on which occasion I must not omit to state that the Prince said everything that the most cordial feelings of gratitude towards, and confidence in Great Britain might be supposed to dictate. After my having required and obtained the assurance that the salute I proposed firing on the occasion should be returned His Royal Highness himself emphatically ordering that

it should be gun for gun but from other ships than his own on account of the Queen being on board and Her Majesty's state of health.[2]

Salutes were of such importance that they would only be fired after negotiations had taken place and absolute certainty existed that the salute would be returned 'like for like'. The negotiation, for example, avoided the danger of a ship entering port and, without warning, starting to salute: it could be mistaken for an attack, thus provoking the forts guarding the port to fire back in earnest.

On Sidney Smith's return at 4.30 p.m. the *Hibernia* hoisted signal no. 21: 'The Squadron is to salute with the number of guns shown after this signal is answered; each ship to begin when the second gun is fired onboard the Admirals ship', followed by no. 21. The Portuguese fleet, as agreed, replied, gun for gun.

The royal family was distributed as follows: on the *Príncipe Real* – the Queen D. Maria I, the Prince Regent D. João, Prince of Beira D. Pedro, his brother Infante D. Miguel, and Infante of Spain D. Pedro Carlos;[3] on the *Afonso de Albuquerque* – Princess of Brazil D. Carlota Joaquina with her daughters[4] infantas D. Maria Isabel Francisca, D. Maria da Assunção, D. Ana de Jesus and Princess of Beira D. Maria Teresa; on the *Príncipe do Brazil* – the widow Princess D. Maria Benedita and Infanta Maria Ana,[5] both sisters to the queen; and on the *Rainha de Portugal* – D. Carlota Joaquina's daughters infantas D. Maria Francisca de Assis and D. Isabel Maria.

The number of Portuguese that undertook the voyage to Brazil has been estimated, by different historians, as between 5,000 and 15,000. Many important members of the Court, as previously mentioned, in spite of every effort could not find a place on board. It would appear, therefore, that had there been more space, the number of passengers would have been even greater.

No complete list of passengers has been found. Antônio Marques Esparteiro[6] lists, in great detail, the names of officers of each ship and those who travelled as passengers, as well as the complement of each vessel. Assuming that all ships sailed with a full complement, an unlikely occurrence, a total of 7,000 can be estimated. In addition each merchantman would carry a crew of some 40 to 50: a total of say, some 1,000. The eight line-of-battle ships would each have been carrying between 100 and 300 passengers and the British squadron some 100. The smaller naval ships and the many merchantmen, 20 to 30 each. The total number therefore would appear to be closer to 12,000.

Lord Strangford's movements that day are not mentioned either in *Hibernia*'s log or in Sir Sidney's letter to the Rt Hon W W Pole of 1 December.[7] He claims in a letter to the Rt Hon George Canning of 29 November[8] that, subsequent to crossing the bar in company with the Prince Regent, he left for the *Hibernia* but immediately returned with Sir Sidney Smith and presented him to the Prince Regent.

Thomas O'Neil, a marine officer from the *London*, wrote as though he saw everything from a 'bird's-eye view'.[9] In fact, by the early afternoon of the 29th, O'Neil was far away: firstly in the *London* and subsequently on board the much smaller *Solebay*, preparing to land and take the fort of Bugio. The movements of Lord Strangford and Sir Sidney appeared in the *London Gazette* of 22 December. This was most probably the source for O'Neil's information.[10]

Lord Strangford's assertion that he was largely responsible for the Prince Regent's decision to transfer his Court to Brazil met with considerable resistance and doubts subsequent to the event. The detailed report, supposedly written on the *Hibernia* on 29 November,[11] supports the main basis for this claim. Although it is indicated in the margin of the report that it was sent to England via the Packet *Townsend*, which sailed for England on 3 December, there are allegations that it was composed in the apartment of the Rt Hon George Canning in London on 19 December, and published three days later in the *London Gazette*. The initial inference in his report that he had returned on 28 November to Lisbon and had then met with and persuaded the Prince Regent to embark, had to be later corrected.[12] He admitted that his influence had been decisive, but only during the many months that preceded 29 November. In fact, Lord Strangford was embarked and far out to sea during the period when the decisive news that influenced the State Council reached Lisbon. This was the invasion by the French army (23rd) and, on the 24th, the delivery of the all important copy of *Le Moniteur* of 11 November.

Sir Sidney was anxious and concerned over the condition of the ships with royal persons on board beginning a long and dangerous voyage, if not properly seaworthy and provisioned with food and water:

> I took the Admiral[13] apart and asked him what it was as to efficiency or for the long voyage: He frankly and at once said, "in no state for either," and indeed to the eye it appeared but too evident that preparations had not been made, probably from the counteracting influence from the Party in Power who wished to deter the Prince from embarking and to render it impossible for him to proceed. They have multitudes of helpless men, women and children refugees and heaps of baggage (as at the evacuation of Toulon) on board, very few seamen, neither water or provisions for a voyage of any length, and on my explaining to the Admiral that though I was of course able and willing to relieve immediately distress in any ship I could not furnish them supplies to the extent required without rendering the squadron under my orders as inefficient as he stated his to be. He said, "then we must go to England for we have no where else to go to." He did not state this as arising from any wish in the Prince to deviate from the proposed route to the Brazils [sic], nor do I believe His Royal Highness to entertain any such idea.[14]

The initial reaction from both Sir Sidney and Thomas O'Neil, that the Portuguese ships were in a desperately poor condition, was probably an exaggeration. Perhaps the contrast with the Royal Navy's strict regard to 'spit and polish', as well as the chaos of having an untold number of civilian passengers on board, led them to this opinion. In fact, relatively small quantities of victuals were transferred, and no water. Neither are there any complaints of shortages recorded. Since all HM ships, on return from a voyage, had to account to the agent victualler at the port for provisions consumed and returned, a careful account was kept; so the quantities shown are probably correct. As to the state of the ships, although severely battered by the successive winter storms which caused considerable damage, all the ships arrived at their destination. This reflects the qualities of the officers and crew and the design and construction of the vessels – the experience of several centuries of sailing regularly across oceans in varied weather conditions.

Sir Sidney's next concern was with the close blockade and the danger to merchant ships that were still leaving the Tagus. It was of the utmost importance strategically, that both the St Julião and the Bugio forts be taken immediately. Because of their position at the Tagus bar, they could impose terrible damage to any ship entering or leaving the river. If they were captured by the invading French army, which must be inevitable and of the highest priority, then no further crossing of the bar could take place. Bugio was of particular importance, for as an island fort it could be defended against considerably superior forces.

Lord Strangford, on the previous night aboard the *Medusa*, had had no success in convincing D. Araújo to hand over the forts. Now Sir Sidney tried again with the Prince Regent:

> I proceeded to request that the fort of Bugio at the mouth of Tagus should be given to me in deposit as a security for the free exit of the remaining ships, to this his Royal Highness objected on the grounds of it's being unfair on his part towards the Russians with Whom he was at peace, and who had been received on the ground of hospitality. His Royal Highness refused with great delicacy and feeling but was quite fixed in his determination; though he said that he should be glad to see them in my possession if I could obtain them by negotiation with the regency he had established and to which he did not like to give orders under his present circumstances not to commit it and the inhabitants of Lisbon with the French.[15]

Sir Sidney felt that he could not, with good reason, argue against this refusal

> "… but I could not claim it under the additional articles of the convention as my entry into the Tagus to bring the prince out had not been necessary …"[16]

In fact he had hesitated in taking his squadron into the Tagus, not only because of the forts protecting the river but also, following instructions to the letter that no ships whatever should be allowed to enter, had prevented a Russian frigate from joining her squadron lying at anchor in the river. This act might have provoked the Russians, adding to the hazards of going up river.

He realised that one of the reasons the prince did not want to cede the forts was:

> The refusal of the garrison to dismantle them previous to his passing, the soldiers saying they would defend them against the French and I understand there is such a spirit of resistance in the country that if the people were properly led Portugal would be worse then La Pendée or Calabria to the French army.[17]

Sir Sidney decided instead to go ahead and attempt to capture the island fort "… during the momentary interruption or cessation of all authority…"[18] To this end he ordered a task force of marines from various line-of-battle ships to be made ready on board the much smaller and more manoeuverable ships that could get in close to shore, with orders to take and hold the fort of Bugio.

Hibernia ceded a captain, a subaltern and sixty marines – transferred to the *Confiance*. Likewise the *Marlborough* sent a captain, two subalterns and seventy-five marines to the *Redwing*. One of the marine officers from the *London*, transferred to the *Solebay*, was Lieutenant Count Thomas O'Neil who, in 1810, when he returned to England, was to write a detailed albeit romantic account of the period prior to the voyage, the participation of the marines from HMS *London*, and his subsequent stay in Brazil.[19] He wrote:

> Signal was now made from the commander in chief's ship, for the marines of the *London* to repair on board his Majesty's frigate *Solebay*. The officer under whom I had the honour to serve (Major Malcolm), Lieut. Baynon, and myself, together with eighty privates, three sergeants, three corporals, and two drummers, left the *London*, so soon as circumstances would admit, for the frigate; and on our arrival on board, we were given to understand, that our destination was to take possession of Fort Boujai [sic], situated at the entrance of the Tagus… At seven in the morning of the 30th, the frigate was close in with the fort: it blew a tremendous gale, with a heavy sea, that rendered it possible for us to disembark. At eight we saw the French flag flying on every fort… At nine the gale increased, at ten the ship was in imminent danger, expecting every moment to be cast on shore: but Providence protected us, she worked out, and at seven in the evening we considered ourselves out of danger.

The weather had prevented the operation from taking place and so, much against his will, Sir Sidney ordered it to be cancelled. As soon as the French had garrisoned the forts his opinion was that it was no longer practicable to take them by force without in the first place carrying out a series of land operations in order to starve them out.[20] As he foresaw, their capture was one of the first actions that the French command ordered after entering Lisbon on the dawn of 30 November.

An eyewitness on land recalls that the first order from Junot was to arm the forts, so as to prevent the departure of several ships that were being made ready for the long journey, and to defend himself from a possible attack from the British squadron blockading the entrance to the Tagus:

> French Officers were sent immediately to the fortresses at the bar, and troops in spite of their tiredness, marched to the fortresses on the beach, to prevent the departure of those national ships that had not been got ready the day before; under cannon fire they were forced to turn back; such was the prelude to happiness and protection![21]

Field Marshal Francisco de Borja Garção Stockler, Commander of the Forts and Batteries, wrote in defence of his actions during the last few days of November. This note was handed personally, on 12 July 1812, to State Secretary, Count Aguiar:

> The first of the accusations is that, due to my own actions, I obstructed the departure of Portuguese ships from the port of Lisbon that were preparing to follow His Majesty's' squadron on the 29th and 30th of November 1807.
>
> In order to prove the falseness of this first accusation, all that is needed is the document n.1, written and signed by His Excellency the Marquis of Tancos. It clarifies that:
>
> 1st – On the 27th of November 1807 carrying out orders from His Majesty, given to me under the signature of His Excellency the Marquis of Alegrete, I spiked the guns and destroyed all the ammunition and war material belonging to the fortresses under my command and so did everything that I could, in order that they should not obstruct the departure of his Majesty's squadron from the Tagus nor of any merchant ship that wished to follow it. 2nd – That at dawn on the 28th I left, with Lieutenant General Martinho de Souza d'Albuquerque, to meet the French Army in order to greet General Junot, on behalf of the government. 3rd – That on the afternoon of the 29th, the same government gave orders to rearm the Belém and Bom Sucesso fortresses. 4th – That on the 30th General Junot gave orders, through the General of Artillery, the Marquis of Vagos (previously appointed by HRH Governor of the Army of the Court and of the Province of Estremadura),

to the commanders of all the fortresses lining the banks of the Tagus, not to allow any ships to leave the port of Lisbon, until further notice. And 5th – Finally on 1st of December at midday, more or less, I presented myself to the Headquarters at Junqueira, to report that I had completed my duties and it was then that I was ordered to resume the command of these same fortresses that I had relinquished on the 28th.[22]

Confiance and *Redwing* sailed after the fleet and, on 1 December, caught up with it. The weather, however, prevented them from returning the marines before early morning of 3 December. *Solebay* stayed behind as she was now the sole frigate left outside the Tagus bar. *London*'s marines would only rejoin their ship, after a series of adventures, in Rio de Janeiro, on the afternoon of Saturday, 27 February 1808.

Whilst on board the *Príncipe Real*, Sir Sidney asked for and obtained a copy of her signal book. In addition to the practical aspects – the English squadron could now more easily communicate with the Portuguese – the handing over of the signal book, one of the most secret documents on board, had a much more important side. It was a manifestation of total trust and integration.

There was now every reason for temporarily postponing a land operation. As the fleet had left the Tagus the plan to go in and seize it no longer applied. In addition, the country was now occupied by the French, although there was no certainty as to the strength of this force. The difficulties of keeping transport ships off a lee shore added weight to Sir Sidney's decision, in spite of instructions from London, not to send for Sir John Moore's force from Gibraltar.

By early evening of the same day (29th), with a light and variable breeze and under cloudy skies, both fleets set sail in a northwesterly direction. The British flagship reported in her log a total of fifty-six sail in sight. The Portuguese naval fleet included eight sail of the line (*Conde D. Henrique*, *Martim de Freitas*, *D. João de Castro*, *Afonso de Albuquerque*, *Príncipe Real*, *Medusa*, *Rainha de Portugal* and *Príncipe do Brasil)*, four frigates (*Golfinho*, *Minerva*, *Urânia and Thetis*), two brigs (*Lebre and Vingança*), one Corvette (*Voador*), and one Schooner (*Curiosa*). The British squadron, detached from the Tagus, included HM ships *Bedford*, *Conqueror*, *Elizabeth*, *Foudroyant*, *Hibernia*, *London*, *Marlborough*, *Monarch* and *Plantagenet*, and the packet *Townsend*. HM sloop *Confiance* and HM rig sloop *Redwing* were still trying to take the Bugio fort. The remaining ships were merchantmen, of which only a few names have survived: the *Conceição* e *Santo Antônio* – skippered by Master Domingos João da Costa;[23] *Enrique Souza de Gouveia*;[24] *Príncipe*;[25] *Princesa do Brasil* – Captain Domingos José dos Santos (she was carrying eighteen passengers and took fifty-seven days to complete the journey);[26] *Chocalho*,[27] the last ship to leave the Tagus, on the 30th, under bombardment from the forts; and the *Jequiá*.[28] If the flagship could see all the British and Portuguese ships then, by deduction, there were thirty-one merchantmen, in company.

Lieutenant-Captain Lucas Boiteaux wrote that on this date (29th November) there appeared in sight the merchant fleet, arriving from Brazil:

> In the distance the Brazil convoy, made up of many national ships laden with Brazilian produce worth a vast amount… As the Brazil convoy could not reach Lisbon, the Prince Regent ordered the English Admiral to give it protection. Those ships were sent to London, where they remained for about four years, rotting and lost.[29]

Not only had the Brazil fleet been ordered, in September, to suspend departures until further notice, but also there is not the slightest evidence in any of ships' logs or reports of the event described above taking place on that date. The arrival of the ships from Brazil and their detention by the blockading squadrons is noted by an eyewitness, but the date recorded is Monday, 28 December.[30]

The scene of so many ships of the two nations, moving away together from the Tagus, inspired Sir Sidney to write:

> This fleet of eight sail of the line, four frigates, three brigs, and one schooner, with a crowd of armed merchant ships, arranged itself under the protection of his majesty's, while the firing of a reciprocal salute of twenty-one guns announced the friendly meeting of those who, but the day before, were in open hostility; the scene impressing every beholder, except the French army on the hills, with the most lively emotions of gratitude to Providence that there yet existed a power in the world able as well as willing to protect the oppressed; inclined to pardon the misguided, and capable, by its fostering care, to found new empires and alliances, from the wreck of the old ones, destroyed by the ephemeral power of the day, on the lasting basis of mutual interest.[31]

Maria Graham, writing in 1824, adds as a postscript:

> Such are the public accounts transmitted by foreigners to their court of one of the most singular transactions that has occurred in the history of Kingdoms and of courts. Yet such was the state of Europe at that time, so momentous the struggle between the principals in the mighty warfare that was going on, that the ancient house of Bragança left the seat of its ancestors, to seek shelter and security beyond the Atlantic, almost without notice and with less ceremony than had formally attended an excursion to its country palaces.[32]

In order to give the lords of the Admiralty in London a complete picture as to the state and strength of the Portuguese navy, Sir Sidney wrote in his report of 1 December, on board HMS *Hibernia,* twenty-two leagues west of the Tagus:

> I here enclose the list of those left behind. The absence of but one of the four ships is regretted by the Portuguese (the *Vasco da Gama*) she being under repair and ordered to join the fleet as she might be able to follow, or proceed to Gibraltar. Her guns have been employed to arm the *Freitas 64* a new ship and one of those which came out with the Prince. The other three are mere hulks and the one on the stocks the *Principe Regente* [sic] is only in frame.[33]

In fact, the *Martim de Freitas* was the *Santo Antônio e S. José*, built in Bahia in 1763. Thus she was now forty-four years old. She had undergone extensive repairs in 1794, when her name had been changed to *Infante D. Pedro Carlos*, and again in 1807, when she was renamed *Martim de Freitas*.

Whether to please Britain, or concerned with carrying out the article of the Convention that required that all ships not sailing to Brazil should be handed over or, even, mis-calculating the abilities of the French high command in Lisbon, the fact remains that within a few months Captain Magendie, who was then in charge of the Portuguese ships left behind, had managed to form a squadron ten strong. It included the line-of-battle ships *Vasco da Gama*, *Maria I* (renamed by the French, *Cidade de Lisboa*), *Princesa da Beira (*renamed *Portuguesa)* and *São Sebastião* (renamed *Brasil)*; the frigates *Tristão*, *Vênus*, *Princesa Carlota and Benjamim*; the brig *Gaivota do Mar* and the schooner *Curiosa*. This schooner had sailed with the fleet on 29 November but, badly dam-aged by the very first storm, and with victuals for only fifteen days, had been forced to return. On 7 December *Solebay* transferred to her two Portuguese prisoners, taken off a captured ship. She entered the Tagus and was taken by the French.[34]

~ *Monday, 30 November*

During this first night of the voyage the wind dropped and, at the same time, moved right round the compass: at first to east by north, then east, southeast, south-south-east, then variable but with a tendency to southwest. The fleet, responding to the wind, altered course to west by north, then northwest by north. This change in direction and light winds in the crowded seas was responsible for several near collisions. Just after midnight *Hibernia*'s log reads: "…at 1.30 down Cutter towed a Portuguese clear of us, hove to…" At 2 a.m. *Plantagenet* recorded: "…lowered down 2 boats to tow a ship clear – 3 up boats …"

As the wind changed direction so did it also change in strength. At dawn a fair breeze with squalls had developed with cloudy skies. By 9 a.m. it had become a fresh gale, still with some squalls. To face the stormy weather, topgallant masts and yards were lowered and lashed to the deck; mainsails furled; fore and mizzen topsails raised, but close reefed; and staysails set, to help reduce roll. The storm began to take its toll. Early on *Marlborough* split her main topsail, and *Confiance* fared worse. Towing a cutter lent by *Hibernia*, at 4 p.m. a wave filled her. The additional weight put too much strain on the cable. It parted and she broke adrift and was lost. A squall cost the *Hibernia* her fore topmast staysail. As night drew in, the fleet was now scattered over a wide area. Although the sails in sight were much reduced in number, *Hibernia* was still able to report that she could see thirty-eight. The Portuguese Admiral was some six or seven miles away. The British squadron sailed along, keeping close order, as instructed by the Admiral, busily putting on extra lashings against the force of the wind. The rain continued unabated.

In spite of the weather, life on board continued with a degree of normality. *London* reported opening three casks of beef each containing 26 8 lb pieces, two casks of pork with 133 4 lb and 6 lb pieces, one of oatmeal, one of flour weighing 341 lb and a pipe of wine containing 131 gallons. Her crew went about their various duties: "… Carpenters repairing ladders, Armourers making iron work for the launch, Sailmakers about fore topmasts stay sail…"

∼ *Tuesday, 1 December*

The gale force winds swung round; during the morning the winds were mostly south-westerly but moving in the afternoon to south-southeast. At noon, when their position was fixed, the combined fleets were 20 miles north of the latitude of Lisbon and some 120 miles west. In spite of the weather, the ships were largely managing to stay in sight. *Hibernia* reported seeing all the British ships, with the exception of *Elizabeth*, as well as twenty-six Portuguese vessels.

Ashore the people also felt the gale. Many feared for the royal family, at sea and out of sight of land. There was a general belief that the fleet was at that very moment making its way south to the Atlantic Isles and thence to Brazil. A southeasterly or south-westerly wind, accompanied by heavy seas, would therefore make sailing an uncomfortable and highly dangerous undertaking. Based on this incorrect assumption, many historians wrote of the desperate plight in which the passengers found themselves:

> During these first two days of the voyage the squadron faced, in the open sea, exceptionally severe storms; the wind, because of the direction from which it was blowing made life on board, due to the movement, unpleasant; the majority feared that the adventure would end at any moment. Even those Portuguese that had remained behind in Lisbon felt the bad weather. At three o'clock in the afternoon there was such a hurricane that its force was that of an earthquake, making many families flee. It broke countless window panes

and blew away tiles from several city blocks, mainly in the Treasury and the Royal Arsenal areas; the sea suddenly rose twelve hands.[35]

Eusébio Gomes confirms, in his diary, this storm as felt on shore:

On this day there was a violent storm, both on land and at sea; it would take a long time to describe all the damage it caused. In Mafra it was considerable; as it was market day all the stalls were destroyed, with much loss, the same happening in Lisbon.[36]

They could not know that, in fact, the fleets were moving in a northeasterly or northwesterly direction with topsails set, scudding before a following wind. In practice, under gale force winds and with the limitations imposed by square rigging, there was no reasonable alternative; the ships would be subject to pitch, rather than roll. Provided they kept up their speed and avoided having waves breaking on their poops, the danger from the gale would be much reduced.

Since starting the voyage, on the evening of 29 November, the weather had prevented any communication other than by signal, so wrote Sir Sidney.[37] He had signalled Captain Moore of the *Marlborough*, together with *Bedford*, *London* and *Monarch*, to stay by the main fleet '…and render it every protection and assistance …' He was keeping his flagship close to the prince's ship. *Foudroyant* and *Conqueror* had been ordered to remain with those disabled by the weather.

In the early afternoon *Elizabeth* came back into sight. Sir Sidney signalled her to take command of the *Plantagenet* and return to the estuary of the Tagus, and there continue the blockade. *Plantagenet* recorded the signal, sent as numerals:

649 Proceed 61 and 1115 Blockade 2432 Lisbon 61 and (18 19 13 19 21 2 5 18) Saintubes [sic] 1940 Warn 51 all 784 Ships 951 whatever 318 from (256 9 13 7) entering 867 those (621 18) Ports 387 if 864 they 1081 attempt 873 to 306 force 256 entrance 583 oppose 422 it 129 by 306 force 51 all 784 Ships 951 with gun 129 by gun 306 force 721 Rendezvous 2432 the Lisbon.

At 5 p.m. the two line-of-battle ships parted company from the squadron. The return to their station, however, was not easy. *Elizabeth* found "…the ship labouring hard & making a deal of water…" *Plantagenet* split her mainstay sail.

Pumps on board ships were very primitive – a column with saucers fitted at intervals on a chain. It was hard and strenuous work moving the chain, even though several crew members could operate it at the same time. The water was raised to the level of the first deck above the waterline. Ships were built with slightly cambered decks so that the water could run off through openings on the sides. Below decks the camber would enable the water to flow naturally to the foot of the mainmast, where the pump was located.

Sir Sidney wrote on 1 December:

> I have only the *Elizabeth* and *Plantagenet* off the Port of Lisbon;[38] and their Lordships will observe the utter impossibility I am under of as yet sending the *Foudroyant*, *Plantagenet* and *Conqueror* on to Admiral Purvis according to their order of the 14th without leaving the Russians at liberty to come out and pick out the Portuguese straggling ships which I trust will be the less felt as an inconvenience off Cadiz as they appear to have been ordered thither with reference to the Russians being within the straits before it was known they were on my station.[39]

∼ *Wednesday, 2 December*

In the afternoon the gale finally subsided and, although strong winds continued to blow, the fleets sailed close together. During the previous night the course had changed to west-southwest and so they were able at last to head for the island of Madeira, some 130 leagues away. The noon observation showed that the latitude of Lisbon had just been passed.

∼ *Thursday, 3 December*

The wind, moderate in the morning and by the afternoon down to a light breeze, gave an opportunity for various overdue tasks to be performed.

Although four days had passed since the Portuguese fleet had left the Tagus, Sir Sidney had been prevented by the gale force winds from sending news to England. Now, the various ships sent dispatches and private letters to the hired privateer *Trafalgar*, which in the early afternoon sailed for England. *Marlborough*'s and *Hibernia*'s marines were at last returned. The Portuguese Admiral received from the *Hibernia* the thirty Portuguese sailors who had been taken off a prize, on the 27th, as prisoners. As ships were usually short of their full complement, they would have been well received. *Bedford* reported sending a boat on board a Portuguese ship in distress. She may have been the schooner *Curiosa*, which would shortly return to the Tagus.

On board the *Medusa,* D. Araújo wrote to the Prince Regent:

> The Captain of the *Foudroyant,* that is the ship that accompanies us, proposes that we should ask your Royal Highness permission to suggest to Admiral Manuel da Cunha that he should allow the *Medusa*, accompanied by the *Foudroyant*, to go ahead to Madeira, independently of the squadrons, to get some fresh victuals of which we are in need. The captain and

José Egídio suggest that from the Island we can go to Bahia for water that we shall need.[40]

The Prince Regent, knowing full well that the size of the fleet would delay the journey, agreed that the *Medusa* should make her way, on her own, to Brazil; there to announce the forthcoming arrival of the royal family, thus giving the Viceroy time to make the necessary preparations.

Sir Sidney Smith decided that he could only spare four and not six line-of-battle ships from the Lisbon blockade to escort the Portuguese fleet, as required by the Convention signed in London. The presence of the Russian squadron in the Tagus required him to be in a constant state of alert, with the possibility of an action not to be discarded. He had up to now been escorting the fleet with six ships but shortly he would have to return to the blockade. The four line-of-battle ships chosen would remain with the fleet all the way to their destination. That morning he called on board his flagship the captains of HM ships *Bedford*, *London*, *Marlborough* and *Monarch*, in order to give them their orders. These would be the ships that would cross the Atlantic with the Portuguese fleet.

Sir Sidney regretted not having a frigate to send with the squadron. The *Solebay* was promised, just as soon as she rejoined. In fact, as already mentioned, she would only arrive in Rio de Janeiro nearly three months later.

The plans for the continued escorting of the fleet were now complete. Naval regulations required that the most senior captain present should take charge of the squadron to be detached to accompany the royal family. Seniority was strictly calculated from the date of promotion to the post of captain.

Although not the most senior captain present, Graham Moore of HMS *Marlborough* was chosen to lead the squadron, for reasons explained by Sir Sidney, when writing to the Admiralty on 6 December, some 350 miles from Lisbon:

> The important and unusually delicate duties I have confided to him, as detailed in the instructions I have given him, a copy of which I enclose. I feel the most perfect reliance in that officers' judgment ability and zeal in the execution of them, indeed without disparagement to those of the two officers, in the squadron senior to him one of whom, Captain Curzon[41] was detached on the important service of closely watching Lisbon while I have been on this, and the other is not placed permanently under my orders, there are so many, peculiarly applicable qualities in Captain Moore that I should not have felt myself as paying due regard to the Article of the General Printed instructions if I had not selected him.[42]

Captain Moore suffered from ill health and, for this reason, had been forced to leave the service in 1801:

> I am sorry to say his health is so precarious, from having before suffered severely in hot climates, that he does not feel equal to remaining long and I fear Captain Lee is in the same predicament. I shall therefore relieve those two ships; and the two others in succession.[43]

The appointment of a commodore, a temporary promotion when a senior captain was needed to take command of a small squadron, was usually referred to as 'hoisting a broad pennant'. This was the term used by Sir Sidney Smith in the order written by his secretary, Richard Speare, giving Captain Moore the command of the squadron.[44] The broad pennant of a commodore distinguished it from the pennant – a streamer some thirty yards long in the case of a 74 – of a captain. In both cases, and unlike the ensign which was lowered at sunset, pennants and streamers were flown day and night whilst the ship was under commission.

Sir Sidney's orders to Captain Moore, issued just before his departure from the Portuguese fleet, are very detailed and complete.[45] The communication gap, because of the distance of thousands of miles of sea and at least six weeks of travel in either direction, made it imperative that orders had to cover a lengthy period of time with the many phases planned, but also the unexpected. In practice not all circumstances could be foreseen so the utter reliance on the good sense, character and experience of the officers appointed to this post was extremely important.

Although in the open seas, far from land, the fleets were continuously on the alert for a possible surprise attack from one of the Spanish or French squadrons, supposedly in ports that were under British blockade. Communications were slow and unreliable, so it was always possible that one or more squadrons had managed to slip out.

~ Friday, 4 December

At daybreak the first stranger sighted since leaving the Tagus must have caused considerable apprehension. *Conqueror*, at 7 a.m., was signalled to give chase, which she duly did, and five hours later fired a gun and shortly afterwards another, to bring her to. Unexpectedly, she was a Portuguese merchant ship from Rio de Janeiro bound for Lisbon. For disobedience of the order to temporarily suspend all departures (sent out by the Prince Regent with the brig *Gavião* in September) the ship was apprehended and, next day, a lieutenant with forty men were put on board and seventy-seven Portuguese sailors taken off. As the *Conqueror* had sailed so far after her chase, she now reported that the fleets far to the west by north were barely visible from her masthead.

As the weather continued moderate, with occasional rain and a calm sea, the transfer of crew took place to those ships most in need. The frigate *Urânia* recorded in her log: "...at 5 a boat came from the *Príncipe do Brasil* with an officer and took 10 sailors from the complement of this ship..."

~ *Saturday, 5 December*

Now that the weather had improved, final preparations for the voyage could be made. Rear Admiral Sir Sidney Smith and Vice-Admiral D. Manuel da Cunha Souto Maior, both commanders with a lifetime of experience at sea, took stock of the condition of each vessel.

Basically, to undertake such a long voyage with a degree of safety, ships had to be in a reasonable condition both as to masts, spars and sails, and the state of the hull; had to have enough water, as there was a strong probability of an extended voyage due to calm weather, often encountered near the equator; and also sufficient crew to man the ship.

Storm and battle damage was a common occurrence, and ranged from cracked or even lost yards and smaller masts, rigging destroyed, sails split or blown out, and damage to the hull. To counter these occurrences, ships carried spare spars, sail cloth and cordage as well as the necessary craftsmen. Even below the waterline leaks could be plugged with sail cloth. In the event of very severe damage, the ship could still sail on, although slower, with part of a mast or with a spar rigged as a mast.

At first, the *Martim de Freitas* had been considered as not being in a state to face the journey but under further appraisal D. Manuel decided that the *Príncipe do Brasil* and the *Golfinho*[46] were in a worse condition. It was therefore agreed that before undertaking the long voyage, they should go first to England for repairs. Arrangements had been made in Plymouth to receive the whole or part of the Portuguese fleet. As a precaution D. Manuel ordered that the royal passengers: the queen's sisters, the Infanta D. Maria Ana and the widow princess D. Maria Francisca Benedita, should transfer from the *Príncipe do Brasil* to the *Rainha de Portugal.*

However, in spite of these arrangements, Sir Sidney reported that when he separated from the Portuguese fleet on 5 December, the *Príncipe do Brasil* did not accompany him. Although Esparteiro writes that the *Príncipe do Brasil* arrived in Rio de Janeiro on 14 January, a week before that part of the fleet which had sailed directly to Rio de Janeiro, this would appear to be incorrect. *London*'s log shows that she arrived on 13 February, so she may in fact have gone to Plymouth after all.

The *Martim de Freitas* and the frigate *Golfinho*, in spite of the doubts over their condition, obtained permission to go by themselves directly to Bahia or some other convenient port in Brazil. Separated by bad weather on 9 December, they sailed independently of each other for the rest of the journey.[47]

On 3 December Sir Sydney Smith wrote to Admiral Young in Plymouth, informing him of the successful departure from Portugal of the royal family, warning him that some of the Portuguese ships, needing repairs and supplies, might sail to Plymouth before attempting the crossing to Brazil. He also confirmed that the *Hibernia,* with the *Elizabeth, Foudroyant, Conqueror* and *Plantagenet* would, for the present, remain off the Tagus. Although the Portuguese fleet was no longer in the river, the Russian squadron of nine ships was still there: all the more reason to continue the general blockade.[48]

Following the assessment as to the state of the ships, attention was given to their supplies. Water was not a particular problem, in spite of the additional passengers being carried, as they expected to have an opportunity to replenish in Madeira and perhaps also in St Tiago.[49] Consumption, if necessary, could be cut down by half without too much hardship. In extreme cases the ration could be much reduced, when a permanent guard would be put on the water supply.

Even those ships that went directly to Bahia do not appear to have felt any shortage. The Portuguese frigate *Minerva,* which parted company from the *Príncipe Real* on the night of 21 December, may have transferred part of her water supply to that ship. *Bedford* records her normal water consumption of two tons per day during the whole of the voyage. If required, she would have certainly transferred part of her water to any ship in need. She arrived in Bahia, with seventy-five tons in her hold – sufficient for a least another six weeks.

Food, after the transfers from the *Hibernia* and the *Conqueror*, also does not appear to have been a problem. There is no doubt, however, that the quality would leave much to be desired, particularly amongst the civilians not used to shipboard fare – salted or dried to withstand long periods. Ship's biscuit: in fact bread, overcooked to remove the moisture, even though stored apart in a separate tin-lined room was, after a time, subject to weevil infestation.

D. João supported the journey well, prohibiting any complaints or intrigues.[50] D. Carlota Joaquina, of an entirely different temperament, complained bitterly and demanded that D. João improve the cooking arrangements on board her ship *(Afonso de Albuquerque)*. He wrote to her:[51]

> My dear, I hope that you and our daughters are well. I am well as also my mother, our sons and nephew. As to what you tell me about the Kitchen and pantry, you must authorise Count Caparica, together with an able officer of your ship, to make the best possible arrangements, and punish those that do not obey you. God be with you.
> Your loving husband JC.'

Scurvy, caused by the lack of vitamin C – found in fresh vegetables and fruit – had by then been carefully researched and its cause identified. As a result a regular ration of juice from citrus fruits was distributed on board.

The *Príncipe Real* received the Admiral's barge 'complete'. It would come in useful when they arrived at a port and even before, should the Prince Regent decide to pay a visit to another ship when becalmed – a probability when they entered the doldrums.

In addition to the barge, the *Hibernia* also transferred one bale each of jackets, bell trousers, grey jackets, flannel waistcoats, drawers, blankets, shirts, frocks, shoes, stockings and hats – a strange occurrence, as they were sailing to the tropics.

On 5 December, roughly halfway between Lisbon and Funchal (the island of Madeira), Sir Sidney Smith decided that the danger of meeting enemy ships had receded, and that it was therefore time to return to the Lisbon blockade.

Legend has it that before Sir Sidney Smith departed, he indicated that he wished to present the Prince Regent with a gift, but that conditions did not permit a boat to be lowered into the water. The captain of the *Príncipe Real*, Francisco do Canto de Castro e Mascarenhas, after obtaining permission from the Prince Regent, manoeuvered his ship to pass close enough for the gift to be handed across from one yard arm to the other; thus showing to all those present, the skill and prowess of a ship of the Portuguese navy.[52]

This legend must remain a legend! On the day in question, there were light breezes blowing and clear skies. During the day several ships lowered their boats to transfer stores and prisoners. Ships about to undertake a long journey, with the monarch and the regent on board, would be unlikely to take this unnecessary risk of a collision. The logs show unequivocally that the *Hibernia* and the *Príncipe Real* did not come closer than one mile from each other.

The *Marlborough*, *Bedford*, *London and Monarch* had a busy day preparing for their long voyage to Brazil. In the early morning the captains went on board the *Marlborough* to receive instructions from their future commodore.

D. Manuel, on board the Príncipe Real, decided on their rendezvous:

> The first thing I was anxious to have perfectly understood between the Portuguese Vice Admiral and my self was the Rendezvous, which was fixed by him to be first off the west end of Madeira and afterwards off the Island of Palma (Canary Islands) and lastly Praya Bay on the Island of St. Iago [sic], (Cape Verde) and on his assuring me that he would go to the latter.[53]

Preparations went ahead. The *Marlborough* took on board, as ballast, forty-three tons of sea water in the forehold "…to keep the ship by the head…" As she had been at sea for four weeks since leaving Plymouth on 9 November, and as she consumed two tons of fresh water each day the ballast would largely compensate for the water and provisions consumed. The *London* sent over her three boats – the launch, the cutter and the pinnace – to the *Hibernia* to help transfer stores to the *Principe Real.*

In the afternoon at 3.20, as recorded by the *Hibernia,* the royal salute was fired, and returned by the *Conde D. Henrique.* Preparations now nearly complete, *Hibernia* and *Conqueror*, with the sloop *Confiance* and the brig sloop *Redwing* escorting, steered northeast and parted company from the Portuguese fleet.

At nine o'clock that night the Portuguese fleet, with the escort of the four British line-of-battle ships, under moderate southeasterly breezes and cloudy winter skies, resumed its journey. The pace was very slow and would continue so for the next twenty-four hours – no more than one and very occasionally two knots, in a general southwesterly direction.

～ *Sunday, 6 December*

At first light in the morning nearly the whole of the Portuguese fleet was sailing together. *Marlborough* reported that the squadron and fourteen Portuguese men of war were "… in company …"

On this day Graham Moore went on board the *Príncipe Real* to speak with the Portuguese Admiral. He wrote in his private diary:

> Yesterday (6/12) I had a conversation with the Portuguese Admiral on the subject of the public business, and pressed him very much to relinquish his project of touching at St. Iago [sic] in the Cape de Verde Islands as I was sure it could answer no good purpose and would only occasion delay, of all things to be avoided in the state his Ships were in and not being suffi-ciently stocked with water and provisions. I assured him he could not water his Squadron there as Sir John Warren had not been able to make good his consumption of water when he lay there with six Ships of the Line some 15 or 16 months ago. I then proposed to him to send one of his Brigs to Madeira with directions to the Governor to forward the supplies to any of the English Squadron that I might detach there for water and refreshments. This he did very readily and I sent the *London* with orders to complete her own water and fill as many of the Casks from the other three Line of Battle ships as she could conveniently stow on her decks. I ordered Capt. Western of the *London* to rendezvous either at the SW point of Madeira or off Praya Bay in the Island of St. Iago [sic] where the Prince of Brazil determined to go off, without anchoring, for the purpose of getting some stock."[54]

Commodore Moore understood that his orders were to stay with the Portuguese fleet, in particular with those ships that had members of the royal family on board. Their speed would be that of the slowest, so by sending the *London* ahead, he hoped to gain a day or two – the time needed to bring out the heavy casks from the shore and stow them below decks.

In the middle of the afternoon the fleet and squadron hove to for two hours. The *London* received twenty empty water casks from each of her sister ships. The *Marlborough* sent over nine casks of salted provisions to the *Príncipe Real*. The *Príncipe Real*, overcrowded, now transferred to the *London* sixty-nine of her passengers and an unrecorded number to the *Monarch*.

These are the only recorded instances during the long voyage to Brazil of transferring passengers from the overloaded Portuguese ships. It is possible that because of the first few days of disagreeable stormy weather, or because those passengers transferred to the *London* had family living on one of the Madeira Islands, they may have decided not to continue to Brazil. As there is no record of their leaving the ship in Funchal, it is also possible that the transfer was made solely to relieve the overloaded ship, and so make more room for members of the royal family. The full complement of the 84-gun *Príncipe Real* was 950 men. Captain Walker reported that on arrival in Bahia she was carrying 1,054 persons on board. Therefore, if she had managed to gather her full complement, she was carrying 104 passengers.

At ten o'clock that night *London* put on more sail and began to draw away from the fleet. By noon the following day she was a long way off but still just in sight, making five and six knots.

Captain Thomas Western of HMS *London* was ordered, after watering, to rejoin the squadron, possibly off Palma but definitely in Porto Praia (Cape Verde).

∼ *Monday, 7 December*

The wind again began to gain in force, announcing yet another storm on its way. The fresh breeze forced the faster sailing ships alternately to make and shorten sail, so that the fleet and the escorting squadron, now reduced to three ships, should stay together. In the afternoon one of the Portuguese ships was spoken to by *Bedford*; she had sprung her foremast. *Bedford* sent over a boat to evaluate the damage and see what she could do to help.

At dusk the *Príncipe Real* received Commodore Moore, who had come over to obtain information on the Admiral's immediate plans. As it turned out later, this was the beginning of various misunderstandings that eventually resulted in the separation of the fleet. Commodore Moore, when reporting later on the events that were to occur on the following day, revealed the principal objective of that meeting:

> More especially as we were then about 50 leagues from Madeira and he
> had told me the day before that he was afraid to run in the night on account
> of the danger called the eight stones which are laid down to the northward
> of Porto Santo.[55]

∼ *Tuesday, 8 December*

Daylight showed that this was just another winter's day in the north Atlantic: cold, windy, cloudy and wet. Nothing indicated that Portuguese and Brazilian history would have their paths significantly altered by a series of events – some fortuitous, such as weather; others, through human error due to lack of knowledge of local practice, misinterpretation of instructions and failure in communications.

The wind, increasing by the end of the day to gale force, produced very heavy seas and rain. *Marlborough* recorded the variations throughout the day. First the wind came from the east, then the south, then north and finally east again. The ships, under these conditions, had difficulties and, for those responsible for them, a tiring time in trying to maintain some organisation in their manoeuvres. Most of the day was spent tacking. *Monarch* recorded successively, up south by west off southwest, then up northeast off north-northeast. Commodore Moore, fearful that the rapidly worsening weather conditions could play havoc with his ships, scattering them over a wide area; and as the poor visibility could make the ships lose sight of each other, emphasised the rendezvous by signalling with the wooden telegraph: "…rends. Off the SW end of Madeira 2 days after Porto Santo…"

At seven in the evening, seeing that the Admiral had hove to, *Marlborough* and *Monarch* did likewise. *Bedford* slowed to pass by the *Marlborough*, but continued sailing on. Commodore Moore imagined that the *Príncipe Real* and her sister ships would stay hove to until daylight, thus avoiding the dangers of approaching Madeira by night. As the fleet was much scattered by the baffling winds, with only seven ships in sight, a distance of some two miles was kept by the commodore between ships, to maintain the line of connection with the scattered vessels.

As darkness descended, twice the *Marlborough* moved closer to the Admiral, so as to keep the lights of the *Príncipe Real* in sight, but at 9 p.m. she lost contact. Commodore Moore would not have been particularly alarmed by this fact: with the Admiral hove to, he could not be far away at daylight. All night long he would have redoubled the lookout; anxious to locate the Admiral's lights in fear that, in the darkness, there could be a collision.

Outside the Tagus bar, the British ships that had set off on 29 November with the Portuguese fleet were now once again gathering. Their role was outwardly unchanged, but the purpose of their actions was now different: that of preventing supplies from reaching French or Spanish troops, either from ships friendly to those countries, or from neutrals. During the first week five prizes were taken and a number of neutral ships boarded and told not to land their merchandise in Lisbon. In addition they would effectively blockade the Russian squadron, and so prevent it from taking part in the hostilities.

On 7 December, now well to the north of the Portuguese fleet, the sloop *Confiance*, bound for England, parted from the *Hibernia*. Lord Strangford – who had originally planned to follow with the escorting squadron, so maintaining his post as His Majesty's representative to the Portuguese Court – was taken seriously ill and put on board to return to England. Also on board were his servants and the king's messenger. He would only arrive in Rio de Janeiro, to take up his post, on 2 July 1808.[56]

Lord Strangford, accustomed to negotiating with princes, ministers and admirals, felt obliged, on his return to London, to deal with more mundane matters – he was to write to the Rt Hon George Canning asking for reimbursement of those valuables he had left behind in Lisbon:

> I have to entreat your pardon for the liberty I take in representing, that the peculiar Circumstances of my departure from Lisbon, occasioned me to suffer considerable losses in Carriages, Furniture, Books & other Effects; including some very valuable Andalusian Horses with which I had been presented by the Prince Regent. I can aver, in any manner that may be deemed proper or necessary, that those losses do not amount to less than £1077.0.0 & confiding in the justice and generosity of His Majesty, I venture to solicit that I may be authorised to receive that sum <u>Nett</u>, at the Treasury.[57]

Chapter VI

The line-of-battle ships Príncipe Real, Afonso de Albuquerque *and HMS* Bedford, *after several days alone, reunite and sail on, without stopping, to Brazil. Salvador is finally reached on 22 January 1808. After a brief stay in that city the squadron leaves for Rio de Janeiro, on 26 February, arriving there on 7 March 1808.*

∼ *Wednesday, 9 December*

The surprise on board the *Príncipe Real*, which came with daybreak on that Wednesday, 9 December, can well be imagined. Cloudy skies and a fresh breeze ushered in the new day. The officer on duty that morning, as daylight strengthened, allowing him to search the horizon with his glass, would have felt stunned: after so many days in crowded seas they were now utterly alone apart from the frigate *Urânia* sailing faithfully beside them. He would have immediately sent for the captain, Francisco José do Canto de Castro e Mascarenhas, if he was not already on deck. Responsible captains liked to be present at this hour as, after such a long period of darkness, the scenario might have dramatically changed. In turn, he would have sent for Vice-Admiral D. Manuel da Cunha Souto Maior and for Major General Joaquim José Monteiro Torres. The frigate captain, José Manuel de Meneses,[1] would also have been heard in the ensuing discussion of how this separation had taken place and what was now their best course of action.

Envisaging a situation such as this is the reason why, at all times, there are rendezvous agreed in advance. The natural decision, therefore, would have been, within the limits imposed by the direction and strength of the wind, to head for the first rendezvous, which was off the west end of the island of Madeira.

On board the *Afonso de Albuquerque* the surprise would not have been any different. Captain Inácio da Costa Quintela would, no doubt, have been called up on deck to survey and confer with Captain Rodrigo José Ferreira Lobo of her close escort, the frigate *Minerva*.

Here, too, the decision as to course would have been the same: the west end of Madeira.

Captain James Walker of HMS *Bedford*, recalling the previous evening's events, wrote:

> On the night of the 8th ult°, the Fleet separated, I had spoke the *Marlborough*

by Signal at dusk and received the rendezvous from Captain Moore, he was then lying too which I conceived was for the purpose of speaking us as the Admiral was going on and no signal had been. We bore up out of his way, and resumed our course SWbS we soon lost sight of him. That evening and indeed the whole night it blew fresh & squally and the weather so thick we could not see three times the Ships length, we neither saw the Admirals lights nor heard any guns, and as we were 49 leagues from Madeira I naturally concluded he would continue on the same course.[2]

He had been up all night, for his main concern – due to the very poor visibility – was of a possible collision and its terrible consequences so he reported, on 6 January, to their lordships at the Admiralty:

We went all night (except from 10 to 11) under the close reefed Fore & Main Topsails on the cap, afraid to heave too lest we might have been run on board, however the weather clearing a little we lay too from 10 to 11 – at 2 a.m. still nobody in sight we steered SW. till day light, when finding ourselves alone I hove too in the hope that we had outrun them, as I would not on any other reasonable ground account for so extraordinary an occurrence.[3]

Normally, if there is any doubt that another ship might not see or take note of a signal, either because of poor visibility or because of the distance, a warning gun is fired. All attention on board is then turned towards the signalling ship and glasses trained on her. If, however, the signal still cannot be deciphered, then she will put on sail and steer to close the distance. That night, under very poor visibility, the *Príncipe Real* did not enforce any signal she may have made with a gun.

One of the first questions raised by Captain Walker when he eventually went on board the *Príncipe Real* on the 15th was to enquire of D. Manuel as to what had happened:

I found that early on the evening of the 8th, the Admiral apprehensive that we were running too near a danger called the eight stones, which is said to be NNE, about 40 Lgs. from Madeira had steered W.NW. for the night and altered his course, without signal as it was not customary to fire guns when the Royal Family is on board, the natural consequence was that at day light the Admiral in the *Prince Royal* [sic] found himself with only one frigate in company.[4]

In fact it was the queen's health, rather than the fact that the royal family was on board, that was the real reason for not firing a gun, as the Prince Regent had previously explained to Sir Sidney.

The logbook of the *Urânia*, the frigate that never let the *Príncipe Real* out of sight, however, records that on the night of the 8th a reduction in speed took place between five and six in the evening to some two knots per hour. From seven onwards the speed increased and was maintained throughout the night at five knots.

Bedford, sailing at nine and ten knots in the fresh breeze, was first to reach Madeira:

> I made Sail a little before Noon for Madeira which we were then 18 Lgs. from, at ½ past 3 p.m. we made it and at 5 passed within 7, or 8 miles of the W. end of it / the rendezvous/ and hove, but still without seeing the fleet.[5]

Her log reads:

> (Decr. 9th) …3.30 saw the land SWbyW 4 leagues bore up at the west end of Madeira SWbyW 4 or 5 leagues …

On the way she sighted in the distance a frigate. She reported to the Admiralty:

> I continued with our head to the Southwd. Partly lying too or under easy sail waiting for a frigate we saw about 8, coming down upon us, as she approached finding that she was one of the Fleet but alone.[6]

In the afternoon she sighted another frigate, this time escorting several merchant vessels "…6 sail West which proved to be Merchant vessels under convoy of a Frigate …"

As dusk descended the *Príncipe Real* and the *Afonso de Albuquerque*, with their escorting frigates, were each sailing alone well to the north and westward of Madeira; the result of having steered during the night west-northwest with a following wind. *Bedford*, also alone, was at the rendezvous lying off the Western end of Madeira.

~ *Thursday, 10 December*

The strong, mainly easterly winds and squally weather made it difficult for *Bedford* to hold her station off the west coast of the island of Madeira. By noon, the winds were again at gale force, compelling her to close reef the few sails she had unfurled; and take down, and lash to the deck, her topgallant masts. In the afternoon George Green, a sailor, fell into the sea but a boat, quickly lowered, picked him up. The *Príncipe Real* and the *Afonso de Albuquerque*, with their frigates, continued unescorted and still separated.

∼ *Friday/Saturday, 11/12 December*

Early in the morning the *Príncipe Real* and the *Afonso de Albuquerque* finally joined company with the frigates *Urânia* and *Minerva*: a small squadron of four vessels of the more than thirty-five ships that had left the Tagus, less than two weeks before, and now carrying almost the whole of the royal family.

Too far from the west coast of Madeira, they found it impracticable, with the easterly wind, to make for the rendezvous, so sailed on to Ferro.[7]

Next morning, *Bedford* had drifted to a point some twenty leagues off the west of Madeira. The unwavering easterly wind made it difficult to regain the island. As they had been at the rendezvous for thirty-six hours without seeing any of the ships they were to convoy, or any sister ships, Captain Walker decided, after taking his bearings at noon, to sail on to the second rendezvous. He changed course, now making for Ferro – an island in the Canaries some eighty leagues distant. The weather continued with fresh breezes blowing mainly from the southeast and still cloudy. For the remainder of that day and the following one he pressed on, mostly at five and six knots, increasing on the morning of the 12th to eight and nine knots.

∼ *Sunday/Monday, 13/14 December*

At the speed she had been making it did not take *Bedford* long to cover the distance to her destination, again arriving before all others. At daybreak of the 13th the island of Palma, the most northern of the group comprising the Canaries, came into sight south by west, some six leagues away. During the day the wind dropped to a light breeze and the sun came out, as Palma went slowly by. At six, Ferro came into sight. Once again *Bedford* took up her station, waiting and hoping to pick up the fleet. At this point she had no means of knowing that the two most important ships being escorted had also separated and, although now sailing together, did not have the escort of a British warship.

The *Príncipe Real* and *Bedford* were now close to each other. At seven that evening *Urânia* noted in her log that the island of Ferro could be seen. At the same moment *Bedford* records that Ferro continued in sight. However close, they were out of sight of each other.

On the morning of the 14th, just after she had been exercising her great guns, *Bedford* saw three sails to windward, increased in the afternoon to four.

Exercising the main guns for speed in delivering broadsides and accuracy was a necessary feature of shipboard life, and a certain quantity of powder was allowed by the Admiralty for this purpose. Captains not infrequently purchased additional powder from their own pocket in order to increase the frequency of practices. Repayment was hoped for in prize money; promotions; and glory, won in battle.

Bedford now made all speed towards the distant sails, but it would be a whole day before she could record: "...joined company with part of the Portuguese Squadron which had the royal family …" Captain Walker later reported to the Admiralty:

> On the 14th, in the morning off the Island I had the satisfaction of seeing 4
> Sail to windward the wind being then W.S.W. which I joined the next day,
> and they were the Ships now in company.[8]

～ *Tuesday/Wednesday, 15/16 December*

On the afternoon of the 15th *Bedford* went alongside the *Príncipe Real*, and Captain Walker went on board. Now that she was the lone escort, all responsibilities imposed by the Convention fell on *Bedford*. She took these very seriously, as Captain Walker reported:

> I paid every attention in my power to the Royal Family which my Duty &
> inclination suggested and his Royal Highness has been graciously pleased
> to express his satisfaction on my conduct.[9]

With the last of the gales over and now only two degrees from entering the tropics, good weather with warm and pleasant breezes was the order of the day. On the 16th *Bedford* reported that her sailmakers were busy making an awning. This would give shade on the open deck and help cool the air going down to the lower decks through the ventilation gratings.

As the weather grew better and passengers did not have to worry so much about keeping dry and warm, anxiety receded, both about the weather and from a possible attack from a French squadron. However, this was soon replaced by restlessness and complaints of the lack of space, food, cleanliness and recreation:

> When the storms passed a general outcry arose on board, because of the
> lack of comfort; one complained that his favourite teapot, that made the
> best tea in the world, had remained behind in Lisbon; others that they had
> left behind a chest filled with indispensable belongings; yet others regret-
> ted having embarked.[10]
>
> On realising that they were far from the enemy and from their unhappy
> country, peace returned. They noticed that everything was missing, that the
> food was of the worse quality, that their baggage had been (mistakenly)
> exchanged.[11]

～ *Thursday/Friday, 17/18 December*

The monotony of the journey was broken on the 17th. It was the queen's birthday. Three times during the day – at dawn, noon and sunset – the Portuguese ships fired the royal salute in her honour.[12] *Bedford*, not wishing to be left out of these celebrations, at daylight hoisted the royal standard and further demonstrated her participation, in a traditional British naval ceremony:

> On the 17th, the birthday of the Queen, which they celebrated with three Royal Salutes at Sunrise, Noon and Sunset I thought it highly expedient that His Majesty's Ship should make every demonstration of our partic-ipating in their celebration of it and a little before Noon I took in all the Sails, Manned the Yards the People being all uniformly dressed, with their hats off and the Marines under presented Arms, and 12. I fired a Royal Salute.[13]

The next day, identical celebrations were repeated "…being the Feast of the Tutelar Saint of the Queen…" On board *Bedford* the officers will have been pleased with the reaction: "…The Prince expressed himself highly gratified, on both occasions …"[14]

Captain Walker, facing highly unusual duties and circumstances, worried whether he was doing the right thing and wrote:

> I beg leave to hope Their Lordships will approve of my conduct therein. – To obviate any remark of my having done the thing by halves I explained that we never exceeded 21 Guns in celebrating our Royal Masters Birth day.[15]

~ *Monday, 21 December*

After several days of very slow progress a northeasterly wind sprang up and, for a week, they were sailing at six and seven knots per hour.

The keen desire to get to his new world dominions, the steady northeasterly wind, and an adequate supply of victuals and water may well have been the reasons that made the Prince Regent decide, on 21 December, to sail directly to Brazil. On that morning the *Príncipe Real* signalled *Bedford* to close, so as to pass within hailing distance.

Bedford records:

> At 5 was hailed and informed that the Prince had ordered a frigate to port Praya, to announce his royal highness having gone on and to order all the ships to proceed to Rio de Janeiro and wished Captain Walker to remain with him. This was an important change from the previously agreed plans:

> The Prince intended at first to have called at Porto Praya and it was settled that I should anchor and bring him out refreshments while he lay too, in the offing, but having a strong NNE wind we passed to the Eastwd. of all the

Cape de Ver Islands [sic] and did not go within 60. Lgs. of St. Iago [sic], and he dispatched a Frigate there to order all the Ships that might arrive to follow him to Rio de Janeiro and desired me to continue with him, indeed he has always expressed the greatest wish that I should remain by him, which I should have felt it my duty to do.[16]

During the night of 21 December the frigate *Minerva* was dispatched to Porto Praya, the main town on St Tiago Island. She would arrive there with her news before the *Marlborough* (24th). Before leaving she was informed as to what longitude the *Príncipe Real* and the *Afonso de Albuquerque* expected to cross the equinox.[17]

The equinox is that point where day and night have an equal number of hours. The expected longitude where this imaginary line would be crossed was, therefore, a reference point for the ships watering in Porto Praya. Out of sight of land it was impracticable to select a rendezvous as before. This was therefore as good a reference point as it was possible to have, under the circumstances.

Life on board the ships settled down again, as there was still much sailing to be done – in total length of time they were but half way.

∼ *Thursday, 22 December*

Bedford noted in her log; 22 December:

A.M. sailmakers employed repairing the mainsail people working up junk.[18] Armourers at the forge, p.m. got the remains of cheese up to air and examining it found part of several cheeses decayed and unfit for use condemned pr survey one hundred & fifty two Pounds rotten & stinking & unfit for men to eat which was thrown overboard being a nuisance to the ship.

December 23rd:

"...a.m. washed the lower Deck sent the boat on board the Portuguese Admiral 12 moderate & fair..."

December 24th:

6.30 departed this life John Alioand (s), 8.40 committed the body of the deceased to the deep with the usual ceremony p.m. Punished Hugh Davis with 24 lashes for neglect of duty and disrespect Neal McDougall (s) with 24 lashes for neglect of duty and mutinous expressions and Tho Mirrins (s) with 3 lashes for neglect of duty.

As they approached the equator their speed dropped alarmingly. Little did they know that sailing on a parallel route, not very far to their west, they would soon be overtaken by the *Marlborough* and her convoy.

Frustration on board must have been rampant, for the squadron was now caught up in the doldrums. Although much reduced in area during this time of the year, it meant that headway was minimal. This situation was to get even worse as time passed, as was reported by Captain Walker: "…We were a great deal detained by calms baffling winds and heavy rains on the north side of the Line and were 10 days in going 30 lgs…"[19] A line-of-battle ship, under a stiff breeze, could cover that distance in a mere twenty hours.

Distraction over the ever-lengthening journey included social visits from one ship to another. From the number of times that *Bedford* was putting her boats in the sea, no doubt this was taking place. On most days one of *Bedford*'s boats would go over to the Admiral for a few hours.

One of the most disagreeable aspects of calm weather, with little movement to the ship, was the question of sewage. As there were no septic tanks or anything similar, as time went by all dejects tended to accumulate in the sea around the ship – a nauseating as well as a stinking mass, made worse as the weather grew hotter.

Another disagreeable aspect was the lack of hygiene on board. Tobias Monteiro wrote:

> So great was the invasion of lice, that all the women, including the Royal
> Princess, had to cut her hair. When they were seen arriving with their heads
> shaved, all the fair sex of Rio de Janeiro took it to be the height of fashion
> and, within a very short time, the abundant heads of hair of the cariocas,
> fell one by one to the scissors.[20]

Even on land, as bathing was not a regular custom, lice were a constant problem. Trained monkeys could be hired to pick (and eat) the lice from infested heads! Long hair was taken as a sign of wealth, from the cost of its upkeep.

The tropical weather set in, with thunder, lightning and heavy rain in the afternoons, but little wind.

~ *Friday/Saturday/Sunday, 1/2/3 January 1808*

At 10 a.m. on 1 January, at the height of the calm and windless period, *Bedford* reported seeing from the top of her mast a strange sail in the southeast.

A keen lookout, in the crow's nest of the topmast, could spot a topgallant or even a royal on the horizon when the ship was still hull down, in good visibility, some twenty miles or more away.

Next day at 7.30 a.m. she reported that the strange sail was still there, and at noon she could see two sails in a southerly direction. At that moment *Bedford* was sailing ahead of the ships that she was escorting, so as to be able to return to them if need be. The *Príncipe Real* was north by west, the *Afonso de Albuquerque* north-northwest and the *Urânia* close to the Admiral, also north by west. That night she burnt a blue light. On the 3ʳᵈ the two strange sails had moved to southwest by west.

There was very little that *Bedford* could do: not only was the wind slight so that even relatively short distances required a great deal of time to cover, but being alone she could not leave the ships she was escorting, to investigate strange sails.

It is probable that, allowing for inaccuracies and the fact that the ships were spread over a wide area, she was in fact seeing ships that were being escorted by the *Marlborough*. During these three days the *Commodore*, sailing a more westerly course, overtook the squadron that *Bedford* was escorting.

Their relative positions, at noon each day, were as follows:[21]

	Bedford		**Marlborough**	
	Latitude	**Longitude**	**Latitude**	**Longitude**
1 January	2°58'N	21°48'	3°21'N	23°00'
2 January	2°39'N	21°52'	2°34'N	22°57'
3 January	2°19'29"N	22°09'	1°43'N	23°44'

The positioning of a ship at midday does not provide absolute accuracy, as indicated by the records of the ships sailing together with the *Marlborough*:

	London		**Monarch**	
	Latitude	**Longitude**	**Latitude**	**Longitude**
1 January	3°18'N	22°57'/22°54'	3°23'N	22°38'
2 January	2°26'N	23°04'	2°27'N	22°38'
3 January	1°46'21"N	23°05'04"	1°50'N	23°10'

Additional evidence is the entry in *Marlborough*'s log for the night of 2 January: "...Saw a blue light NE – at 11.15 burnt a blue light – Squadron in Company..." *Bedford*'s log for the same night reads: "...burnt a blue light..."

This is the only night of the voyage, subsequent to 8 December and until arrival in Brazil, that a 'blue light' – typical of Royal Navy ships – is recorded by any of the four vessels. It would appear that *Bedford* burnt a blue light because she had strangers in sight.

The comparison of positions between *Bedford* and *Marlborough* also shows clearly the considerable difference in speeds. Although close by the wind could be different, it is more probable that *Bedford*'s slow progress was due to the sluggish pace set by the *Afonso de Albuquerque*.

~ *Monday, 4 January*

Another stranger now appeared, this time a brig sailing southeastward. *Bedford* altered her course slightly to intercept her and, next day, overtook her. She was a Portuguese brig carrying salt from Lisbon to Rio de Janeiro. A slow sailer, having set off on her journey on 14 November, she knew nothing of the more recent events.

Meanwhile in Bahia, according to records, the very first ship from the merchant fleet that had set out from Lisbon on 29 November had just arrived. She was a merchantman from that town, the *Príncipe*.[22] When she docked in Salvador, on 4 January, she brought news of the transfer of the Court. It appeared to the then Governor, João de Saldanha, 6th Count of Ponte,[23] that her news was authentic – from the details of the meeting with the British squadron outside the bar and from the copy of the decree that had been published stating D. João's intention to leave for Brazil. This news was immediately sent to the Viceroy, Marcos de Noronha e Brito, 8th Count of Arcos,[24] in Rio de Janeiro. Prophetically, the *Principe*'s news was that the Prince Regent was coming to Bahia.

~ *Wednesday, 6 January*

As from the 4th Captain Walker daily exchanged information on their position with the Admiral. The wind, from the south-southeast, had gained some strength so it would appear that they were now clear of the doldrums and sailing, but still slowly, at two and three knots.

Captain Walker's first report on the voyage was written on this date. He adds in a postscript:

> I had written the above letter in the hope of falling in with somebody near the Line, bound to England or the West Indies. As no such opportunity occurred I have thought it right to send it from thence.[25]

The probable sailing route for a vessel going to England from the southern hemisphere was past the West Indies, then up the coast of the United States, only crossing over at a high latitude where she would count on the westerlies.

On board *Bedford* the slow journey was beginning to have its effect on the crew. The captain's log reported on the 7th:

> Punished J. Walker (s) with two dozen lashes J. Tetley J. Fox W. McCurdy Dennis McKelly David Scott Thos Nichols J. McKindly with I dozen each for frivolous provoking complains about provisions Thos Jackson (s) 4 dozen for mutinous expressions.

～ Saturday, 9 January

The equator was crossed at 10.30 a.m. The distance to Cape Frio was, at noon, estimated at 1,670 miles. The southeasterly wind still meant slow progress – no more than forty or fifty miles a day.

Captain Walker, always solicitous, now offered his ship:

> As the heavy sailing of the *Alphonzo* [sic] materially retarded us and the Prince's Ship was getting sickly having 1054 persons onboard, I thought it my Duty to make a tender to his Majesty's Ship for the accommodation of Her Royal Highness and suite in the event of the Prince wishing to push on to Rio de Janeiro or as the wind kept hanging to the S.E. of our being obliged to put in here (Bahia), which offer he was pleased to receive most graciously and proposed it to the Princess who was pleased to say she only declined it lest it should have mortified too much the Captain of the *Alphonzo* [sic].[26]

～ Saturday/Sunday, 16/17 January

After a further week without any sign of change or improvement in their progress, on the 16th the *Príncipe Real* signalled to Captain Walker and the Admiral informed him of a change in their plans. Instead of Rio de Janeiro they would head instead for Bahia, much closer and, at that moment, some 162 leagues away.

Next day, just before noon, *Bedford* made a signal to the Admiral that she had sighted a strange sail in the southwest. As the day passed and as they came down the coast of Brazil the strange sail moved to a position west half north, moving closer until she could be identified as a brig of war. She was in fact the Portuguese brig *Trez-Corações*. The Governor of Pernambuco,[27] on learning that the royal family had left Portugal and would be sailing past this part of the coast on their way to Rio de Janeiro, decided, as a gesture of goodwill, to send out the *Trez-Corações*, laden with fresh fruit and vegetables, to cruise in that area and try to intercept the *Príncipe Real*. By the afternoon the brig's position was due west between the squadron and the land. The southeasterly wind made it very difficult for her to close the distance that separated them. In the early hours of next morning she was finally successful in her mission; *Urânia* intercepted her. *Trez-Corações* now joined them for the remainder of the journey.

～ Monday, 18 January

On the 18th the Queen of England's[28] birthday was commemorated. She was born in 1744. At 11 a.m. Squadron Major General and Chief of Division Joaquim José Monteiro Torres went on board *Bedford*. Captain Walker wrote:

Having as I had the Honour to state in my first letter felt it to be my bounden Duty to join in the celebration of the Birth day of His Majesty's august ally. I thought I should have been wanting in my Liege Duty to my own Sovereign if I omitted to celebrate the 18th. Inst in like manner and I therefore fired a royal Salute in which I was joined by the Frigate. The other Ships had hoisted their colours at Sunrise, His royal Highness sent the captain of the Fleet to compliment His Majesties Ship on the occasion, he was received with the honours due to a Rear Admiral and Saluted with 13 Guns on his leaving the Ship when the Prince ordered the Frigate by Signal to return the salute with an equal number of Guns. I beg leave Sir to hope Their Lordships will approve of my conduct in this, as the peculiar nature of the case led me to deviate from the established custom.[29]

As soon as the saluting formalities were over, Captain Walker changed course to intercept a strange sail close by, south by east:

2 made sail fired a shot to bring too the stranger 3.45 wore ship & hove too boarded the stranger which hoisted Portuguese colours from St. Catherines [sic] bound Paramaiha [sic].

∼ Wednesday/Thursday, 20/21 January

For several nights now a moderate breeze had sprung up, so that the squadron was able, for a few days, to sail at six and seven knots. On the morning of the 20th the Admiral ordered the squadron to change course, from southwest to west, and turn in towards the coast. In the afternoon the *Trez-Corações*, which will have been stationed to the west, fired a gun: she had sighted land. At 6 p.m. *Bedford* reported seeing land from the masthead, west by north, some nine or ten leagues away.

Next morning *Bedford* sounded with the deep sea line, but found no bottom at 110 fathoms. In the early evening she tried again and found a sandy bottom, at 28 fathoms.

Measuring the depth of water over which a ship was sailing when near to land was an important duty. Not only were there many parts of the world still uncharted, but also the depth and consistency of the bottom often were useful guides to determine the position. The weighted line was cast forward by a seaman stationed at the bows and allowed to sink and, hopefully, to touch the bottom before the ship had gone past. At the stern another seaman held the line. Tallow on the weight would pick up a sample of the bottom. Tags, tied along the line, ensured that the depth could be quickly read.

That afternoon the *Urânia* fired a gun and brought to a strange sail. They were now no more than 100 miles from their destination.

~ Friday, 22 January

On land the squadron had been sighted and messengers dispatched to warn the Governor in St Salvador. He wrote of the arrival:

> On the 22nd of January at 2.00 a.m. I was given the news that large vessels had been seen on the north coast, on the 21st at 4.00 p.m. I doubled the watches and next a report was received of a sighting of three line-of-battle ships, a full rigged ship and two brigs, almost certainly British; until midday this was the belief, but when their flags became visible, the royal standard could be seen. I immediately gave orders to remove the shot from the guns, so as to be able to fire the merited salutes.[30]

On the afternoon of 22 January 1808, after fifty-four days at sea, the squadron entered the bay of St Salvador and moored. *Bedford* records:

> 1.25 made the signal with a gun for a Pilot… 4 standing in to the bay of St. Salvador… 6 came too with the best bower in 12 ½ fathoms furled sails unbent the small sails and moored ship a cable each way.

Now that they had safely arrived, their concern was for the remaining ships of the fleet, in particular the line-of-battle ships carrying other members of the royal family, ministers and members of the Court.

Before the separation of the squadron both the *D. João de Castro* and the *Medusa* had obtained permission to set off for Brazil independently.[31] Commodore Moore in his report confirmed this: "…two of them viz *Meduse* [sic] and *Dom Juan de Castro* [sic], having been separated before you detached me on this service…"[32]

The *D. João de Castro* arrived, in early January, in the Enseada de Lucena (Paraíba), making more water than she could pump out[33] and with damage to her masts and rigging.[34] On 17 December she had talked to the *London* and said she did not require any assistance. Since no gales are recorded after this period she must either have been caught in a local tropical storm, or else was too proud, or did not realise the extent of the damage she had received in the gales prior to that date.

The *Medusa*,[35] badly damaged in the gale off the island of Madeira, limped into Receife, arriving there on 13 January 1808. During the last few days she had been escorted by the frigate *Medea*, belonging to merchants of Rio de Janeiro:

> …that on the night of the tenth, near the Island of Madeira we lost the main mast and took with it the mizzen; subsequently we suffered terribly from the rolling which made us lose the top sail, so we remained only with

bowsprit and the mast of the fore sail; we were short of all spares at that difficult moment, but spent ten days setting up a small jury-rig, with light winds, we arrived here on the 13th of this month…[36]

D. Antônio de Araújo, travelling on this ship, when writing to the Prince Regent blamed the damage on the condition of the masts and rigging: "…The mainmast was not carrying sails, and broke because it was completely rotten, the cables unworthy, everything has happened to put our lives in danger…"[37] It is probable that in trying to keep their course in strong southeasterly winds, they overstrained the masts and rigging. It was the *Medusa* with her news that had given the Governor in Pernambuco the idea of sending the *Trez-Corações* to intercept the *Príncipe Real*. On 25 January, D. Antônio de Araújo wrote that on the 20th he had received news that the ships carrying the royal family had, on the 17th, crossed the latitude of Receife. The ship that had brought the news, as already mentioned, had been boarded by *Bedford* during the afternoon of Sunday the 18th.

～ *Saturday, 23 January*

On their first morning in port, a Dutch man-of-war in the harbour of St Salvador attracted *Bedford*'s attention:

> On our arrival here we found a small Dutch Man of War Brig the Fly which the Prince seized and he has determined to send her to England which I had presumed to suggest to His Royal Highness concluding His Majesty's Government would be naturally anxious to learn our arrival in the Brazils [sic].[38]

The destiny of the other members of the royal family and of the ships that had set out together from the Tagus, was still unknown:

> The Prince means to sail for Rio de Janeiro where we hope to meet the rest of the Fleet, only one of the Portuguese ships a 64 had arrived here before us and had sailed again before our arrival and they know nothing of the other Ships.[39]

The Portuguese fleet had three 64s: the *D. João de Castro*, the *Afonso de Albuquerque* and the *Martim de Freitas*. The *Martim de Freitas* is the ship referred to. She arrived in Bahia on 10 January and, after taking on board provisions for twenty days, left again for Rio de Janeiro. She is reported by the *London* as arriving on 26 January, the delay – on this last leg of the journey – being due to variable winds at latitude 18 degrees.[40] Her captain, D. Manuel de Menezes, shortly after arrival met a tragic death: on leaving the *Rainha de Portugal* after a dinner, and whilst getting into his barge, he fell in the sea and was drowned, his body appearing three days later.[41]

This nobleman was the brother of D. Gregório Ferreira d'Eça e Meneses, Count of

Cavalleiros, who later also met a tragic death. Whilst accompanying the royal family on a picnic to Tijuca he went to take a closer look at the Cascatinha waterfall, slipped and fell headlong down the rocks. His body was later found in pieces.

Now, lying in port after the long journey, preparations had to go ahead to prepare the ships for the continuation of their journey. In practice, this meant taking on board water and food, replacing broken masts and spars, and repairing and replacing cordage and sail cloth. Also, water casks had to be stowed on board; sand brought in in large quantities; the wooden decks scraped clean; live bullocks killed on board; and vegetables and fresh fruit brought in. In the afternoon of the 23rd work stopped, as the royal family was going on shore. *Bedford* recorded: "…the Prince went on shore mand the yards & fired salute of 21 Guns at 4…"

~ *Sunday, 24 January*

In the afternoon the queen also went on shore, and again a royal salute was fired.

Bahia had in the past built several ships for the Portuguese navy, so wood and skilled workmen were available for repairs. Captain Walker wrote that *Bedford* was getting every attention:

> His Royal Highness has been pleased to give orders that every possible attention should be paid to his Majesty Ship by the Dock Yard who instantly set about making us a new Main Yard (the former having been sprung in the Gale off Madeira) and a Topmast and ample supplies of Bullocks fruits and vegetables sent on board every day, with craft to water the ship.[42]

~ *Thursday, 28 January*

On this date D. João signed the Royal Warrant, which permitted Brazil to trade with all foreign nations. By this act he was putting into practice what had been agreed in principle in the Convention with Britain, but in a much more extensive way. At the same time it was a way of reducing the tension produced by so many laden merchant ships waiting in the harbour ready to sail but with nowhere to go. The importance of this act, at that time and for future generations, cannot be underestimated: "…this royal warrant[43] one could say was the Magna Carta and the principal source of wealth from Brazil…"[44]

~ *Saturday, 30 January*

A busy day as D. João, grateful for the weeks of careful convoying, decided to honour the captain and crew of *Bedford* by paying them a visit.

Bedford's log reads:

> Light winds & fair Wr. hoisted the colours 6 the standard at the main 9 fired a royal salute 9.10 the Prince with part of the royal family visited the ship

hoisted the Portuguese standard at the fore… p.m.1.30 the Royal Family quitted the ship fired a Royal salute and hauled down the standard 3 Mand the yards came on board the Portuguese Admiral with Captains 6.30 mand yards the admiral quitted the ship.

His report to the Admiralty gives further details of this visit:

His Royal Highness having expressed his intentions to visit His Majesties Ship came onboard yesterday with all the Royal family except the Queen, and Breakfasted. They staid above three hours and visited every part of the Ship. They were pleased to express themselves highly gratified. We fired a Royal Salute on their coming and going, and obtained the Prince's permission to hoist the Royal Standard of Portugal at the Fore, while he was onboard, and ours was flying at the Main with the Pendant over it.[45]

O'Neil also describes this visit to *Bedford*, from a letter received from a member of *Bedford*'s crew:

The good people here pay the greatest attention to the British officers. The Royal fugitives having announced to Captain Walker their intention of visiting the *Bedford*, which took place the third day after landing, they left the shore under a royal salute from batteries and from the ships, and were received on board with the greatest respect, where a cold collation had been prepared for them. His Royal Highness visited every part of the ship, and expressed his approbation of the cleanliness which prevailed throughout.

Captain Walker's attention to the Prince has been very great, not only to the ship which His Royal Highness was on board, but also to every one of the Portuguese men of war. In grateful acknowledgement of his assiduous attention, the Prince has presented him with a gold medal of a very ancient Portuguese order of Knighthood. His Highness consults with him on all occasions, and seems glad to receive his advice.[46]

D. João was so satisfied with the outcome of the voyage and the help received from Britain in general and her Admiral and captains in particular that, following the custom on such occasions, he decided to decorate them. A problem, however, existed in that the three military orders in Portugal were all religious, and could only be conferred on Catholics. He decided, therefore, to revive the only non-religious order, the Order of the Tower and Sword, originally instituted by D. Alphonso V in 1459.[47] Even whilst in Bahia he ordered two medals to be struck, inscribed 'Courage and Loyalty', to be given to "two well-deserving subjects of my faithful and ancient ally, the King of Great

Britain". Presumably these were for the captain and the first lieutenant of *Bedford*.

Daily routine continued on board *Bedford*: receiving meat, fresh fruit and vegetables to feed the marines and the crew, so as not to use the supplies brought from England; bringing in water and bread to replenish supplies used up during the journey; and substituting masts and yards damaged by the weather.

The attraction of the port, for the sailor, was evident from these entries in the log:

> Punished Mario Penush 36 lashes for attempting to desert… punis Hy Mcgee with 24 lashes for leaving the boat on duty… received Joseph Pereira a deserter… received four deserters taken by Portuguese soldiers viz Daniel Cameron Jonathan Cook Alexander Mc Clean and James Power – likewise four pressed men & one boy…

～ *Monday, 8 February*

This day the captured Dutch brig set off for England with the news of the convoy's safe arrival. Captain Walker had written to the Secretary to the Admiralty on the 6th to the effect that, so far, all was well:

> I take the opportunity of to acquaint You for the information of Their Lordships, with our having got so far our voyage to the Brazils [sic] in company with *Prince Royal* [sic] of 80 Guns in which the Queen of Portugal, the Prince of Brazils [sic], and his two Sons are embarked in the *Alphonzo D'Albuquerque* [sic] of 74 in which the Princess of Brazils [sic] and four of her Daughters are and the *Urânia* Frigate, and that we are all well…

Now he wrote, from St Salvador, of their safe arrival:

> As I had no opportunity of transmitting my letter N.1 of 6th Inst. before our arrival here, I have thought it right to send it by this conveyance in its original shape and have now the honour to acquaint you for Their Lordships' information that we arrived in this bay on the 22nd. Inst. all well in Company with the *Prince Royal* [sic] the *Aphonzo D'Albuquerque* [sic] and the *Urânia* frigate.[48]

An estimate of the length of time the brig took to reach England can be made from the fact that these two letters only reached the Admiralty on 10 May.[49]

On the same day another brig sailed for Rio de Janeiro with the news of their arrival. Commodore Moore wrote:

> We had no news of His Royal Highness until the 12th. February, when a Brig from St Salvador brought letters from His Royal Highness to the

Princess Dowager informing her of his arrived there on the 22nd. of January with the *Príncipe Real, Afonso d'Albuquerque, Uranie* [sic] Frigate, and His Majesty's Ship *Bedford*.[50]

∼ *Wednesday, 10 February*

On the evening of the 10th the *D. João de Castro*, still somewhat battered and leaking, came in and anchored: she was in no condition to continue the voyage to Rio de Janeiro. It was decided that she should remain in St Salvador for repairs in the competent dockyard. Her passengers and crew were transferred to the *Ativo* and to the merchant ship *Imperador Adriano* for the remainder of the voyage.

One of the most important members of the Court, excluding the royal family, was the Duke of Cadaval.[51] A passenger on the *D. João de Castro*, he was taken ill during the journey. He was to remain in St Salvador at the residence of a rich merchant, Manoel Joaquim Alves Ribeiro, in the rua das Mercês. He passed away on 14 March 1808 and was buried in the convent of St Francis. His widow and children then moved to Rio de Janeiro.

An idea of the extent of the trust that the Prince Regent placed in Captain Walker can be gauged from the fact that he ordered that the treasures, which had been brought so far on board the *D. João de Castro*, should be transferred to *Bedford* for the remainder of the voyage. Her log reads, Sunday 14th: "...& 51 chests treasure from the Portuguese ship *John de Castro* [sic]..." Monday 15th: "...received three bullocks vegetables & fruit and thirty chests of treasure... p.m. received eleven chests of treasure" Wednesday 17th: "...three cases of treasure from the Portuguese ship..."

∼ *Thursday, 11 February*

On this day the Prince Regent crossed the bay and was saluted by *Bedford*, by manning the yards.

The problem of desertions continued; some members of the crew trying, and being caught, for the second time. Monday 15th: "...Punished Jonathan Smith (s) Daniel Cameron with 5 dozen Hugh Davies with 4 dozen and Jonathan Smith with 4 dozen for desertion..." Monday 22nd: "...received Alex Patterson and Daniel Houghton & John Wilson deserters..."

The additional responsibility of carrying treasure chests and to discourage deserters may well have been the reasons that made Captain Walker, on the morning of the 17th, unmoor *Bedford*; and in the evening moor his ship in a new position, with a cable each way in eight fathoms. After the 17th no further desertions are recorded.

∼ *Tuesday, 16 February*

The *Medusa* finally came in from Recife and at 5.30 in the evening anchored in the bay. Towards the end of January she had sailed from Receife to St Salvador but due to contrary winds had been unable to round Cape St Agostinho and so had anchored, waiting for a change of wind. However, her cable parted and, not having another heavy anchor, she returned. Whilst waiting to make a new attempt her masts were replaced with those of a merchant ship.[52]

Now that all the ships were together, final preparations began for the departure for Rio de Janeiro. On the 23rd *Bedford* received on board several passengers who would be travelling with her. A quantity of hay was brought on board. She reported slaughtering eight bullocks and three pigs during the voyage to Rio de Janeiro.

~ *Wednesday/Thursday, 24/25 February*

Early in the day the process of unmooring began. First the starboard anchor, the best bower, was raised and brought in. She then hove short with her port anchor, the small bower, attentive to the Admiral's signals. At 12.30 the yards were manned and a royal salute was fired as the Prince Regent and royal family returned to their ships.

Thursday the 25th, as the wind was unfavourable and the skies grey with rain clouds, the departure was postponed. In the afternoon the Prince Regent returned ashore.

~ *Friday, 26 February*

At 10 a.m. the squadron, composed of the line-of-battle ships *Príncipe Real*, *Afonso de Albuquerque*, *Medusa* and *Bedford*, the frigate *Urânia*, the *Trez-Corações*, the *Activo* and the *Imperador Adriano*, finally got under way. At noon they hove to, waiting for the tide, but shortly after were on their way again and by 4 p.m. were out of the bay and in open seas.

As the squadron sailed down the coast towards Cabo Frio, a lookout was kept for any strange sail. At first light on the 29th two strange sails, which had come up during the night, were sighted west-southwest. One of the Portuguese ships was sent to intercept them. *Bedford*'s log shows that her captain was in constant touch with the Admiral by signals and even, on the morning of 1 March, by boat. During the last three days of the journey, for reasons of safety, the squadron hove to during the night. As they were sailing quite close to islands near the mainland, every precaution had to be taken before resuming their journey at daybreak. At least once a day *Bedford* sounded the bottom.

~ *Sunday/Monday, 6/7 March*

At 1.15 p.m., between showers of rain, the lookout at the masthead at last saw land. They were some eight leagues from Cabo Frio. Next morning *Bedford* recorded:

> Standing in for Rio de Janeiro observed the shipping fire a salute... 4.30 p.m. shortened sail & came too with the best bower in 15 fathoms found laying here HMS *Marlborough*, *London Monarch* and *Solebay* frigate with part of a Portuguese Squadron... 6 Moored ship NW& SE a cable each way the fort on the South most point...

Chapter VII

Commodore Moore, with the remainder of the fleet, sails to St Tiago. HMS London joins them there. The voyage to Rio de Janeiro and arrival there on 17 January 1808. Awaiting the remainder of the fleet and the arrival of the Prince Regent from St Salvador.

~ *Wednesday, 9 December*

The ships that sailed directly to Rio de Janeiro also had an eventful voyage. On the night of 8 December, when the fleet separated, the *Príncipe Real* had hove to. The arrangements of her sails would have indicated this to an experienced captain. Graham Moore wrote:

> On the evening of the 8th, the weather being hazy and squally with rain and the appearance of blowing from the NE. the Admiral's ship hauled to the wind on the Starboard Tack and brought to.[1]

Commodore Graham Moore later wrote of his feelings on finding that the principal members of the royal family, for whom he had been given responsibility to escort to Brazil, were no longer with him: "…it certainly occasioned me excessive vexation, tho', from the circumstances attending it, no produce or vigilance on my part could…"[2]

He was not able to discover, until much later, what had happened that night:

> The Portuguese Ships being at this time much scattered and only seven of them in sight, I hauled to the wind about 2 Miles to windward of the Admiral with *Monarch* and *Bedford* for the purpose, as it was almost dark of keeping the line of connexion with the scattered Ships and supposing, as he had brought too at that time, that he meant to lie by for the night… It came on to blow hard with squalls of rain, we bore up close with the Admiral but at 9 P.M. we lost sight of his Light. In the morning, blowing a gale of wind and very hazy wr. we found the *Monarch* and two Portuguese Line of Battle Ships in company. We have since found that the Portuguese Admiral bore away after dark and steered WNW, without

signal, and accordingly next morning found only the Portuguese Frigate *Uranie* [sic] in company, which happened to be quite close to him when he bore away.[3]

The fact however, remains that *Marlborough*'s log showed that she was tacking throughout the night, but with no forward speed. *Monarch's* log, on the other hand, records that she was tacking until 11 p.m., then a forward speed of two knots. The only Portuguese log available, that of the *Urânia* – which remained close to the *Príncipe Real* – notes a speed of five knots as from 7.00 p.m.; yet *Marlborough* maintained the *Príncipe Real* in sight until 9.00 p.m., in spite of extremely poor visibility "not more than three ships' length". These inaccuracies cannot be explained and would have certainly been taken up officially, but for the safe arrival in Brazil of every single ship of the fleet.

In the early morning, after a brief wait for the ships that were scattered to come together, they set off towards the first rendezvous. *Marlborough's* log records:

> At 8 not finding any of the other Ships altered the course to the S ward hauled up the Fore Sail – hauled to the wind for the line astern to come up made the Portuguese signal to close – bore up under Main top Sail and Fore Stay sail – at Noon the *Monarch* and 2 Portuguese ships in company.

These would have been the *Rainha de Portugal*[4] and the *Conde D. Henrique*.[5] He later reported to the Admiralty:

> As soon as the day light convinced us of the separation I bore away for Madeira making the Portuguese Signals and enforcing them with Guns for the Portuguese Ships, *Reyna de Portugal* [sic] and *Conde Henrique*, of 74 guns each, to close and follow us.[6]

As *Marlborough* had been hove to all through the night and, as the speed at which she could progress was that of the slowest ship that she was escorting, she would not see Madeira that day. At noon, after taking her position, she exchanged latitude and longitude with the *Monarch*.

As night descended the *Rainha de Portugal* and the *Conde D. Henrique*, escorted by the *Marlborough*, slowly made their way southwest towards Madeira. The *London*, which had sailed on ahead, was now nearing Porto Santo, a small island to the northeast of Madeira.

~ Thursday, 10 December

At daybreak next morning, *Marlborough* signalled *Monarch* to look out south. Soon after, the island of Madeira came into sight, and *Monarch* was recalled. All that day Madeira remained within sight. At night the squadron hauled to the wind, so as to remain near to the Island: as an easterly gale was blowing it was not easy to remain close to the western side of the island. *Bedford* was not far away, but out of sight, further to the west.

London was on the eastern side of the island. Some idea of the struggle she was having in trying to get into Funchal to anchor can be imagined from her log:

> Strong breeze & squally Brazen H. NW I Mile Standing down per Funchal Roads, at 5 haul'd to the wind on Larboard tack & Kept Tacking off & on blowing too hard to Anchor Split Fore Sail & carried away F. topmast Sprung Stay & Larb. M Topsail Sheet Block a boat came from the Shore with the Consul, at 7 Stood off under close reef Topsails & Courses down T. G. Masts… Funchal Town N 4 Miles.

Next morning, in spite of the gale, she regained Funchal roads and anchored "… with the best bower… veered a cable & a half. Saluted the Garrison with 15 Guns which was returned…" The next two days would be spent getting water from the shore, hoisting it on board with improvised tackle, and stowing the casks.

Voador, detached to accompany the *London*, could not keep up:

> On December 6th I received orders from His Royal Highness to follow the English ship, the *London*…next day the other ship separated from me, as she was much faster, in spite of trying with all possible sails set. On December the 9th I saw the Island of Madeira, but under a very violent storm that kept me running for forty eight hours.[7]

As she had 181 soldiers on board in addition to her own crew of 135, she was fearful that she might run out of food and water so decided to sail, without stopping, directly for Rio de Janeiro.

~ Friday, 11 December

Off the island of Madeira, after a night-long wait without success, at daybreak, the Portuguese made a signal to close, which was answered by the *Marlborough* with three guns. It was now decided that they should go to the second rendezvous, off the island of Palma in the southeast, some seventy-nine leagues distant. Commodore Moore wrote:

Her Royal Highness the Princess Dowager of Brazil having, in the most condescending manner, directed the Portuguese Senior Captain to follow all my orders and assuring me that she relied on my discretion in doing my utmost to rejoin His Royal Highness.[8]

As Madeira approached, Sir Sidney Smith's orders were obeyed. "…Got a main Top Sail Yard up – bent the Sail set it treble reefed – Hoisted a Broad Pendant…" A commodore was now commanding the squadron.

~ Sunday, 13 December

The high land of the island of Palma, some ten leagues distant, came into sight. The second rendezvous had been reached. There was still no sign of the other ships.

Continuing with Graham Moore's private diary:

> I took the opportunity this day of the weather being fine to go on board, with Capt[n] Lee of the *Monarch*, to see the Senior Captain of the two Portuguese Ships and to pay our respects to the widow of the late Prince of Brazil whom I have mentioned before and who is embarked onboard *La Reyne de Portugal* [sic]. I took this opportunity of explaining and apologising to the Portuguese Captain for the liberty I had taken in assuming the command by making signals to them… assuring him that I was ready and anxious to do every thing in my power to forward the great object of getting safe with the Fleet and the Royal Family to Rio de Janeiro. He said he was quite satisfied, and said that he would attend to all our signals and whatever arrangements I might choose to make.
>
> I then settled, a very few of the most necessary Night Signals with him, and we parted. The old Princess was exceedingly desirous of making the best of our way to Rio Janeiro, and was averse to stopping at St. Iago [sic] or any where else, but when I had a little conversation with her and represented to her the certainty of our being there joined by the Squadron with the rest of the Royal Family, she was apparently satisfied. She presented two of the little Princesses to me, who, she said, had been miserably ill with the sea sickness and she said she feared St. Iago [sic] was unhealthy. I assured her there would be no delay at St. Iago [sic] but what was absolutely necessary viz to effect the junction of the dispersed Ships of the Squadron. I then took my leave.[9]

~ Monday, 14 December

At daybreak, a strange sail could be seen northwest by north, some ten miles away. *Marlborough* made *Monarch* a signal to chase her. She proved to be the Portuguese

Thetis – a frigate being used as a store ship – under the command of First Lieutenant Paulo José Miguel de Brito.[10] She joined the squadron as it lay off Palma, waiting to see whether any other ships would appear. In addition to a hundred passengers she carried nine carriages and a large quantity of assorted luggage.

~ Tuesday, 15 December

At noon the next day it was decided to go to the third rendezvous. Under a moderate breeze, the squadron set sail and steered southwest. Before long Palma could be seen in the distance and Ferro, the most southerly island of the Canary Archipelago, passed by some four leagues away.

The next leg of the journey, some 240 leagues, would take several days. The wind maintained at moderate to fresh nearly all the way, the weather improving as they moved further south. On board the ships their logs record the daily routines: "… scrubbed hammocks… issued lemon juice and sugar to the ship's company… exercised Marines at small arms… Sail Maker making a Quarter Deck Awning…"

The *Thetis*, a slower sailer, had difficulty in keeping up, and by the third day she was some six or seven miles behind. *Monarch* sailed close to the *Marlborough*, some half a mile away. The two Portuguese line-of-battle ships, also, were always close by.

~ Thursday, 17 December

HMS *London* was still without her marines. As already mentioned, *Solebay* was the only frigate left at the Tagus bar, so had stayed behind. On the 17th the *Solebay* had detained a Portuguese ship, the *Oliveira*. Her log records: "…1.30 saw a Strange Sail to windward, set Top Gallant Sails at 2 tack'd in chase… At 4.30 fired Two Shots at the Ship to windward with Portuguese Colours… 5.30 boarded her …" Thomas O'Neil later wrote a full account:[11]

> The *Solebay* detained several Brazil Portuguese merchant ships, on board one of which (the *Olivira* [sic], Capt. Belham) I was ordered, December 16th, with twenty marines, accompanied by Lieut. Kirwin of the Royal navy, the frigate having no seamen to spare.
>
> At the risk of the marines lives we arrived on board, and were instantly given to understand, that they were in the greatest distress for provisions, being destitute of bread, meat, wine, and spirits, and having only sixteen gallons of water, and twenty quarts of rice. The gale continued to such a degree, that no further communication could be had with the ship we had left.
>
> We were now forty-nine persons on board, and had nothing to subsist on but the scanty articles above specified. The gale increasing, the

Lieutenant was obliged to put her before the wind, as she was in such a bad state; we all expected to go to the bottom every moment. We saw no more of the frigate, or any part of squadron, until Christmas-day; during which interval, our only sustenance was three spoonfuls of boiled rice per day for each person.

On the 25th of December, in the morning, we saw the squadron from the mast-head; made signals of distress, and fired several guns, but the distance was too great to be observed. Throughout the 24th and 25th, we took no food, our scanty stock being expended. At seven A.M. we passed under the stern of a British man of war, and hailed her. A Lieutenant from her came on board, to whom we described our urgent distress, and craved relief. The officer returned to his ship, and after some time had elapsed, we were hailed by the captain, who ordered us to proceed to the Admiral, without contributing to our wants! This ship had the look-out during that night, but for the honour of the British navy and the nation, she shall be nameless.[12]

The *Olivira* [sic] joined the squadron early in the morning and Lieut. Kirwin repaired on board the commander in chief's ship. As soon as the Admiral was acquainted with our distress, his benevolence was far different from the apathy of the former, and he ordered everything necessary for us.

Had it been our misfortune to have parted from the squadron, previous to our speaking to the Admiral, every soul on board would have inevitably perished.

At ten the *Solebay* came within hail; and on Capt. Sprole being made acquainted with the situation that we had been in, he applied to the Admiral to have us instantly removed on board the frigate; which request the Admiral granted. As soon as circumstances would admit, in the evening of the 26th, we returned to the frigates, and were informed that the *London, Marlborough, Bedford and Monarch*, had parted company, and were on their passage, convoying the prince to Rio de Janeiro. Thus were my commanding officer and myself, together with the detachment, left without any other apparel than what we wore; a situation of the most unpleasant nature.

Our distresses were represented to the Admiral, who informed us that the frigate must take dispatches out to the Brazils [sic], and that we were all to remain on board; every assistance that lay in his power should be rendered to us, and the moment he was ready, we were to sail.

1808. January 18th – Signal being made for the ship to close, the captain went on board the admiral's ship, and received his orders. We parted company at three, and made the island of Madeira on the 16th; we took in a supply of water, and sailed on the 18th. We passed the Canaries on the 23rd, and saw the rock of Teneriff, and the Cape de Verd [sic] Islands. We put into Port Epre [sic], in the island of Santa Jago [sic], and took in more water, and sailed thence for Rio de Janeiro, where we arrived on the 29th of February, and found the *London*, *Monarch* and *Marlborough*, with part of the Portuguese squadron; the *Bedford* and the remainder had parted company with the Prince Regent in a gale of wind, but had arrived in St. Salvador, which place his Royal Highness was obliged to put into, being destitute of all kinds of provisions. [In fact, as already shown, there was no shortage of victuals or water.]

On the same day we rejoined the *London,* it was a most gratifying sight to us when we first beheld her lying at anchor, having then been absent thirteen weeks without any change of apparel, except what had been given us by the liberality of the officers on board the *Solebay.* Here, however, I experienced a new disappointment; I found my chest had been forced, and every article of my linen, that was of any value, had been taken away. There were several hundred emigrations on board the *London*, chiefly females; but through the generosity of the officers, they obtained every necessary in their power to afford. [An exaggeration on the part of O'Neil; *London*'s log records, taking on a total of 69 passengers.]

The marine commanding officer of HMS *London,* Major Malcolm wrote to Sir Sidney Smith asking him to intercede with the Admiralty, to define the position of *London*'s marines with regard to prize money. His concern was that, not being on board the *London*, they would not share in any prize money attributed to her; and on the other hand, not being officially part of *Solebay*'s crew, they might miss out there as well. Sir Sidney, in turn, wrote to the Admiralty on 5 January, recommending that they should share in the prize money to be attributed to the *Solebay*.[13]

∼ Friday, 18 December

Once again Graham Moore writes on the worries of the princess, on board the *Rainha de Portugal*:

Yesterday morning I had a message from the former Princess of Brasil, stating her wishes that I would not go to Port Praya, but spare them what Provisions I could and send the Store Ship in when we made S[t]. Iago [sic]. I sent to inform her that I had hardly any Stock of Fresh Provisions, any part of what I had at her Royal Highness's service when ever she ran short, but to other people there was too small a quantity to be of any sensible relief. That I judged it absolutely necessary to touch at Port Praya, as it was the Rendezvous the Portuguese Admiral had given where he assured me he would go, and where I confidently expected to meet the Portuguese Ships as well as the *London* and *Bedford*.

She was apprehensive of the unwholesomeness of S^t. Iago [sic]. I told the Officer who brought the message that it was much against my advice that the Admiral determined on going to S^t. Iago [sic], but as he gave me that Rendezvous I thought we certainly should go there, where, if we found that he had already been, we would proceed on our Voyage to Rio de Janeiro, otherwise remain there "till he should arrive".

~ *Wednesday, 23 December*

At first light the island of Sal, the most northwesterly of the group, came into sight bearing west to northwest. The squadron had been sailing between the African coast and the Atlantic Islands.

In succession Boa Vista and Maio islands could be clearly seen. At the end of the afternoon the squadron hove to for the night, so as to wait for daylight, before entering Praya Bay on St Tiago Island, to moor.

~ *Thursday, 24 December*

Early in the morning the *Marlborough* signalled the Portuguese ships to close, and the *Monarch* to examine a ship at anchor west of Maio. She proved to be an American.

In the afternoon the ships approached Praya Bay to anchor:

At 2 came to with the best bower in 7 fm^s. In Port Praya Bay. S^t. Iago [sic] – veered to half a cable the E^t. P^t. of the Bay bearing ESE the W^t. p^t. SW½W and the Fort flag staff NNW½W the *Monarch* and 3 Portuguese in company.

The *Thetis* missed her anchorage and had to put out to sea again. At anchor in the bay they found the frigate *Minerva,* sent by the Prince Regent, with the news that he was going on without stopping and they should follow him to Rio de Janeiro: she had arrived that morning.[14] Commodore Moore must have been relieved to hear that the ships carrying the royal family were safe and that they were being escorted by the *Bedford*.

Captain Moore's report fills in further details:

On the 24th Dec. We anchored in Port Praya with the Four Men of war and *Thetis* frigate (fitted as a Store Ship) one of the Portuguese squadron that had separated on the night of the Eight and which rejoined us off Palma, and found there the Portuguese Frigate *Minerve* [sic] (one of the squadron) by which I learnt that she had fallen in with the Portuguese Admiral off Ferro on the 13th where he was also rejoined by the *Afonso D'Albuquerque* (the Ship in which Her Royal Highness the Princess of Brazil was embarked) some days after the separation, and His Majesty's Ship *Bedford*. The Viscount of Anadia, the Minister of the Marine, who was embarked in the *Minerve* [sic] had permission from His Royal Highness to proceed to Port Praya for refreshments and was directed by His Royal Highness to inform me that he had altered his mind and did not mean to touch at Port Praya but to proceed direct for Rio de Janeiro, and that he had requested the Captain of the *Bedford* to remain with him.[15]

No time was lost. That very afternoon, the launch from the *Marlborough* and all the boats from the *Monarch* were hoisted out and empty casks sent on shore.

～ *Friday, 26 December*

The next day *Thetis* finally managed to enter the bay and anchor. All day was spent loading water. *Marlborough* supplied the *Rainha de Portugal* with seven tons in fourteen butts. She herself took on board twenty-three tons of water.

The *London* had not yet arrived. On 12 December she had finished watering. That evening she tried to sail out of Funchal, but had to desist:

> Strong breeze & Cloudy – at 9 More moderate & Rain 11.30 Wind Shifted to SE prepared for weighing, and made the Signal with a Gun… at 12 Blew a hard gale so that we could not have a head.

During the early hours of the morning she tried again, but without success. Fearing now that the wind would increase and that she would be delayed in reaching St Tiago, she tied the anchor cable to a buoy marked 'HMS *London*', which would be left behind and, under double reefed topsails, courses and staysails, she managed to manoeuvre out. The anchor she had left behind was replaced by one of the two spares she carried on board, stowed beside her mainmast.

As she had watered without losing too much time, she decided to go to Palma rather than direct to St Tiago, to see whether she could fall in with the fleet. She would not know as yet of their separation. She reached her destination on the 15th but *Marlborough* and company were already past Ferro, the most southern of the Canary Islands, on their way to the Cape Verde islands. At daylight next morning, eleven leagues northwest of Palma, she sighted a line-of-battle ship sailing alone. As she expected to see several ships together, she took every precaution:

At 5 & at 6 Tack'd Saw a Ship SW gave chase 8.30 in 2 reefs down jib & driver – Clear'd for action – Chase a Ship of war 9.20 Tack'd Chase Shew'd Portuguese Colours & hove too at 10 hove too & out Boat found the Portuguese Ship of the line *Don de Castro* [sic] Don Manuel John of Louis & Seilbez Com^r [sic].[16] 10.40 in Boats & Set Courses & T. G^t. Sails S°. P^t. of Palma SbE½E 14 Leagues – Fresh breezes & Rain Parted Company from Portuguese as she wanted no assistance.

Her preparations for battle had been unnecessary.

On the 18th, having decided that sufficient time had been spent at the rendezvous, *London* set off for St Tiago; arriving there on the evening of the 26th.

Hauled to the Island to make it more clearly… got the spare anchor over the side. Strong breeze and cloudy… hauling round Ex. P^t. of Praya Bay at 7 shortn'd Sail & anchord with small bower in 6½ fms. but it did not hold. Let go the best bower and brought up to a whole cable & 2/3 on the best Bower.

∼ *Saturday, 26 December*

The *London* recorded that she found the following in the bay: "…the *Marlborough Monarch* 2 Portuguese 74s 3 Frigates & a Brig…" These would have been the *Rainha de Portugal* (74) and the *Conde D. Henrique* (74); the *Minerva* (frigate 48), and the *Thetis* (frigate 36). The third frigate must have been the *Golfinho*.

During the day *London* transferred the water she had brought, whilst *Marlborough* supplied the frigate *Minerva* with twelve casks of pork and nineteen casks of beef.

∼ *Sunday, 27 December*

The following morning they were ready to leave. Because of the fresh breeze blowing from the east-northeast, and the number of vessels in harbour, a series of manoeuvres became necessary. *London* wrote in her log:

At 7 Commd, made Sig to weigh in not having room to cast clear of 2 masts out Launch & carried out Stream Anchor & Cable under Weather in 6 fm. & into Larb hawse – at 11 hove up the Stream anchor foul of a Rock- after some time heaving with a great force the Cable parted in the Hawser cast the right way & made Sail left behind the anchor & 16 fms. of the Cable, as t'was blowing strong & no probability of being able to weigh it with the Launch… hove too & in Boats fill'd & made Sail after the Commodore & squadron.

It was the second anchor she had lost on the voyage.

Monarch did not have any difficulty in weighing, but *Marlborough* put out an anchor to turn her head in the right direction:

> At day light made signal to weigh with a gun run the Kedge & Hauser out to the N. word to cast the Ship – at half past 7 Whed. And made sail... hove to *Monarch* and 2 Portuguese Line of Battle Ships in company and one frigate.

These were the *Rainha de Portugal*, *Conde D. Henrique* and the frigate *Minerva*.

With her wooden telegraph *Marlborough* now signalled the new rendezvous:

> "... 17, 9, 14, 9, 1, 13, 5, 9, 17 and 14..." Rio de Janeiro was some 823 leagues away, according to *Marlborough*, after calculating her position at noon. The *Thetis* was left behind to complete her water.[17]

~ Monday/Tuesday, 28/29 December

The next two days saw the squadron making good progress, sailing day and night at seven and eight knots. However, as they approached the line the wind dropped so that speed was immediately affected.

~ Friday, 1 January 1808

By 1 January, speeds of no more than one or two knots per hour could be maintained. Commodore Moore had every hope of catching up with and sighting the remaining ships. The information supplied by the *Minerva* as to the point where the *Príncipe Real* would cross the equinox (latitude 15° east of Cadíz) enabled him to calculate, quite correctly as it turned out, that the squadron being escorted by *Bedford* was sailing closer to the African shore, on a parallel course but further to his east. Early every morning *Monarch* was signalled to take up a station far off, to the southeast, in order to extend their field of vision. At dusk she was recalled, in case during the night she lost sight of them in the vast expanse of sea that stretched around them to the horizon.

Commodore Moore wrote:

> Yesterday being New Year's day and almost calm, I went on board the *Reyne de Portugal* [sic] to enquire after her Royal Highness and to present captain Western of the *London* to her. She was in tolerable health and spirits and presented the two young Princesses to us the Daughters of the Prince of Brazil the eldest of whom (she was then 7) is rather pretty

and seems to agree very well with the voyage. I was very happy on being informed that, in spite of the crowd on board these Ships, they continue quite healthy.[18]

∼ *Monday, 4 January*

Little did they know that in the last three days they had overtaken *Bedford* and the vessels she was escorting.

The slow progress in good weather continued until 4 January, when a fresh breeze sprang up. That night they crossed the equator, and the doldrums were now left behind. As the squadron sailed south much time was spent in navigation for, after leaving St Tiago (Cape Verde), they were hoping to make landfall in Cabo Frio, having crossed over 2,000 miles of open sea. Longitude was taken with the chronometer and the noon sighting helped to establish their position. The variation of the compass was calculated and checked, as was the setting of the current.

∼ *Wednesday, 13 January*

Commodore Moore on this day changed tactics. Instead of sending the *Monarch* southeastward to look out for the remaining ships he sent her southwestward to look out for coastal shipping and, as they approached the coast, to watch out for high land.

∼ *Thursday, 14 January*

Next day the *Monarch* was successful for in the early afternoon, after a chase, she brought to a Portuguese coaster from Rio Grande.

∼ *Friday, 15 January*

They now altered course, from southwest by west to west-southwest, to bring them closer to land. Cape Frio, according to their calculations, was but 200 miles away.

∼ *Saturday, 16 January*

In the morning the *Monarch* at last sighted land. Their navigation demonstrated that although they were at the beginning of the nineteenth century, accuracy was possible. That afternoon she recorded: "…7.40 bore up Squadron in company Cape Frio NW by N 4 or 5 Miles …" Later that same afternoon the *Monarch* intercepted a brig of war, the *Balão*, sent out by the Viceroy, Count of Arcos, to cruise outside the bay of Rio de Janeiro. From her they learnt that the ships carrying the royal family had not yet passed by.

～ *Sunday, 17 January*

During the early hours the squadron hove to not far from the entrance to the harbour of Rio de Janeiro, to avoid entering during darkness. In the afternoon the Portuguese ships entered harbour, followed in the early evening by their escorts. This moment, after so many days of sailing in the open sea and with all the discomforts of the journey, must have been especially welcome. *Marlborough* recorded:

> Running for the Harbour of Rio Janeiro… came to with the small bower in the above Harbour 6½ fms and moored with the Stream Anchor and Cable the N ward and the Island Cobra bearing South, and NNE… *London, Monarch* and 2 Portuguese Ships in Company.

London adds further details:

> 6 Stood for the harbour with a Strong Ebb Tide & Portuguese harbour Master came off – 8 Anchord with best bower in 17 fms S. Jago [sic] P. WNW 1 Mile – Com ½ Cable Commodore *Monarch* and 2 Portuguese Anchord further in – all the Forts Salute & Town Illuminated at night.

On 20 January the town was illuminated for the festivities of St Sebastian, her patron saint, the full name of the town being St Sebastian of Rio de Janeiro. Commodore Moore wrote to their Lordships at the Admiralty:

> On the 17th of January, exactly three weeks from Port Praya, the Squadron arrived at Rio Janeiro all in good health altho' the Portuguese Line of Battle Ships were crowded with Men Women and Children, each having near Eleven hundred people on board, of all descriptions.[19]

In addition to the crew, this meant that each ship was carrying some 400 to 500 passengers.

The *Marlborough* almost certainly found the brig *Voador* already in harbour. Her official report records sighting Pernambuco on 5 January and, on crossing with a small local boat, sending in dispatches and all the news to the naval superintendent of that District.[20]

Antonio Marques Esparteiro wrote that she arrived in Rio de Janeiro on the 14th of January.[21]

～ *Monday, 18 January*

Although the journey was over there was much to be done. In the morning all three

British ships, after taking on pilots, changed their moorings. *London* moored with her two large bow anchors, in sixteen and a half fathoms of water. Her description of her position was such that, if needed, it could be found even to this day:

> Flag Staff on P. S Yago [sic] WbS ½ Mile – Great Church with 2 Steeples on with a White Rock off S^t. Yago [sic] P^t. MSW½S 3 Cables length – Sugar Loaf at the Entrance on with Isl'd Vergnaum [sic] S½E Santa Cruz Fort SSE Village of Domingo [sic] ENE.

Topmasts, yards and their rigging were now brought down. It was reasonable to expect that they would be some time in harbour but should it prove necessary they could unmoor and sail away to open sea whilst putting back the rigging.

In the afternoon the Queen of England's birthday was celebrated with a 21-gun salute. There was as yet no news of the remaining ships carrying the royal family; Commodore Moore and his officers could but speculate what might have happened to delay them.

~ *19/31 January*

By the second day all had settled down to port routine: replenishing water supplies and maintain them at maximum capacity; and receiving fresh supplies of meat, vegetables and fruit for immediate consumption. The preserved victuals, which had come out with them from England and were not so readily available locally, would be kept in case they were needed for a further voyage. Sir Sidney Smith had already written to the Admiralty, on 6 December, on this matter:

> I need hardly suggest to their Lordships the necessary of sending a supply of provisions and stores from England to that new naval station, and if a responsible person was sent from the Victualling board as M. Ford was with me in Sicily to make contracts and purchases in the country it might be more economical, very conductive to health, and would save the commanding Naval officer from much irksome responsibility and detail.[22]

Only cheese and butter appeared to present conservation problems, as *Marlborough*'s log records:

> Condemned per Survey 264 pounds of Cheese, being rotten and unfit to eat, all of which cheese was thrown overboard into the Sea, and 84 pounds of Butter, rancid and unfit to eat, all of which Butter was left in charge of the Piorser [sic].

The *London* records minor problems with their supplies, and a shortage discovered in the flour cask: "…opened I of Flour 31 Mark'd 353 lbs found it 56 lbs Short eat by the Mice…" Occasionally the weather was the cause: "…opened a cask of oatmeal no. 11 12 Bushels 3 of which round the Sides of the Cask was bad by getting wet…"

Just as important was the appearance of the ship. As recorded, each ship now set about employing her crews to restore the pristine condition expected from a warship: caulkers caulking the wales; and between the decks, painters painting the hull; sailmakers carrying out repairs; and others blacking and tarring the stays to give them better protection against the weather.

As she was about to replenish her water supplies, *Marlborough* began to pump out the forty-three tons of sea water she had taken on as ballast at the beginning of December. Although only two days in harbour, she records the first cases of seamen attempting to leave the ship. "…Punished Rob. Fox and Tho. Marr Seamen with 60 lashes each for attempting to Desert…"

In Rio harbour, *London* records the arrival of the various ships that had left Lisbon on 29 November. 20 January: "…Arrived a Portuguese Man Of War brig…" 22nd: "…Arrived a Portuguese frigate …" The *Golfinho* records on the 26th: "…Arrived a Portuguese Ship of the Line…" The *Martim de Freitas* records on 9 February: "Arrived a Portuguese Man of war brig…" 11th: "arrived a Portuguese man of War Brig…"

On arrival the *Martim de Freitas* wrote a report of the voyage. Just before departure the dukes of Cadaval were transferred to the *D. João de Castro*, their families and belongings remaining on board. They reported that they were short of medicines, artillery material and gear. She sailed with a crew of 416 men (therefore short of 234). Subsequent to separating from the fleet, as a measure of precaution, allowances of water and victuals were reduced to three-quarters.

The frigate *Minerva*, which had left St Tiago on 27 December, being a slower sailer, separated from the main body of the fleet and only anchored in Rio de Janeiro on 31 January.[23]

~ Thursday, 11 February

The brig arriving on the 11th had come from St Salvador, with the good news that the queen, Prince Regent, and other members of the royal family had arrived there safely.[24] Up to that moment, the princess dowager had not set foot on shore for, out of respect for the queen and the Prince Regent, she did not wish to do so before them.

No better description exists of the expected arrival of the royal family than that written by Luiz Gonçalves dos Santos (Padre Perereca),[25] here reproduced at some length:

As soon as it became known, in this city of Rio de Janeiro, that the Prince Regent Our Lord was in Bahia, our minds were laid to rest and the fears set aside as to the cause of their delay; seeing the dangers faced by the most serene princess and Infantas remaining embarked during a time of the year when thunder is frequent, and sometimes really dreadful and fatal, at the same time recognising the discomfort that these ladies were experiencing, being enclosed for so many days in the cabin of a ship and not knowing for how long the Prince Regent Our Lord would be delayed in Bahia, at the request of the nobility and aristocracy, already to be found at this port, the most serene princess and Infantas decided to disembark and take shelter in the royal palace. At the disembarkation the troops lined the quay to receive Their Highnesses and a large crowd, made up of all ages, had a great deal of pleasure and general satisfaction with the presence of such august important people. To the sound of salutes, from the ships and batteries, on the 2nd of February, at ten o'clock in the morning, the ladies accompanied by their ladies-in-waiting and preceded by the nobility and aristocracy disembarked on the key, in front of the palace, and went to the royal residence where they kindly received all who, with just motive, came to kiss their hand.

~ Saturday, 13 February

The last of the ships travelling independently came in on the 13th: "…Arrived a Portuguese 74…" The entry in the log that she was a 74 enables us to identify her. The Portuguese naval fleet that came out of Lisbon on 29 November included eight line-of-battle ships. Four of them were still, at that moment, in the northeast (the *Príncipe Real*, *Afonso de Albuquerque*, *Medusa* and *D. João de Castro*). Two had come in to Rio de Janeiro with Commodore Moore and were now moored in the harbour. The remaining two were the *Martim de Freitas* (a 64) and the *Príncipe do Brasil* (a 74). The *Martim de Freitas*, coming from St Salvador, where she had briefly called in, arrived on 26 January. The *Príncipe do Brasil* is unlikely to have taken an additional four weeks to complete the voyage so she probably went to England for repairs, as had been arranged between Admiral D. Manuel and Sir Sidney Smith.

~ Wednesday, 24 February

At dusk, the lookout on the *London* sighted a cutter outside the bay: "…saw a Cutter outside with a Blue Ensign repeated the Signal to recall her She Stood to the East…" All on board knew that it was highly unlikely that an English cutter[26] would be sailing alone in the Atlantic. The cutter, with her oversize sail area to give her speed, must be out scouting for a much larger ship.

∼ *Saturday, 27 February*

In the morning the frigate *Solebay* could be seen, anchored outside the bay, waiting to come in. In the afternoon the *London* recorded: "…4 anchord here the *Solebay* received our Officers and party of Marines from her/sent on Board when off Lisbon 29th November last…" She brought, for Commodore Moore, from Sir Sidney Smith "…Letters and Orders of different dates to the 10th of January …"[27]

∼ *Monday, 7 March*

At last, the much-awaited squadron arrived from St Salvador. *London* records:

> 10 Saw the *Pce of Brazil* [sic] with 3 sail of the Line and other Vessels com[g] in…at 11 they enterd the Harbour mouth and the Portuguese laying here saluted… 12.40 Mann'd Ship – 2 saluted the Prince with 21 Guns and on His Anchoring Cheer'd him – as did all the English and Portuguese Ships… Anchored here the *Bedford*.

Luiz Gonçalves dos Santos continues:

> In fact, as soon after day-break of this happy and forever memorable 7th of March, the agreed signal was made, at the bar, announcing the arrival of the royal squadron; the whole town showing a lively happiness became agitated with uproar and confusion… From ships that happened to be in the port, as soon as the royal squadron appeared on the horizon, gigs set off to meet His Royal Highness…
>
> As soon as the royal squadron approached the bar, all the Portuguese and English warships anchored in this beautiful bay, adorned themselves with a thousand flags, pennants and streamers of many colours, (that made a beautiful and enchanting scene); the fortresses hoisting their flags, welcomed the royal standard with a twenty one gun salute…
>
> Two motives occurred that dissuaded the crowd from going out to the bar to meet His Royal Highness; firstly the breeze that started to blow early and secondly, everyone remained in their place, persuaded that His Majesty would disembark as soon as the ship anchored.
>
> It was between two and three in the afternoon, of a fresh, beautiful and forever gratifying 7th of March… and across the bar there came in with majestic grace the ship *Príncipe Real*, followed by all the others, and once more the air was filled with the noise of the cheerful and repeated salutes from the fortresses and warships…
>
> As soon as the ships anchored in front of the town, notice was given

that the Prince Regent Our Lord would not disembark that afternoon, saving, for the next day, his solemn entrance to this capital; so that the most distinguished, by their standing or office, without delay made for the gigs and other boats for the royal vessel, anxious to have the honour of kissing the august hand of the Prince Regent Our Lord, and Their Royal Highness.

Thomas O'Neil records:

This morning a signal was made from the heights for five sail of the line. At twelve came in sight the *Príncipe Real* [sic], *Alfonso* [sic], *Rainha de Portugal* [sic], *Conde Henrique*, and the *Bedford*. His Royal Highness led the line, with his standard flying at the main. Signal being given from the *Marlborough*, (Commodore Moore) to prepare for a general salute; at one we saluted, which was returned by the forts. The Commodore and Captains then proceeded in their boats to congratulate his Royal Highness and family on their safe arrival.

The Viceroy came off in the state barge to tender his resignation, when an officer of the *London* was sent on board to offer his assistance and was with the regent when the Commodore and Captains waited on him. His Highness was deeply affected, and expressed in the strongest language the satisfaction he felt in the kind attentions he received from every one in this part of the world ... Commodore Moore was most graciously received, a circumstance that must afford infinite satisfaction to every one who has the honour of being known to an officer, whose character is held in such high estimation in his Majesty's service: the Captains were also received with every demonstration of respect.[28]

That night was spent in preparations for the disembarkation which would take place next day, and for the ceremonies that would follow.

～ *Tuesday, 8 March*

Luiz Gonçalves dos Santos continues, in his inimitable style of describing the scenario:[29]

Having the Prince Regent Our Lord decided his disembarkation for the afternoon of the next day, 8th of March, in which he would make his solemn entrance to his new court. It was his pleasure to go with his august family, and all his court to the cathedral, there to offer to the Almighty for the good fortune of his journey... The whole town received, with total

pleasure and satisfaction the news that the Prince Regent Our Lord would participate in a solemn procession to the cathedral on the afternoon of the next day, so that on this long stretch, the people would have the best opportunity to see their prince and his august...

At four in the afternoon, with the yards manned and all the ships firing a 21-gun salute, the Prince Regent, accompanied by his family, except the queen, went on shore:

Finally the long-awaited day, March the 8th, dawned as clear and beautiful as the previous one and, with everything ready for the reception of Their Highness, at four in the most beautiful and tranquil afternoon with happy and repeated salutes from the Portuguese and English and loud hoorays from the sailors from their places on the yards, the Prince Regent Our Lord disembarked from the ship that had brought him, the *Príncipe Real*, accompanied by their most Serene Highness prince of Beira, Infantes and Infantas; and by all the court that had left Lisbon, and of other distinguished people, that had gone from shore to fetch him on board, or that had disembarked from the ships... In the midst of this frightening confusion of so many repeated different sounds, disembarked all the royal persons: and together with the Prince Regent Our Lord, prostrated themselves before a rich altar, which had been erected on the upper part of the ramp, where the Chapter of the cathedral was to be found, dressed in silken cope of white gold, and there His Royal highness kissed the Holy Cross...

The temple was properly decorated, and bright with the profusion of lights, as soon as His Royal Highness and his august family entered, a large orchestra broke into melodious hymns... the musicians sang the hymn 'Te Deum Laudamus'... On the conclusion of this sacred ceremony, Their Highnesses rose up and kindly gave their hands to be kissed to all those who approached him, without preferences, and without leaving out anyone... After a short delay ...surrounded again by cheers from the crowd, that was patiently waiting to see again, Their Highnesses the Prince Regent Our Lord, together with the Serene Highness prince of Beira, took a richly decorated coach, the same occurring with the remainder of his family, in other coaches...

Commodore Moore wrote to the Admiralty:

I have great pleasure in informing you that His Royal Highness the Prince
Regent, the Queen and all the Royal Family arrived here on the eighth of
this month with the following Ships, viz. The *Prince Real* [sic], *Afonso
d'Albuquerque*, *Meduse* [sic], *Uranie* [sic], His Majesty's Ship *Bedford*
and a number of Store Ships and Merchant Ships.

The Royal Family have been received in the Brazils [sic] with every
mark of affectionate attachment by all ranks of the Inhabitants, who seem
to me full of Zeal and Loyalty to their Sovereign. The Prince and every
person of the Royal Family are in perfect health. He made his public
Entry yesterday into the city of Rio Janeiro and walked through the principal streets in procession to the Church of St. Rosario to return thanks to
the Almighty. He appeared highly gratified by the universal and enthusi-
astic joy with which he was hailed by an immense concourse of all ranks
and descriptions of the inhabitants.[30]

That evening, and also on the following one, the royal family returned to their
ships for the night.

~ *Thursday, 10 March*

On this day, accompanied by the queen, the royal family parted company from their
ships for the last time. *London*'s log noted:

At 4 the Prince of Brazil left the P. Admls Ship, when the Standard was
haul'd down and the Admirals flag hoisted. The fleet Saluted him with
21 guns: Mann'd ship and Cheered him.

Luiz Gonçalves dos Santos recalls [31]:

Having the Prince Regent Our Lord disembarked on the 8th and made his
solemn entrance into this town with all the pomp and applause described
above, he reserved for the afternoon of the following day the disembarkation and public reception of the Queen, his august mother and Our
Lady, which did not take place during that afternoon due to the sick-
ness of Her Majesty, but on the afternoon of the 10th...at five o'clock in
the afternoon Her Majesty disembarked from the *Príncipe Real* and was
taken in a brig, accompanied by her august son, the Prince Regent Our
Lord, and her serene grand-children, the prince of Beira, D. Pedro; and
Infantes D. Miguel and D. Pedro Carlos... All the fortresses and war-

ships both Portuguese and English saluted on her Majesty leaving her ship, and again on reaching the shore... and received under a canopy... was carried in a armchair, in a procession... Her Majesty the Queen Our Lady was taken to her room; there appeared at the window of the palace, the Prince Regent Our Lord accompanied by his family, the court and the ladies occupying the remaining windows along the front that overlooks the square.

Eventually D. João and his family moved into their home, originally built for a rich local merchant Elias Antônio Lopes – the Real Quinta da Boa Vista.

Chapter VIII

After entering Lisbon, on the dawn of 30 November 1807, Junot moves, together with French and Spanish troops, to take over Portugal. The people, after the initial shock, begin to react. The few British citizens that remain behind suffer the impositions of the conqueror. By the time the Prince Regent reaches Rio de Janeiro, Junot is well established in Portugal.

I n Lisbon, apprehension over the departure of the Prince Regent and the Court was mingled with the expectation of an unknown future.

Junot, now completing a month since starting the forced march, continued to face the problems caused by the distance travelled and the weather.

The 3rd division was considered lost, the spent cavalry and artillery wandered astray to lonely places, led by disloyal guides, or else was detained by the floods. The rain poured down and everywhere streams broke out.[1]

The lack of resistance worried him. He could not believe the Portuguese would hand over their country without first trying to defend it. Could this lack of activity mean that they were preparing an ambush for his depleted and weary troops?

The news from Lisbon would lead one to believe that everything was ready for the resistance. A messenger arrived at that moment announcing that 1,400 troops and all the people would rise up and march behind the first crucifix that was raised in front of them.

~ Monday, 30 November

The last obstacle to be won was the River Trancão, in Sacavém. In the early hours of the morning of the 30th the crossing finally took place. Lisbon now lay before him.

An anonymous observer recalls:

When the squadron left on the 29th, that night part of the French army was in the vicinity of Lisbon; the 1st Division marching without baggage, only with their rucksacks; exhausted from the brutality of their marches and incapable of fighting, had it been necessary. It was made up of more or less ten thousand; very thin, very ragged, the greater part without shoes, ill, limping and dying of hunger, their guns rusty and broken and incapable of firing a shot; rucksacks made from goat skins, a gourd for water tied to their waist, a filthy white canvas uniform; those were the possessions, dress and military discipline of the French soldiers that marched across Portuguese territory, declaring friendship and security of protection and happiness.[3]

The anonymous writer continues:

The General in Command, Junot, arrived with an escort of French horses and another of the Royal Police Guard that had gone to wait for him, and made his way to the palace of the Baron of Quintella, in the square in the Alecrim road, where he established his General Headquarters.[4]

It was the dawn of 30 November. Junot had arrived. The Portuguese fleet had sailed, just eighteen hours before.

The Palace of Bemposta had been prepared to receive him. However, he preferred the opulent home of the Baron of Quintella. His stay was free of expenses; and, even then, he received from the Senate a monthly allowance of twelve thousand cruzados.

One of the principal objectives of his mission, announced prematurely by Bonaparte: to capture the royal family of Portugal, had failed.

Junot even then tried to sell to the more humble, the image of a France totally protective. He ordered that a proclamation[5] should be displayed explaining the reasons for the invasion. If any citizen believed it, the way the invaders acted readily made him see that reality was very different.

The sacrifice of those who had stayed behind had begun. On the eve of the departure, the demand for provisions had made prices rise by 60 per cent. Many weeks would go by before they returned to normal.

On the same day that he arrived, Junot went to the opera and occupied the royal box. The purpose of this action was for the public to see the nobles, and for those who had not accompanied the Prince Regent, to come to pay their compliments:

Crowds filling the roads and closed offices provoked confusion that threatened a collapse; the patriotic citizen, the honoured and loving head of the family could only lament, seeing around him oppressors disguised as protectors. In this state of things and of grief...

That same day, the Superintendent General of the Police gave orders that commerce had to accept French and Spanish currency.[6]

After the departure of the royal family, the Nuncio attempted, in vain, to obtain his passports so as to leave Portugal and follow the Prince Regent. After much effort it became clear that Junot would only give authorisation for him to return to Rome by way of Spain. The Nuncio, accommodated in the almshouse of the Italian Capuchins, waited for the moment to leave for Aldeia Galega, on the far bank of the Tagus, where his coach awaited him. His intention was to travel as far as the River Guadiana and, from there, find a vessel that would take him to Brazil. The river marks the frontier between Portugal and Spain, in the Algarve.

An alternative presented itself. A Portuguese ship, the *Estrela do Mar*, had managed, at a high price, permission to leave the Tagus. It was arranged that the ship would wait for him – during three days – some two leagues outside the bar. On the night of 18 April the Nuncio set off in a small rowing boat. After several hours of searching in a very choppy sea and not finding the Portuguese ship, he decided to approach an English frigate, the *Ninfa*, to go on board. Next day, after signals had been exchanged, the Admiral of the English squadron, Sir Charles Cotton, invited him to transfer to his flagship, HMS *Hibernia*. On the 22nd he set sail for England in the *Estrela do Mar*, escorted by an English frigate, the *Mediator*. Due to the condition of the merchant vessel *Estrela do Mar*, after three days it became necessary to transfer the Nuncio to the *Mediator* and, after putting several men on board the merchant vessel to carry out emergency repairs, take her under tow. On 11 May they entered Plymouth. They next departed, on board HMS *Stork*, on 11 July and after spending a few days in Madeira they sailed on 30 July for Rio de Janeiro on a voyage that took forty days.[7]

In Lisbon French troops continued to arrive, nearly always at night. They looked for large buildings, with ample capacity for their quarters. Not only did this make it easier to maintain order and discipline, but at the same time protected them against the as yet unknown reaction from the people.

~ *Wednesday, 2 December*

Several Divisional Generals arrived, amongst them De Laborde, Loison, and Kellerman; also some of Brigade, establishing themselves in the houses and palaces of the absent nobles and principal merchants.

They evicted from the convents of St Francisco da Cidade, Paulistas and Jesus all the members of the orders who had relatives that could take them in; this so as to accommodate the French soldiers, who had converted the monasteries into barracks.

~ Thursday, 3 December

The French troops continued to arrive. They now numbered more than 11,000. The Portuguese that remained behind were as yet not used to this reality. The number of generals in Lisbon rose to fifteen. It was the beginning of a disastrous era as far as commerce was concerned as:

> ...Commerce was called upon to provide a loan of two million cruzados, before the end of the month; this was the beginning of the plunder... Commerce was affected to a great extent by the threat of total ruin, with the ships taken by surprise in France, with those that went to Britain because of the economic blockade and, with the investment of our working capital in the four corners of the world.

~ Friday, 4 December

Gradually Junot started to take over public administration. He began in the most important sector, by substituting the president of the Royal Treasury Luiz de Vasconcellos e Sousa, and naming in his place M. Hermann, with the title of Interior and Finance Minister. Next, he sent a French inspector to the arsenal. He gave orders to list all the assets of those nobles and others who had accompanied His Royal Highness, in order to confiscate them. He directed M. Joufre to make an inventory of the assets belonging to the royal household.

The English hospital, located at the Travessa dos Ladrões, was chosen to serve as a prison for those Englishmen who remained in Lisbon. Assets that belonged to them, and which were with the Portuguese, had to be handed over; or else they ran the risk of being fined at a rate ten times the value of the merchandise discovered.[8]

Before crossing the frontier the previous month Junot had tried to justify the invasion, especially to the more simple peasant, though none the less astute: "... At last there appeared this day the first proclamation that he, Junot, had divulged in Valença de Alcântara on entering the Kingdom that, until the departure of His Royal Highness, had been kept hidden from us..."[9]

~ Saturday, 5 December

The assets belonging to British subjects, and goods manufactured in England, were the object of special attention during the coming weeks: they would be confiscated by the new authority.

An edict prohibits hunting and the use of firearms, with severe penalties: "... huntsman found... will be taken to be a vagabond, slayer of the highway and, as such, will be taken before a Military Tribunal to be set up for this purpose..."

~ Sunday/Monday, 6/7 December

As the occupation troops increased, so did their need for accommodation.

> "...and divided and quartered the French troops in the monasteries of St. Bento, St. Domingos, Camillos, Carmo, Trindade, Carmelitas bare-footed, St. Vicente de Fóra; the Spanish in St. Francisco de Paula. The carriages belonging to the royal household and to those who had left with His Royal Highness were spoiled by the daily use of many Generals and French public servants."

A new proclamation was displayed, prohibiting any soldier of whatsoever nationality of frequenting "...Inns and places of Drinks..." after seven in the evening, subject to severe penalties for the innkeeper who disobeys. It also forbade the use of any:

> "...Kind of firearm, especially at night, and every person that is arrested and is proved to have used a firearm, whatsoever kind it might be, will be judged by Military Commission and taken to be an assassin."

On this day, those Portuguese that were near the Tagus saw the arrival of the schooner *Curiosa*, which had sailed with the squadron on 29 November: "...she came followed by a storm and making water, and soon after the French took possession of her and she no longer hoisted the Portuguese flag..."

In spite of the rigorous blockade by the English squadron, two small ships from Taninfe and Hamburg managed to come in. This fact caused sadness, as it was a reminder of the rich commerce of another era.

~ Thursday, 10 December

The Patriarch Cardinal, frightened by the people's reaction, published a pastoral letter asking that all co-operate with and respect "...the army of his Majesty, Napoleon the Great, Emperor of the French and King of Italy, that God has destined to sustain and protect religion and make the people happy..."

~ Friday, 11 December

Junot and other officers went on board the Russian squadron anchored in the Tagus. The hoisting of the French flag at the Royal Arsenal caused the people much anger, but their reaction went no further.

~ Sunday, 13 December

The first hostile demonstration from the people occurred on this day. Afterwards, it was remembered as the beginning of the revolution that expelled the French. They were provoked by the nearly 6,000 French soldiers lined up in the Rocio Square, and the presence of Junot and his officers, to receive honours and salutes; and even more when the French flag was hoisted on the Castle followed by a 20-gun salute, answered by the fortresses at the bar. At five in the afternoon the crowds demonstrated for the first time, with stones, sticks and small arms, shouting, "Long live Portugal and death to the French." The confusion was intense, especially in the Chiado and on the Carmo pavement. Many fled to the Church of Sacramento, and twice soldiers discharged their guns into this holy place. It was eight o'clock at night before peace returned to the town. In this first clash four French soldiers died and a Portuguese woman with a bullet wound died next day.

~ Monday, 14 December

The demonstrations of the previous day continued, and the French guard was reinforced everywhere. The people waited, hidden, to attack solitary soldiers. The balance at the end of the day was nine Frenchmen killed and many wounded, as well as three Portuguese dead and four wounded.

~ Tuesday, 15 December

Next day the roads in the capital were quiet, partly because, frightened by the previous day's demonstrations, the army had doubled the guard in places where they were most vulnerable, and began patrolling the roads in the centre.

~ Wednesday, 16 December

Letters received reported that Spanish soldiers had entered Oporto and, on 13 December, had had a proclamation displayed – signed by D. Francisco Taranco e Llano, Lieutenant General of the Royal Armies of His Catholic Majesty – similar to the one in Lisbon by Junot.

~ Saturday, 19 December

After a great deal of insistence, some of the neutral ships that were in the harbour when the invasion occurred managed to get their passports and leave.

A large number of Spanish officers from Além-Tejo were seen entering Lisbon.

~ Sunday, 20 December

In the Rocio Square, troops paraded for the second time. It was said that it was to frighten those who still held hopes of reacting against the occupation.

With the passing of the month, various edicts were published in order to take over public administration, but not without certain confusion.

> The Spanish General from Além-Tejo also issued decrees in the name of his Monarch, giving jobs, charming ministers, etc. In this way this small kingdom found itself with three owners, two strangers and one legitimate that was His Royal Highness.

~ *Monday, 21 December*
In order to avoid the crowd gathering and demonstrating, Junot forbade the celebration of masses and the chiming of bells on Christmas day.

~ *Tuesday, 22 December*
In accordance with the Treaty of Fontainebleau, which stipulated that on the division of Portugal the south would go to Spain (Prince of Peace), Junot ordered that the income from Além-Tejo and Algarve should not go to the Treasury, but be placed at the disposal of the Spanish General, the Marquis of Soccorro.

The titular bishop of the Algarve, D. José Maria de Mello, ordered a pastoral letter to be divulged; the contents similar to that issued by the Patriarch Cardinal.

~ *Monday, 28 December*
News arrived that several ships, proceeding from Brazil, had been taken by the English blockading squadron. The Prince Regent had given orders, taken by the brig *Gavião* on 7 September, to suspend any sailing to Portugal. These ships were either unaware of them, or had disobeyed them. Commerce, already suffering the effects of the invasion, became even more disheartened.[10]

~ *Tuesday, 29 December*
Lucas de Seabra da Silva, Superintendent General of the Police of the Court and Kingdom, fearing that some people could look for excuses in order to go out at night, published an edict: "…that person as from the 1st of January onwards take through the streets any kind of cattle, from the time of the 'Ave-Marias' until seven o'clock in the morning, subject to the loss of this same cattle …"

The first listing of those who would contribute to the forced loan was published. It totalled 800,000 dollars. At the head of the list, each with a contribution of 32,000 dollars, were the Baron of Quintella, Chief Justice Antônio Rodrigues Caldas and Jacinto Fernandes da Costa Bandeira.

∼ *Friday, 1 January 1808*

On this day a large banquet and ball was held at General Headquarters. In addition to French officers, there were present senior officers from the Russian squadron and several families from Lisbon.

∼ *Saturday, 2 January*

The English blockade, after one month, created shortages of food: even bread was in short supply. In order to ease this situation, which was becoming critical, the King of Spain decreed that foodstuffs and provisions could be brought in or be taken out free of taxes.

Martial law was declared. A warship anchored in front of Commerce Square would fire a gun every morning and night as a signal of curfew.

∼ *Monday, 4 January*

The Government decreed that all Brazilians who wished to leave could do so, needing only to obtain their passport. They should indicate the country they would be travelling to, departing in neutral ships. Many families, claiming they were Brazilian, managed to escape.

∼ *Tuesday, 5 January*

There was considerable movement of troops at the coast as the English squadron came in closer and, through fishermen, obtained information as to what was happening on shore.

As a result, fishing boats were prohibited, under severe penalties, of maintaining contact. By painting letters and numbers on their hulls, identification was made easy.

∼ *Sunday, 10 January*

Once again Junot ordered the troops to the Rocio, for a parade and manoeuvres:

> They made the generals manoeuvre the troops, and Junot inspected them as was usual; at this moment General Kellerman fell to the ground, as his horse shied, and he remained for a time unconscious; they took him to Nicola's Bar and, after several drinks, he recovered completely. Various officers participated of this scene; they cheered the General with their glasses and, on leaving (as it was the practice), they all went to see the General remount; for this reason forgot the unimportant (the drinks). The owner of the bar was left without payment: similar cases were always happening.

~ Thursday, 14 January

Today Junot went, after lunch (which was always at eleven o'clock and similar in food and drink to dinner), to the foundry and had the panels with scenes, representing the house of Bragança, taken down and broken; he gave orders that in the future the coat of arms should not appear on the casts; he took with him five Frenchmen with axes and with daring words, characteristic of him, pronounced that the Legitimate House would cease to reign; this vile act took place with more than usual ostentation and he returned in a happy mood, as if he had achieved a Victory.

~ Friday, 15 January

The whole town awoke to the noise of powder carts and guns being taken to the beaches at the bar. A regiment of Swiss and another of artillery followed. The rumour was that the English squadron had a number of transport ships beyond the horizon, ready to disembark soldiers on the beach. It was not true.

~ Saturday, 16 January

Once more Junot went to the foundry and ordered that the Portuguese coat of arms over the doorway, made of stone, should be destroyed. He invited some Portuguese workmen who were in the vicinity to carry out this task, offering them 6,400 réis: "… the poor groaned with hunger… however, there was no one who should accept the vile offer, so that French soldiers had to do it…"

~ Sunday/Monday, 17/18 January

"…During these days shoes for the French army were taken from the shoemak-ers' shops; blankets and linen sheets from the drapers; all this with the greatest violence…"

~ Tuesday/Wednesday, 19/20 January

Portuguese regiments were depleted by a dramatic reduction of men bearing arms. Thus the enemy further consolidated its supremacy.

~ Friday/Saturday, 22/23 January

Officers and sailors of the ship *Princeza* and others who had been arrested by the English blockade were left on shore. Immediately they were imprisoned and taken to General De Laborde for interrogation about the English squadron, and then released. The ship was taken to England.

~ Sunday, 24 January

The preparations against a possible invasion by the English continued on the beaches by the bar.

~ Thursday, 28 January

From Mafra came news that a man had been shot for killing two Frenchmen with a scythe.

~ Monday, 1 February

On this day, exactly two months after the occupation, confident of their complete control of the territory and that the Treaty of Fontainebleau could now be implemented, an important step was taken:

> Two rows of Grenadiers were placed, from the General Headquarters to the Rocio, along the Chiado and Calçada Nova do Carmo, roads that lead into the great square: Junot came out and made his way to the Regencia Palace, where he remained for some time... the news spread that the Regency was going to be abolished or extinguished, and that Napoleon had ordered that Junot should be made Governor General of the Kingdom. At five o'clock he gave orders for the edict to be released...[11]

Immediately, another edict was published, extinguishing the Regency Council established by the Prince Regent before leaving. At the same time, he created the Council of War and the Council of Government. Some public employees were maintained at their posts; French and Portuguese were appointed to occupy jobs requiring trust.

~ Tuesday, 2 February

The publication of the edict,[12] signed by Napoleon in Milan on 23 December, left the people sad and bitter. It ordered the people to make a donation of one hundred million francs (forty million cruzados) as a contribution towards the war, as well as the confiscation of the assets of the royal family and of those nobles who had accompanied them. The donation of two million cruzados already paid would be taken into account.

In 1808, by order of Junot, a delegation of the Three States was formed with the objective of going to Bayonne to greet the Emperor and to ask him for a reduction in his demands as to the war contribution. The delegation included the marquises of Marialva, Penalva and Valença; the two marquises of Abrantes (father and son); D. Nuno Alvares Pereira de Melo (second son of the House of Cadaval) and Count of

Sabugal and Viscount of Barbacena. Received in Bayonne by Napoleon, and with the negotiations having begun, a popular uprising against the invaders erupted all over the country. The position of the delegation became untenable, and so the delegates became prisoners of war and were taken to Bordeaux and then to Paris. They were only able to return in 1814.

～ *Thursday, 4 February*

Domination was not complete – here and there occurred spontaneous reaction to the invasion:

> News has been received of a small scale mutiny in Caldas, between the soldiers of the Oporto Regiment and the French, with several deaths; General Loison with four thousand men and six pieces of artillery was sent to make enquires and punish.

An English boat was seen near the port of Setúbal.

～ *Saturday, 5 February*

The English squadron, after the episode of the Brazil merchant ships, started to take a more active attitude. On this and on the following days an English boat patrolled near to the bar.

～ *Saturday, 9 February*

The position of nobles, clergy and others who had remained in Lisbon was very delicate. If on the one hand they were called to make 'donations' (a lesser punishment than confiscation); on the other, they would be summoned, as happened on this day at three o'clock, to greet General Junot and to render him obedience. The people looked on, indignant: were these people traitors?

～ *Wednesday, 10 February*

From Caldas came news that the Oporto regiment, on garrison duty, had been surrounded and disarmed. Nine Portuguese were executed.

～ *Saturday, 13 February*

The English squadron at last got into action.

> At three o'clock in the morning, the English came in boats and pinnaces and boarded one of the gun-boats that were on duty in St. José de Riba-Mar with its commander and a crew of 60 men; they took her prisoner, without being noticed by the look-outs at the fortresses and even less by

the warships. This news made General Junot furious; the bar was reinforced with the line-of-battle ship *Vasco da Gama*, the frigate *Carlota*,
the brig *Gaivota*, the frigate *Beijamim,* the schooner *Curiosa*, and another
two smaller boats, not counting the floating battery; all anchored between
the tower of Belém and the fort of Area.

∼ *Monday, 15 February*

The captured gunboat appeared, flying the English ensign, in the midst of the squadron. A pinnace (with a flag of truce) brought five Frenchmen, wounded when the
boarding took place on the 13th.

∼ *Tuesday, 16 February*

Once again the English squadron showed that they were on the alert as:

> There anchored in Cascais eleven English ships, this visit made many rush
> to different observation points… the guards and garrisons at the bar were
> doubled; and for two days, fearful of a landing, they remained under arms…

∼ *Wednesday, 17 February*

A considerable movement of troops occured in the direction of the Além-Tejo and in
the area of Elvas. The number of men distributed between Lisbon and Oporto was
reduced to 8,000.

∼ *Friday, 19 February*

Much against the wish of the Portuguese people, the English ships anchored in
Cascais made sail, not to enter the Tagus but to return to the high seas.

∼ *Sunday, 21 February*

In the Rocio the troops paraded once more: this time French and Portuguese (Infantry
Regiments 1, 4, 10, 13 and 16) – the latter without their colours. They were inspected
by French generals, by the Marquis of Alorna and by Gomes Freire. It was current
gossip that the Portuguese troops were to be sent abroad, as was French policy. They
would be replacing the French troops now in Portugal and, at the same time, elimi-
nating the possibility of an uprising.

∼ *Monday, 22 February*

Again there was grumbling. Having publicly stated that Brazilians could apply for
their passports and leave their country and, having stamped their passports and permitted embarkation on the brig *Real João*, suddenly, and without explanation, the
passports were cancelled.

~ Friday, 11 March

An incident occurred that captured the imagination of the people of Lisbon.

A chicken belonging to a certain Sr. Costa laid an egg and, to the general surprise, the letters VDSRP could clearly be seen on the shell. The initials were interpreted as representing 'Hooray for D. Sebastião King of Portugal' *(Viva D. Sebastião Rei de Portugal)*. The news of this miraculous egg rapidly spread, attracting a crowd to Sr. Costa's house in the Rua das Taipas, stretching from there to the river bank, to receive the much awaited saviour. It was presumed that the saviour would come dressed in the uniform of the British navy! In the year 1578 D. Sebastião led an expedition to Alcacer-Kebir and during the battle that look place on 4 August he disappeared, leaving not the slightest trace. In accordance with Portuguese legend, D. Sebastião did not die and will one day return to save his country. His return is still awaited!

They say that the egg, on a silver salver, was presented to Junot at a banquet and that everyone appeared anxious to inspect the phenomenon.[13]

Chapter IX

EPILOGUE

The British squadron in Rio de Janeiro. Cruise to St Salvador in search of the Rochefort squadron. Arrival of Sir Sidney Smith. Commemorations on the birthday of His Majesty George III. Escort duty to the royal farm in Santa Cruz. HMS London *returns home.*

∼ *March 1808*

The arrival of the royal family in Rio de Janeiro heralded a new role for the British squadron, now augmented by the frigates *Solebay* and *Surveillance*, which had come in on 9 March.

In the meantime Vice-Admiral Sir Charles Cotton[1] had been sent out to Portugal to replace Sir Sidney Smith. However, before handing over, Sir Sidney was sent to Gibraltar, Porto Praya and Madeira to look for French vessels that might be cruising in these areas. The French squadron had managed to slip out of Rochefort although the port was under blockade, and its whereabouts was unknown.

On 29 February, whilst in Gibraltar on board the *Foudroyant*, Sir Sidney received orders to take under his command the *Agamemnon* and the *Confiance*, to proceed to Brazil in the *Foudroyant*, and there hoist his flag as Commander-in-Chief:

> The orders of the Admiralty were dated January the 25th 1808; but what with the stoppage at Gibraltar, where he was ordered to communicate with Lieutenant-General Sir John Moore, and calling at other ports, together with the change of ships at sea, the *Foudroyant* being much out of repair, it was not before the 17th May that he reached the magnificent harbour of Rio de Janeiro, in his Majesty's ship *London*.[2]

On 14 March Commodore Graham Moore, from Rio de Janeiro, wrote to his new Commander-in-Chief, Vice-Admiral Sir Charles Cotton:

> I have to inform you that His Majesties Ship *Surveillance* arrived here on the 9th instant, having onboard Francis Hill Esq. Secretary of Legation and

Chargée des Affaires; Captain Sir George Collier, delivered me your order dated the 11th December last, directing me to put myself under your command, together with sundry orders of Council and Proclamations. He also delivered to me your Letter of 25th January, containing the important intelligence communicated to you by Vice Admiral Sir I. T. Dinkworth, respecting the sailing of the Enemy Squadron from Rochefort, on the 17th January, which Letters, and orders he received from Captain Grant of the *Raven* at St. Iago [sic]. – As from the state of the defence and natural strength of this Harbour, together with the whole of the Portuguese Squadron being here except the *Don Juan de Castro* [sic] at Bahia (St. Salvador), I think this Harbour perfectly safe from any attack from the Rochefort Squadron, I have been waiting for a land Breeze to carry the Squadron under my command, consisting of the Ships named in the Margin (M*arlborough*, *Monarch*, *London*, *Bedford* and *Surveillance*), to sea, to endeavour to fall in with them. His Royal Highness the Prince wishes me to go to Bahia, as the Town of St. Salvador is open to an attack from the Sea, and might be put under contribution, if that were a sufficient object for the Enemy to risk their Squadron. I am rather of opinion that their object is Rio de la Plata, to throw what Troops they may have on board into Monte Video, I shall be guided by circumstances, and the intelligence I may receive in following them, the force under my command being, I hope, equal to fight them.

I have to inform you that pursuant to an Order from the Right Hon. The Lords Commissioners of the Admiralty I have taken the *Surveillance* under my command.[3]

On the afternoon of Wednesday, 16 March *London* took on a pilot, ready to cross the bar and put out to sea. In the evening lack of wind prevented the squadron from leaving and so the pilot was returned to shore. At dawn the next morning, with a land breeze blowing, the squadron, together with the Portuguese brig *Voador*, sailed for Bahia. The squadron cruised along the coast in their search for French ships.

∼ *April 1808*

As Commodore Moore had predicted, they were unsuccessful: on 8 April they moored one mile from shore at the southern end of the town of St Salvador.

The next few days were spent preparing for the return journey. On the 12th the Governor, the Count of Ponte, went on board the *London* for a visit; the regulation 13-gun salute was fired, both on embarking and on leaving the ship.

On 18 April the squadron set off for the return journey, arriving at Rio de Janeiro, without incident, on 8 May.

~ May 1808

On 12 May the *Confiance* finally came in and joined her squadron; followed on the 17th by the *Foudroyant*, bringing Sir Sidney Smith, accompanied by the *Agamennon*[4] and the brig *Pitt*.

~ June 1808

Sir Sidney Smith now invited the Prince Regent and the royal family to dine on board the *London*, in celebration of the king's birthday. Thomas O'Neil, who was present, describes the preparations and the event:

> May 24th – Orders came on board the *London* from the commander in chief, to employ every artificer in the fleet to prepare the ship for the reception of the Royal family, who had been invited by him to dine on board the 4th of June, in commemoration of (my most grandiose sovereign) his Britannic Majestys birthday; and which invitation they had condescendingly accepted. Accordingly, all the guns from the middle deck and upper cabin, as also from the quarter-deck, were removed. The cabins were decorated with the English, Portuguese, and Spanish colours,[5] and a picture, containing the likeness of all our naval heroes; and, in honour of the Royal visitors, the deck was covered with French Flags.
>
> The Royal table was placed in front of the upper cabin, and tables for the reception of the nobles attending the Royal family, were set the full length of each side of the quarterdeck. A platform was raised from the main to the foremast, the railing of which was ornamented with English, Portuguese, and Spanish colours. In the centre, a table was placed with one hundred and sixty covers; the awnings, the full length of the ship, were lined with English and Portuguese ensigns, the borders of which were festooned with different coloured signal flags; the sides of the ship on the quarter-deck were covered with the Royal standards of England, in front of which was his Britannic Majesty's arms over the Royal table. On the poop was raised a marquee, for the reception of the attendants of the illustrious visitors; and no pains were spared to render the appearance of the ship most nautically magnificent.
>
> On the 4th of June, the standard of England, in conjunction with that of Spain, were hoisted. At two o'clock, the Regent and his family embarked, under a royal salute from the ships and batteries; and upon his Highness's arrival on board, the standard of Portugal was hoisted at the fore, when they were received with sincere demonstrations of heartfelt respect. His Highness remarked that the decks were covered with the colours of the

French nation. The Admiral answered in the affirmative, and the Prince replied, he was indebted to his faithful ally and his brave subjects, which enable him to trample them under his feet; a reply which feelingly evidenced his grateful sentiments for British friendship.

At four o'clock the Royal family seated themselves at table, the Admiral superintending, until commanded by his Highness, to sit at the table which was placed at his right hand, with Mr. Hill, the British minister, the nobility taking their places according to their rank; and the Royal Family were attended by British naval officers.

In front of the table was placed the memorable standard which the Prince had flying onboard the *Principe Real*, when he was compelled to quit his native country; the arms of Portugal and Spain were suspended over the Royal guests, and when the English and Portuguese officers were seated, nothing could exceed the happiness his Highness and family manifested, and the whole of their misfortunes seemed to be forgotten.

On this festive occasion, various appropriate toasts were given... His Highness the Prince Regent, the Princess of Brazil, and the Princesses, severally gave – "The King of Great Britain, and may he live till time be no more!"

The Prince of Spain gave – "Prosperity to the British arms, who are fighting for my family's cause."

The Infantas gave – "May our father and his family ever retain the esteem of all his British Majesty's officers."

These were returned with Royal salutes. At sunset, his Royal highness requested that the Royal standard, which had been flying on board the *London*, might be brought before him. This request being complied with, his Highness commanded that the standard should be laid on the deck, and then addressed the Admiral in the following impressive manner:

"Admiral, the honour that you and the British officers have this day conferred on me my family, is more than we ever expected... But to you, Admiral, I and my family owe our liberty, and my mother her crown and dignity. We are this day come on board the *London*, to celebrate his British Majesty's birth-day; and on this joyful occasion my Royal standard has had the honour to fly in conjunction with that to England. It now lies on the deck; and permit me to return you and the officers thanks for all the services you and they have conferred on me, my family, and my faithful subjects."

"As a mark of my respect, accept this standard from me; and from henceforth, quarter the arms of my house with those of your own: it will remain as a memorial for your posterity that your exertions preserved us from falling into the snare which Bonaparte had laid for our destruction."

This address was honoured with a salute from all his Majesty's ships… although the entertainment was the most magnificent that was ever given on board any of his Majesty's ships, yet when a sovereign addressed the British Admiral in such terms of respect, it was sufficient to cause a retrospective sigh to be heaved at the calamities his Highness and his family had been compelled to undergo, and the loss of their ancient hereditary dominions. But the Admiral revived their cheerfulness, by recommending the British officers to drink "Prosperity to his Royal Highness and his dominions"; which was most graciously received by the Royal visitors.

At eight in the evening, these illustrious personages left the ship, and invited the Admiral, Captains, and officers, to attend them to the opera; which had been previously commanded on the occasion, in honour of the day, boxes having been prepared for their reception.[6]

The *Naval Chronicle* records the event:

At Brazil, on the 14th June 1808, Sir Sidney Smith gave an entertainment to the whole Portuguese royal family and court onboard his majesty's ship *London*. On quitting the ship, the Prince Regent presented to the rear admiral, with his own hand, the standard of Portugal, to be borne as an augmentation to the coat of arms and declared the revival of the order of the sword, instituted by Don Afonso V surnamed the African in 1459, of which order Sir Sidney Smith is to be created grand cross.

All the English captains before the Tagus under his command, on the 20th of November, to be commanders, and the first lieutenants of each ship, knights of the same; also Mr. Hill his majesty's secretary of legation to that court. His royal highness conferred medals on the four captains composing the squadron detached by Sir Sidney Smith to accompany the Portuguese fleet to Brazil…"[7]

In addition to the honours given by the Prince Regent, Sir Sidney Smith received a country estate with six slaves.[8]

The Admiralty in London was pleased with Sir Sidney's conduct of this unusual mission.

I lost no time in laying your dispatches brought by Captain Yeo of his majesty's ship *Confiance*, and by the *Trafalgar*, letter of marque, before my lords commissioners of the admiralty; and I am commanded by their lordships to express their high approbation of your judicious and able conduct, in the management of the service entrusted to your charge, and in the execution of the various orders you have received from time to time.

Their lordships are strongly impressed with the propriety of the whole of your conduct towards the royal family of Portugal: the respectful attention which you appear to have shewn to the illustrious house of Bragança, has been in strict conformity to their lordships' wishes, and they have directed me to express their complete satisfaction at the manner in which you have in this, as well as in every other respect, obeyed their instructions…"[9]

The members of the Court, military officers, clergy and others were not forgotten by D. João, as recorded by Melo Morais:[10]

Recognising the haste with which the grandees of this, his court, had left their homes and possessions, he deemed to provide them with allowances taken from the Royal Treasury; determining with which they could decently live on, in accordance with their social position. The Naval and Military officers were given positions of employment, or taken into the Brazilian Military Corps. The clergymen received livings or jobs, to earn sufficiently to live. He created posts and departments to accommodate all who were lacking in sustenance. He awarded decorations, posts, jobs and dignity, to a large number of inhabitants in Bahia and in Rio de Janeiro.

～ 1809

The *London* stayed on and, on the following January her log showed that she escorted the Prince Regent to Santa Cruz.

During the second half of the sixteenth century the Jesuit Order was bequeathed the nucleus of what was to become an immense agricultural estate – Santa Cruz – on the coast west of Rio de Janeiro. In 1759, under the influence of the Marquis of Pombal, the Jesuits were expelled from Portugal. As a result Santa Cruz became crown property. It was here that D. João spent the summer of 1809 and, as agreed, whenever he left harbour a British man-of-war acted as escort.

Finally, on 5 March 1809 *London* left Rio de Janeiro, escorting the merchant vessels *Jane*, *Clarkson* and *Fingal* on their return to England. She reached Cawsand Bay on 21 May, almost exactly eighteen months from the date she had sailed. She moved up to Chatham dockyard and was paid off. In 1811 she was broken up.

At the beginning of 1811 the French troops were expelled from Portuguese territory by Britain. This victory was followed by others in Spain and, eventually, in France. Finally, following Waterloo, Napoleon was conclusively beaten; removed from the scenario where he had been the major figure for so many years. He was taken to the island of St Helena, to spend the rest of his days in exile.

Although his motherland was no longer occupied, D. João remained in Brazil. On his mother's death in 1816 he succeeded to the throne with the title of João VI. In 1821, after spending thirteen years in Brazil, he returned to Portugal.

In 1822 Brazil declared her independence from Portugal. Following protracted negotiations, carried out on behalf of Portugal by British Ambassador Lord Stuart, the separation was ratified.[11]

The cycle came to an end with the death of D. João in 1826. When he set off in 1807, he could not have imagined that such a sizeable part of his reign would be spent in Brazil.

Appendix A:

A short biography of the principal personalities, both Portuguese and British, involved in the transfer of the Court to Brazil.[1]

CHAPTER I

~ *D. Maria I: 26th Queen Of Portugal And Algarves; Princess Of Brazil*[2]

D. Maria I, 'the Devout', was born in Lisbon on 17 December 1734, and was baptised by the Patriarch of Lisbon, D. Tomás de Almeida with the names of Maria Francisca Isabel Josefa Antônia Gertrudes Rita Joana. Her wedding took place, at the Palace of Nª Sª da Ajuda, on 6 July 1760, to her uncle, the Serene Infante D. Pedro (later king, 3rd by name). He was born in Lisbon on 5 July 1717, and passed away in the Royal Palace of Nª Sª da Ajuda on 5 March 1786.

The queen, D. Maria I, began to reign on the death of her father, D. José I, on 24 February 1777, and was crowned on 13 May of that same year. She died in Rio de Janeiro on 20 March 1816, at the age of 81 years. She reigned for thirty-nine years. The queen, for health reasons, in fact ceased to reign on 10 February 1792.

~ *D. João Vi: 27th King Of Portugal; 1st Of The United Kingdom Of Portugal, Brazil And Algarves; Titular Emperor Of Brazil; 8th Prince Of Beira And Of Brazil*

D. João VI, 'the Merciful', on baptism received the names João Maria José Francisco Xavier de Paula Luis Antônio Domingos Rafael. He was also 21st Duke of Bragança, 18th of Guimarães, 16th of Barcellos, 20th Marquis of Villa Viçosa, 24th Count of Arrayolos, and 22nd of Ourem, Faria and Neiva. He was born at the royal residence of the Quinta de Queluz on 13 March 1767.

During his lifetime, he was given decorations by almost every country in Europe. Amongst them, he received the prestigious knighthood of the Order of the Garter of England and the Golden Fleece of Spain.

Because of the grave illness of his mother, Queen D. Maria I, he took over the administration of the country, as Regent *de facto* and in her name, on 10 February 1792.

In 1799 he began to rule as Prince Regent until, with the death of his mother, he suc-ceeded to the throne. He began to exercise his right as monarch on 20 March 1816. He was crowned King of the United Kingdom of Portugal, Brazil and Algarves in Rio de Janeiro on 6 February 1818. He died, after his return to Portugal, on 16 March 1826.

D. João VI, in the series of Portuguese kings, became known as 'the Merciful' in the recognition of the many manifestations and proofs of his goodness of heart and magnanimity of soul. He was married, whilst still a prince, on 8 March 1785, to the Serene Infanta of Spain, D. Carlota Joaquina de Bourbon.

∼ D. Carlota Joaquina Queen Of Portugal And Algarves; Queen Of The United Kingdom Of Portugal, Brazil And Algarves; Titular Empress Of Brazil; Princess Of Beira And Of Brazil

D. Carlota Joaquina de Bourbon was the eldest daughter of King D. Carlos IV of Spain and Queen D. Maria Luiza Thereza of Bourbon, Duchess of Parma. She was born at the residence of Aranguez (Spain) on 25 April 1775, and died at the royal residence of Queluz on 7 January 1830. She was married at the age of 10, but only went to live with the prince in 1790, when she was 16

∼ D. Pedro IV, 28th King Of Portugal; 1st Emperor Of Brazil

His Royal and Imperial Highness, D. Pedro IV, 'the Liberator', was 22nd Duke of Bragança, 21st Marquis of Villa Viçosa, 25th Count of Arrayolos and 23rd of Ourem, Faria and of Neiva.

He was born in the royal residence of the Paço de Queluz on 21 October 1798 and was baptised in the royal chapel of that residence, Pedro de Alcântara Francisco Antônio João Carlos Xavier de Paula Miguel Rafael Joaquim José Gonzaga Paschoal Cipriano Serafino de Bragança e Bourbon. He became Infante of Portugal and Prince of Beira on 11 June 1801, and of Brazil on 20 March 1816. Amongst his many titles he was also Grand Prior of Crato and later Prince of the United Kingdom of Portugal, Brazil and Algarves. He was acclaimed Emperor of Brazil, and crowned on 1 December 1822. In 1825 he founded the Order which carried his name, now known as the Order of the Southern Cross and later he founded the Order of the Rose.

D. Pedro IV succeeded his father, King D. João VI, to the throne of Portugal on his death in 1826. He became D. Pedro IV, King of Portugal, but only for seven days, for he had previously decided that it was impracticable to rule Portugal whilst living in Brazil. He renounced the crown in favour of his eldest daughter D. Maria II da Glória. His only brother, Miguel, complained that whereas Pedro had two kingdoms, he had none. In order to conciliate the situation it was agreed that D. Maria da Glória should marry her uncle Miguel and that he should become Prince Consort.

Arriving in Portugal from Austria, ahead of his future wife, Miguel persuaded the Council of the Three States that he was the legitimate successor and so was crowned King of Portugal in 1828.

In 1831 D. Pedro decided to leave Brazil in order to defend the rights of his daughter. He then abdicated his imperial crown of Brazil in favour of his eldest son Pedro, then a child of six (who at the age of 15 was crowned D. Pedro II, Emperor of Brazil).

With the title of Duke of Bragança, whilst on the island of Terceira (Azores) he proclaimed and took over the regency, in the name of the queen, as father, tutor and natural defender of the rights of his august daughter to the crown of Portugal. It was the beginning of the fight to oust his brother that resulted in a bloody civil war which was to last two years (1832-1834); but, he was successful. On his death on 24 September 1934, his daughter, although only 15, was proclaimed of age and began to rule.

He was married for the first time on 13 May 1817, to the Archduchess of Austria, D. Maria Leopoldina Josefa Carolina, who was born on 22 January 1797, and who died in Rio de Janeiro on 11 December 1826. She was the second daughter of Francisco I, Emperor of Austria, and of his second wife, the Empress D. Maria Thereza Carolina, Princess of the Two Sicilies. He married for the second time on 2 August 1829, to D. Amélia Augusta Eugênia Napoleon Beauharnais. The Widow Empress died in Lisbon on 26 January 1873.

~ D. Miguel I 29ᵗʰ King Of Portugal

D. Miguel Maria de Patrocínio João Carlos Francisco de Assis Xavier de Paula Pedro d´Alcântara Antônio Rafael Gabriel Joaquim José Gonzaga Evaristo de Bragança e Bourbon was born at the royal palace of Queluz on 26 October 1802 and died in exile in Bronnbach (Germany) on 14 November 1866.

In 1824 he was unsuccessful in deposing his father, D João VI, from his throne.

After receiving a royal pardon he was forced into living abroad.

The Council of the Three States, at a meeting on 25 July 1828, excluded D. Pedro and his descendants and decided that the legitimate succession to the crown of Portugal should belong to the Infante D. Miguel and so proclaimed him king.

After a civil war and much bloodshed, D. Pedro was successful in retaking Portugal in the name of his daughter, thus ending D. Miguel´s reign, which had lasted almost six years.

He married Princess Adelaide de Loewenstein-Wertheim-Rosenberg on 24 September 1851. She died on 16 December 1909.

~ Count Of Barca

D. Antônio d´Araújo de Azevedo, 1ˢᵗ Count of Barca (1815), was born on 14 May 1754 in Ponte de Lima, and died in Rio de Janeiro on 21 June 1817. He was the son of Antônio Pereira Pinto d´Araújo de Azevedo, Seigneur of the Tenure of Sá and of the house of Laje; and his wife D. Maria Francisca d´Araújo de Azevedo.

He followed a diplomatic career, first as Minister and Ambassador Extraordinary to the Court in The Hague (1787) and later Minister to the Court in St Petersburg (1801), where he spent three years. On being recalled, he took over responsibility for Foreign Affairs and War.

Over the years he managed to build a very fine library of books, maps and prints which he later donated to the National Library of Rio de Janeiro.

On arrival in Brazil in 1808, D. João changed all his ministers. The Count of Barca then dedicated himself to his garden, known as Hortus Araujensis, where he cultivated 1,500 indigenous and exotic species; later he would bequeath it to the newly inaugurated Botanical Gardens of Rio de Janeiro.

Recalled once more, in 1814 he took over responsibility for the Navy. In 1817, at the same time, he answered for all the various ministries. His health, which was already frail, did not resist. The Court of Barca did not marry and did not leave descendants.

~ Lord Strangford [3]

Percy Clinton Sidney Smythe, 1780–1855, was the 6th Viscount Strangford and Baron Panhurst (1825). Born in London, he was educated at Trinity College Dublin. Strangford joined the Foreign Office and was sent in 1802, at the age of 22, to Lisbon as Secretary of the British Legation.

During this, his first assignment, he learned Portuguese sufficiently well and gained certain notoriety by translating and having published in the *Edinburgh Review* 'Poems from the Portuguese of Camões'. Byron, highly critical of the translation, wrote: "It is also to be remarked, that the things given to the public as Poems of Camoens, are no more work to be found in the Portuguese, than in the Song of Samon." He even expressed his opinion in verse:

> Hibernian Strangford! With thine eyes of blue,
> And boasted locks of red, or auburn hue,
> Learn if thou canst, to yield thine author's sence,
> Nor vend thy sonnets on a false pretence.
> Mend! Strangford! Mend thy morals and thy taste;
> Be warm, be pure, be amorous, but be chaste:
> Cease to deceive; thy pilfered harp restore
> Nor teach the Lusian Barb to copy Moore.

During 1807 he was Minister to the Court of Portugal and, as such, was deeply involved in the negotiations that led to the royal family migrating to Brazil, under escort of HM ships. His influence in the event was, perhaps, less than he tried to make believe. Because of severe illness he was forced to return to London. Nominated to the post of Minister Plenipotentiary and Special Envoy to the Court in Brazil, he arrived in Rio de Janeiro on 22 July 1808.

In 1815 D. João, judging that the degree of influence that he had over internal matters had reached unacceptable levels, had him recalled. He left under a cloud, having upset D. João by refusing to accept a gift of twelve bars of gold, normally given to retiring ambassadors.

He became Ambassador in Stockholm (1817), Constantinople (1820) and St Petersburg in 1824. In 1825 he was active in the House of Lords with the title of Baron Panhurst. In 1828 he returned to Brazil, as Minister Extraordinary, to try and reconcile D. Pedro to his brother D. Miguel. In this he was unsuccessful. In 1829 he left for the last time. He died in London on 29 May 1855.

～ Marquis Of Funchal

D. Domingo Antônio de Sousa Coutinho was born in Chaves in 1760, and died, a bachelor, in England in 1833. He was the son of D. Francisco Inocêncio de Sousa Coutinho, Governor and Captain-General of the Kingdoms of Angola and Benguela, and Ambassador to Madrid. He was the brother of the first Count of Linhares.

After graduating from the University of Coimbra, with a law degree, he began his diplomatic career in Denmark. Subsequently he served in Turin, Rome and London, where he spent many years. As an Anglophile, he was a political enemy of the all-powerful Francophile, Count of Barca.

～ Count Of Galvêas

D. João de Almeida de Mello e Castro, 5th Count of Galvêas, was born on 22 January 1756, and died in Rio de Janeiro on 18 January 1814. During his life he held many posts, including:

Official of the royal household, Gamekeeper of the royal forests of Villa Viçosa and other properties belonging to the House of Bragança, State councillor, Minister and State Secretary for Foreign Affairs and War, Interim Minister of the Navy and Overseas (whilst residing in Brazil). Portuguese Ambassador to the Court in Vienna, Austria, Special Envoy and Extraordinary Minister to the Court in London, the Hague and Rome, Counsellor of the Finance Council, President of the Finance Committee and of the arsenal of the Armed Forces. He was married to D. Isabel José de Menezes, fifth daughter of the first counts of Cavalheiros.

～ Pina Manique [4]

D. Diogo Inácio de Pina Manique was born on 3 October 1733, and died on 1 July 1805. He graduated in law at the University of Coimbra in 1758. In 1780 he was appointed to the important post of General Superintendent of the Police of the Court and Realm. He accumulated, at the same time, the posts of: General Superintendent for Contraband and Tax Avoidance, Accountant at the Finance Ministry, General

Administrator of the Sugar Custom House, Judge at the Court of Appeals, Inspector of the Council of Administrators of the Pernambuco and Paraíba Company.

Endowed with a very strong personality, energetic and entrepreneurial, he was the most powerful and able administrator during the last two decades of the eighteenth century. He was particularly active against the infiltration of political liberalism into Portugal.

He was the founder of various institutions, amongst them Casa Pia in Lisbon, the College of Art in Rome, and boarding houses for medical students in London, Edinburgh and in Denmark.

Through inheritance or donations, by the sovereigns under whom he served, he was: Alcalde of the Vila of Porto Alegre, Seigneur of the Vila of Manique do Intendente, Councillor Commander of Santa Maria de Oureda, in the Order of Christ, Tenure of St Joaquim, in the Villa of Coina.

In 1759 he received the honour of being nominated shield bearer and Knight of the Royal Household. He married D. Inácia Margarida de Brito Nogueira in 1773.

~ Count Of Linhares

D. Rodrigo de Souza Coutinho Teixeira de Andrade Barbosa was born at Chaves on 4 August 1745, and died in Rio de Janeiro on 26 January 1812. His varied career included: Plenipotentiary Minister in Turin in 1778 and 1796, Minister of the Navy, President of the Royal Treasury, Minister for Foreign Affairs and of War, whilst in Brazil. He was made Count of Linhares in December 1808.

He was married in Turin on 8 May 1789 to D. Gabriela Asinari de San Marsan, This lady held many titles and honours, including: Dame of the Orders of St Isabel and of St Louise of Spain; of the Luminous Cross of Austria; of St John of Jerusalem, Dame of Honour to Queen D. Carlota Joaquina, Lady-in-waiting to the Infantas D. Maria Isabel and D. Maria Francisca (when they were married in Spain), Lady-in-waiting to D. Leopoldina.

She was the daughter of D. Francisco Filipe Valentim Asinari di San Marsan. Marquis of San Marsan, Master of the Horses and Cavalry General, to the Prince of Piedmont and his wife, D. Úrsula Gabriela, Princess of Cistena.

~ Duke Of Abrantès

The former ambassador to Portugal and commander of the French invasion troops, Jean Andoche Junot, was born in Burgundy from a farming family. At an early age he became one of Bonaparte's prodigy generals and, in 1807, was named Duke of Abrantès. In 1800, whilst he was Governor of Paris, he married the sixteen-year-old beauty Laure Permon (1784–1838). After his defeat in Portugal he never recovered his career on the battlefield. In 1813, separated from his wife, who had had an affair with the famous Austrian minister Metternich, he committed suicide during a bout of madness in his father's home. The Duchess of Abrantes, although without funds, kept her title and successfully made the transition to the new era (that of Louis XVIII). The writer Balsac encouraged her to write her memoirs, *Souvenirs d'une Ambassade*, which were published in eighteen volumes between 1813 and 1835.

~ Count Of Mafra [5]

D. Lourenço José Xavier de Lima was born on 15 May 1767, and died a bachelor on 11 January 1839. He was the son of the first marquises of Ponte do Lima.

He became a diplomat, serving first in Turin, then in Vienna. In 1801 he was appointed Minister to the Court of St. James (England). In August 1803 he was posted to Paris as Portuguese Minister.

Held to be a sympathiser of Napoleon's policies, he was not able to see through the strategy developed by the Emperor of the French and consequently his interpretation of the events taking place was mistaken, as subsequently became apparent.[6]

With the declaration of war in 1807 he was expelled from France, and returned to Portugal.

Later his life became complicated as his debts mounted. In 1814, to escape from his creditors, he had to take refuge in England. There the Ambassador D. Pedro de Souza Holstein, who was later to become Duke of Palmela, hired him as secretary, thus giving him diplomatic immunity.[7]

~ Marquis Of Alorna

D. Pedro de Almeida Portugal was 3rd Marquis of Alorna – son of the second marquises of Alorna and sixth count of Assumar. He was born in Lisbon on 16 January 1754 and died on the 2 January 1813.

He married, on 19 February 1782, D. Henriquetta, daughter of the second count of St Vicente.

He joined the cavalry regiment and was made colonel on 31 July 1793. In 1797 he was named Head of the Lusitanian Legion of Light troops.

Because he commanded the Portuguese Legion that was to fight abroad and, later, returning with Massena to invade Portugal, the Regency in Lisbon that same year extinguished his title and cancelled his decorations and honours. Subsequently he was condemned to death. After his death in Kongsberg, through the efforts of his sister, his sentence was quashed.

~ Count Of Ega

D. Ayres José Maria de Saldanha Albuquerque Coutinho Mattos e Noronha, 2nd Count of Ega, was born in the town of Funchal on the island of Madeira on 29 March 1755, and died in Lisbon on 12 January 1827.

He was married, for the first time, on 5 March 1786 to D. Maria José do Carmo Xavier de Almeida, who died in November 1795.

He held many important posts and honours, including:

Member of the Council of the Three States, Inspector General for Army Provisions, Ambassador at the Court in Madrid (1805), Nobleman attached to the Royal Household, Gentleman of the Bedchamber of Queen D. Maria I and of the King D. João VI.

On 9 February 1800 he married for the second time to D. Juliana Maria Luiza Carolina Sofia de Oyenhausen e Almeida, Countess of Oyenhausen-Gravemburg, who was born in Vienna on 1 September 1784, and died in St Petersburg on 14 November 1864. This lady, of exceptional beauty, was courted by Junot. The ensuing love affair became notorious in Lisbon and so put her life at risk, subsequent to the departure of the French, in 1808.

The counts decided to leave Lisbon and, after many adventures at sea, they went to Paris, where Napoleon granted them an annual pension of 60,000 francs. In Portugal the Count of Ega, in 1811, was condemned to death and deprived of all his assets and honours. In 1823 this sentence was quashed, whereupon he returned. He lived, withdrawn from politics, until his death. D. Juliana, his widow, married again to Gregório Alexandrovitch, Count of Strogonoff, in Russia.

∼ Marquis Of Angeja

D. José Xavier de Noronha Camões de Albuquerque Souza Moniz, 4th Marquis of Angeja, also held the titles of Marquis Relation, 10th Seigneur of the Villas of Angeja and Bemposta and part of Pinheiro, 7th Count of Villa Verde, 10th Seigneur of the same Villa.

He was born on 24 April 1741, and died on 27 December 1811. On 23 January 1768 he married D. Francisca Thereza d´Almeida, who was born on 22 September 1754 and died on 5 January 1810. She was the second daughter of the 2nd Marquis of Lavradio and fifth counts of Avintes.

He held the posts of: President of the Court of Appeal and of the Council of Administration of Tobacco, State councillor of the Supreme Military Court and that of Justice, in Rio de Janeiro, Lieutenant General of the Army, Governor of the Arms of the Court (Lisbon).

∼ Marquis Of Pombal

D. Henrique José de Carvalho e Mello, 2nd Count of Oieras and 2nd Marquis of Pombal, was born in 1748 and died in Rio de Janeiro on 26 May 1812. In 1764 he married D. Maria Antônia de Menezes, daughter of D. José de Menezes of the house of the counts of Caparica.

~ Marquis Of Belas

D. José Luiz de Vasconcellos e Souza was born on 6 June 1740, and died in Rio de Janeiro on 16 April 1812. He was the son of the first marquises and fourth count of Castello Melhor.

An active and intelligent man, he was: Member of His Majesty's Council, Administrator of Justice, Judge of the Court of Appeal, Fiscal Procurator of the Council of Three States, President of the New Law Code, Delegate on the Council of Tobacco, of Control of the Plague and of the Audit of the Debts of the Royal Treasury, Director and Inspector General of the Royal College of Nobles, President of the council of the same college, Extraordinary Ambassador to England during different periods, President of the Court of Appeal (whilst in Brazil).

On 29 November 1783 he married D. Maria Rita de Castello Branco Corrêa e Cunha, Dame of Honour to the Queen D. Maria I, who was born on 5 April 1769 and died on 3 May 1823.

By his marriage he became 1st Marquis of Belas and 6th Count of Pombeiro. His wife, in addition to her titles as 1st Marquise of Belas and 6th Countess of Pombeiro, was: 18th Seigneur of Pombeiro, 14th Seigneur of the Tenure of Castello Branco in Santa Iria within the limits of Lisbon, 12th Seigneur of Belas, 12th Seigneur of Villa Franca de Xira, Dame of the Office of the Captain of the Royal Halberdier Guards, Dame of Honour of the Queen D. Maria I, Dame of the Order of St Izabel.

~ Count Of Anadia

D. João Rodrigues de Sá e Melo, 1st Viscount and 1st Count of Anadia, was born in Aveiro on 11 November 1755, and died in Rio de Janeiro on 30 December 1809. He married D. Maria Antônia de Carvalho Cortez de Vasconcellos, daughter of D. Manoel Antônio Cortez de Vasconcellos, nobleman of the royal household. He was a member of the Treasury council, Plenipotentiary minister to the Court of Berlin and member of the Royal Academy of Science in Lisbon.

~ Marquis Of Aguiar

D. Fernando José de Portugal e Castro, 1st Count and 2nd Marquis of Aguiar, was born in Lisbon on 4 December 1752, and died in Rio de Janeiro on 24 January 1817. He was the third son of the third marquises of Valença and ninth count of Vimioso.

He graduated from the University of Coimbra with a degree in law, and took up a career in the magistrature, serving in the Court of Appeal in Lisbon and in the House of Appeal.

He was also: Governor and Captain-General in Bahia for fourteen years, Viceroy of Brazil 1804-1806, President of the Overseas Council, Minister of War and Foreign Affairs, President of the Royal Treasury, Member of the Finance Council and of the

Council of Commerce, responsible for the charities of the royal house.

Whilst in Rio de Janeiro he married his niece, D. Maria Francisca de Portugal e Castro, second daughter of the fourth marquise of Valença and eleventh count of Vimioso, born in 1752. She was a dame in the Court of Queen D. Maria I and, in Brazil, lady-in-waiting to Empress D. Maria Leopoldina.

CHAPTER II

~ *Count Of Belmonte*

D. Vasco Manuel de Figueiredo Cabral da Câmara, 1st Count of Belmonte, was born on 29 March 1767, and died on 10 November 1830. On 17 January 1795 he married D. Jerônima Margarida de Noronha, Dame to Queen D. Maria I.

Amongst his many posts and honours, he was: Peer of the realm, Doorman of the royal household, Gentleman of the Bedchamber of D. João, Delegate on the Council of the Three States, President of the Tobacco Council. 16th Seigneur of the Tenure of Belmonte, 10th Seigneur of the Tenure of Otta, 3rd Seigneur of the Tenure of the Maninhos da Villa de Corvillã.

~ *Count Of Redondo and Marquis Of Borba*

D. Thomé Xavier de Souza Coutinho de Castelo Branco e Menezes, the 1st Marquis of Borba and 13th Count of Redondo, was born on 22 July 1753. In 1775 he married D. Margarida Telles da Silva, daughter of the second marquises of Penalva.

In 1807 he accompanied the Court to Brazil and never returned. He succeeded to his father's title on 6 July 1791. On 15 December 1811 his title was raised to that of Marquis of Borba.

His many posts and honours included; Tax inspector of the royal household, 11th Seigneur of Gouvea de Riba Tâmega, Figueró dos Vinhos and Pedrogão, Patron of Santa Cecilia de Vilaça.

~ *Marquis Of Marialva*

D. Pedro José Joaquim Vito de Menezes was the 6th Marquis of Marialva and 8th Count of Castanhede. He was also:

Gentleman of the Bedchamber of Queen D. Maria I, Master of the Horse, Member of the Council of the Penal Code, Director of Military Archives, Colonel of the Mecklembourg Cavalry Regiment, Brigadier of the Army.

He inherited the wealthy house of his father, and had six commanderies in the Order of Christ, one in Aviz, and many others.

Pinheiro Chagas referred as follows to the Marquis in his *Dicionário Popular:*[8]

Following the invasion of our country by Junot's army, the Marquis of Marialva was one of the members of the commission that left Portugal for Bayonne to greet the Emperor Napoleon and to ask him for a reduction in the enormous contribution of one hundred million francs that he had demanded from the Reign; as is well known, the commission only obtained promises and evasive replies and, on the outbreak of the Portuguese revolution, its members became prisoners of France until 1814.

Later he was sent, in the name of the Prince Regent, to congratulate Louis XVIII on his accession to the throne of France. In 1816 he headed the mission that, on behalf of D. Pedro, was to ask for the hand of the Archduchess of Austria, D. Maria Leopoldina, and to marry her by proxy. Presenting himself in Vienna with extraordinary ostentation and luxury, he spent a fortune from his affluent house. Following the wedding, he accompanied the princess to Brazil. Subsequently he was named Portugal's representative to France, and carried out these duties until revolution broke out in 1820. He died in Paris, on 22 November 1823, without leaving a successor. On his death, the illustrious house of Marialva was incorporated into that of the house of Lafões, as the house passed to his sister, D. Henriqueta Maria Julia de Lorena e Menezes, married to the 2nd Duke of Lafões.

The most notable amorous adventure of the last Marquis of Marialva, because of the woman involved, is said to have taken place on the night of 14 June 1794:

> From this mild night, I was repeatedly told, of the predilection of the future empress-queen [Carlota Joaquina] for this graceful young nobleman – of this predilection much was said and much was presumed.[9]

One of the many conjectures arising from that spring evening was the subsequent birth of the Infante D. Miguel.

~ Marquis Of Abrantes

D. Pedro de Lancastre da Silveira Castelo Branco Sá e Menezes was born on 28 July 1763, and died on 25 March 1828. He was married to D. Maria Joana Xavier de Lima, daughter of the first marquises of Ponte de Lima. He was the 7th Count of Villa Nova de Portimão and, on 6 April 1789, he was given the honour of 'Marquis Relation'.

Amongst his many posts and honours, he was: Peer of the Realm, 18th Commander of the Order of Aviz, Commander of Alcanede, Veiros, Etremoz, Alandroal, also in the Order of Aviz, Alcaide of the castles of Avis, Veiros, Alandroal, Cabeção, Benavila, Alcanete and Pernes, Seigneur of the vilas of Góis and Sortelha and of the tenures of Povoa, Esporão, Oliveira do Conde, Góis, Pedra Alçada, Marvila, Valverde, Alcochete and Mafra.

Subsequent to the departure of the Prince Regent, he was named president of the Regency Council, until he was dismissed by Junot. He was a member of the commission of Portuguese noblemen that was imprisoned in France, only returning at the end of the Peninsular War.

~ *Viscount Of Rio Seco*

D. Joaquim José de Azevedo was was born on 12 November 1761 and died in Rio de Janeiro on 7 May 1835. He was the 1st Baron and 1st Viscount of Rio Seco. He was: Treasurer of the Royal Household and of the Royal Chapel, Storekeeper of the royal residences, Buyer of the wardrobes of the crown residences and of the royal stables.

Not wishing to accompany the king on his return to Portugal, he transferred to the service of the 1st Emperor of Brazil, who gave him the Honour of the Empire, the title of Marquis of Jundiaí and the decorations of the Southern Cross and of the Rose.

He married twice: the first time, in Lisbon on 17 May 1787, to D. Maria Carlota Milsaid and the second time, in Rio de Janeiro, to D. Marianna da Cunha Pereira, daughter of the first marquises of Inhambupe.

~ *Marquis Of Vagos*

The 1st Marquis of Vagos and 6th Count of Aveiras, D. Francisco da Silva Telo e Menezes, was born in Lisbon on 1 January 1723, the only son of the first marriage of the fifth count of Aveiras. He died on 5 January 1808.

He was Commander of the Commanderie of St Francisco Ponte de Sor, in the Order of Christ, of Vagos and of Aveiras.

On 22 October 1743 he married D. Barbara Xavier Média da Gama, who was born on 7 June 1730 and died on 27 February 1753. She was the daughter of the fourth marquises of Nisa.

~ *Apostolic Nuncio* [10]

Monsignor Lourenço Caleppi, son of the count of Caleppi, was born on 29 April 1741 in Cervia, a city within the Papal States. Subsequent to the election of Pope Pius VII, in March 1800, he was named Apostolic Nuncio of Nisibi at the Court of Lisbon in February 1801.

In spite of all his efforts, he did not manage to embark on the Portuguese squadron. After a tumultuous journey of many hardships he arrived in Rio de Janeiro on 8 August 1808; that same year His Holiness Pope Pius VII raised him to the cardinalate.

~ *Duke Of Palmela*

D. Pedro de Sousa Holstein, Count of Sanfré, in Piedmont, was born in Turin on 8 May 1782, and died in Lisbon on 12 October 1851.

Amongst his titles, he was: 13th Seigneur of the tenures of Calhariz, Monfalim and

Fonte do Anjo, Hereditary Captain of the Royal Guard of Halberdiers.

He was the son of D. Alexandre de Sousa Holstein and D. Isabel Juliana de Sousa Coutinho (of the House of Alva, later Marquise of Santa Rita).

He married, on 4 June 1810, D. Eugénia Teles da Gama, who was born on 4 January 1798, and died on 20 May 1848. She was the daughter of the seventh marquises of Nice.

He was educated in Geneva and at the University of Coimbra. In 1796 he joined the Regiment of the Garrison of the Court and in the following year he became a captain and an aide to the Duke of Lafões. On the death of his father, who was Ambassador in Rome, he took his place as chargé d'affaires. He was only 21 years old.

In 1810 he was made Plenipotentiary Minister to the Spanish government in Cadiz. He was unsuccessful in nominating D. Carlota Joaquina as Regent, with the right to eventually succeed her brother D. Fernando VII.

In 1812 his services were rewarded with a newly-created title, Count of Palmela. That same year he was sent to London as Ambassador. In 1817, following the death of the Count of Barca, he was named Minister of Foreign Affairs.

He was one of the principal followers of D. Pedro, Duke of Bragança, in his fight to restore his daughter Queen D. Maria II to the throne. In 1833 the Regent, D. Pedro, made him Duke of Faial – a title later changed to Duke of Palmela.

CHAPTER III

~ Sir William Sidney Smith 1764–1840, Rear Admiral Of The Blue

A 'larger than life character', Sir Sidney joined the navy at 13 years old and served in several engagements, attracting, by his talent, the attention of Lord Rodney.[11] In 1796 he was captured attempting to make off with a French privateer at the mouth of the River Seine, and spent two years in French prisons before managing to escape. In 1799, following his 63-day defence of Saint Jean de Acre[12] against Napoleon's army, he became a national hero, second only to Nelson. His weakness, however, was his character, which inspired suspicion and resentment. "Possessing in the highest degree the essential military qualities of courage, resourcefulness and imagination, he combined with them presumption, vanity, and exaggerated self-will," wrote Admiral Earl Spencer.[13] His restlessness and his flamboyant and invincible self-confidence leading to a total disregard of orders, frequently antagonised his superiors. "There seems to me such a want of judgment in our friend Sir Sidney, that it is much safer to employ him under command than in command," were words attributed to Lord Barham.[14]

On 17 May 1808 he arrived at Rio de Janeiro on board HMS *Foudroyant*, escorted by the *Agamemnon* and the brig *Pitt*, to take up the post of Commander-in-Chief of the squadron, based on the Brazilian coast.[15]

For his role in the migration of the Portuguese royal family to Brazil, in 1807– 08, the Prince Regent made him Knight Grand Cross of the Order of the Tower and

Sword and authorised him to add the standard of Portugal to his coat of arms.[16] By a decree of 17 September 1808, the Prince Regent gave him a property on the coast near St Domingos, six slaves and a boat.[17]

Because of his open support for the aspiring plans of D. Carlota Joaquina, his frequent indiscretions, and his opposition to Lord Strangford's policies, he was recalled in 1809.[18] His last mission was as vice-commander of the Mediterranean squadron from 1812 to 1814.

Later, he became interested in the liberation of white slaves held by the Barbary States (Algiers, Morocco, Libya and Tunisia), becoming president of the 'Knights Liberators and Anti-Piratical Society'.

England was slow to officially recognise Sidney Smith's triumphs, even though foreign countries (Portugal, the Ottoman Empire, the Kingdom of the Two Sicilies and Sweden) recognised his contribution and decorated him. Only in 1838, at the age of 74 – two years before his death – did the young Queen Victoria make him Grand Cross of the Order of the Bath. At last he was an English knight. The last few years of his life were spent in Paris, where he died in 1840, and he was buried in a simple grave in the Père Lachaise cemetery.[19]

CHAPTER IV

~ *Sir Graham Moore 1764–1843*[20]

Sir Graham had a long and distinguished career in the navy. He entered the service in 1777, at the age of 13; during the early years in command of the sloop *Bonetta* (1790) and then the frigate *Syren* (1794) and *Melampus* (1795). He saw much action, including the relief of Gibraltar against the French. In 1801, after an eighteen-month tour of the West Indies, his health broke down and he had to leave the service.

On the renewal of war, in 1803, he refused to remain on shore and so was appointed to the frigate *Indefatigable*. On 5 October 1804, leading a squadron of four frigates, he intercepted a like frigate squadron of treasure ships off Cadiz and, on the Spanish Admiral's refusal to surrender, an action took place in which three of the Spanish frigates were captured, and a fourth blew up with the total loss of her men. The treasure, amounting to more than three and a half million dollars (values at that time, today an immense amount – perhaps over one thousand million dollars), was declared to be 'Droits of Admiralty', on the grounds that war had not been declared, and so the officers and crew received a relatively small payment.

Following service as captain of the *Marlborough* he was offered command of the *Royal Sovereign* yacht in 1811, which he declined. Subsequently he was given the command of the Royal Naval Dockyard at Chatham. In 1812 he was appointed Rear Admiral. Knighted in 1815, the following year he became one of the lords of the Admiralty. He was promoted to Vice-Admiral in 1819, and full Admiral in 1837.

From 1839 to 1849 he was Commander-in-Chief at Plymouth. Younger brother to the famous Lieutenant General Sir John Moore, he married Dora Eden in 1812.

Chapter V

~ D. Pedro Carlos Of Bourbon E Bragança Infante Of Spain

Infante D. Pedro Carlos was born in the Palace of Aranguez on 18 July 1787, and died in Rio de Janeiro on 26 May. He was the son of the Infante of Spain D. Gabriel and his wife the Infanta of Portugal, D. Marianna Victoria, daughter of Her Majesty Queen D. Maria I and her husband and paternal uncle, King D. Pedro III.

A favourite of the Prince Regent D. João, in 1810 he married him to his eldest daughter, HRH D. Maria Francisca de Assis of Bragança e Bourbon, Princess of Beira and, that same year, gave him the title of General Admiral of the Portuguese navy. Unhappily, he would die of tuberculosis, in 1812.

He held many condecorations, including: Knight of the Distinguished Order of the Golden Fleece of Spain, Grand Cross of the Military Orders of Christ of St Benedict of Aviz and of the Ancient Order of the Tower and Sword, both of Portugal, Grand Cross of the Distinguished Order of Carlos III and of St John of Jerusalem, of Spain, Grand Prior of the Order of Jerusalem, of Castile and of Leon.

~ Count Of Ponte

D. João de Saldanha da Gama Mello Torres Guedes de Brito, 6th Count of Ponte, was born on 4 December 1773 and died whilst Governor of Bahia, on 24 May 1809. He was 6th Seigneur of Assequins; Commander in the Order of Christ; Governor and Captain-General of Bahia; and a cavalry major. He inherited from his father the sugar mill of Accupe and other properties in the territory of Bahia. He was married on 10 May 1796 to D. Maria Constança de Saldanha Oliveira Daun (1772–1833), daughter of the first count of Rio Maior.

~ Count Of Arcos

D. Marcos de Noronha e Brito, 8th Count of Arcos de Val-de-vêz, was born on the 7 June 1771, and died on 6 May 1828. His lineage of service to the crown of Portugal placed him in an unique position.

He was: Peer of the Realm, Gentleman of the Bedchamber of Queen D. Maria I, State councillor, President of the Council of Ministers, Minister and State Secretary for the Navy and Overseas, Governor and Captain-General of the territory of Grão-Pará and of Rio Negro, Viceroy and Captain-General of Land and Sea of the State of Brazil until the arrival, at Rio de Janeiro on 7 March 1808, of Queen D. Maria I and her son, the Prince Regent, later King D. João VI.

Governor and Captain-General of the territory of Bahia in 1809,

Minister and State Secretary for the Navy and Overseas in Rio de Janeiro in 1817, Lieutenant General of the Army,

Member of the State Commission. Created by D. João VI by decree of 6 March 1826.

This State Council was directed to assist the Serene Infanta D. Isabel Maria in the Regency of the Realm. This same decree would apply following the death of D. João VI.

He married, on 7 August 1791, D. Maria Rosa Caetana de Lorena, who was born on 10 January 1769, and who died on 31 July 1795. She was the second daughter of the sixth count of St Vincente: D. Manuel Carlos da Cunha, who was Vice-Admiral of the Fleet, and the Countess D. Luiza Caetana de Lorena, daughter of the third duke of Cadaval.

~ Duque De Cadaval

D. Miguel Caetano Álvares Pereira de Melo, 5th Duke of Cadaval, 7th Marquis of Ferreira and 8th Count of Tentúgal, was born on 6 February 1765, and died in Bahia on 14 March 1808. His military career began when he joined the Mecklemburg and Castelo Branco Regiment Regiment. In 1801 he was promoted to Field Marshal.

He was a member of the Council of D. Maria I, her Gentleman-in-Waiting and Grand Cross in the Orders of Christ and of the Legion of Honour.

He married, on 7 October 1791, D. Maria Madalena Henriqueta Carlota Emília de Montmorency Luxemburgo, Dame of the Orders of St Isabel and of St John of Jerusalem. She was born on 13 April 1778, and died at Pombal on 29 August 1833. Her father was the Duke of Pinay, Luxemburg and Chantillon.

CHAPTER VI

~ Marquis Of Viana

D. João Manuel de Meneses was born on 27 April 1783. He was the son of the third marquises of Tancos. At an early age he entered the navy, and in 1807 he took command of the frigate *Urânia*, the only ship to escort the Prince Regent during the whole of the voyage to Brazil.

Later, in 1821, now a Vice-Admiral he would command the squadron that took D. João back to Portugal. In 1826 he was promoted to Major-General of the Fleet and Peer of the Realm. In 1808 he married D. Ana de Castelo Branco, daughter of the first marquises of Belas.

~ Luiz Gonçalves Dos Santos (Padre Perereca)

Born in 1767, in the Villa of St Sebastian, he was the son of José Gonçalves dos Santos, from Oporto, and Rosa Maria de Jesus. At an early age his father, a silversmith, went bankrupt and retired to a small farm in the State of Rio de Janeiro. Luiz received holy orders in 1794. His destiny was a lifetime of teaching until he became deaf in 1825. He wrote several books, but his best-known work was Memórias para Servir à História do Reino do Brasil. He died in 1844.

~ Count Thomas O'Neil

Lieutenant in the Royal Marines, he was on board the *London* when she left Plymouth on 11th November 1807, as flagship to Rear Admiral Sir Sidney Smith. He took part in the blockade of the Tagus during that month of November and, on the departure of the Portuguese fleet, he was transferred to the frigate *Solebay*. After many adventures he finally reached Rio de Janeiro and rejoined the *London* on 27 February 1808. During the next few months the *London* cruised to St Salvador and, early in the year 1809, escorted the Prince Regent to his farm in Santa Cruz.

Later that year, on his return to England, he published an account of the journey of the royal family to Brazil. The book is dedicated to the Dukes of Clarence and Kent, sons of George III.

The subscribers listed in the book include all the children of George III, as well as a considerable number of the English aristocracy and Members of Parliament.

Appendix B:

Profile of the Portuguese and British fleets. Daily position of HM ships on their voyage to Brazil.

The Portuguese sailing ships that set out for Brazil in 1807 had changed little from the preceding few decades. Wooden sailing ships had a useful life of some fifty to sixty years in the case of line-of-battle ships; twenty to thirty years for frigates; and less for the smaller brigantines and schooners. Once or twice during their life, larger ships would go into dry dock to be overhauled. The extent of the work carried out can be gauged from the length of time taken – up to two years. On relaunch, often a name change took place.

Damage could be caused by storms, as a result of enemy action or by close manoeuvring in heavy seas; as occurred in a collision between the frigate *Minerva* and the *Medusa* in 1791, killing the chief of squadron José de Melo Bryner. When the winds turned to gale force and land was nearby, a run would be made for shelter. Not infrequently ships that had sailed from Lisbon, finding that a strong westerly wind had begun to blow, would return to anchor in the protected Tagus. On the other hand, if the ship was anchored in a harbour that did not provide shelter, for reasons of safety she would be forced to put out to sea and there await calmer weather. This happened to the *N*ª *S*ª *do Bom Sucesso* in 1780 whilst loading bullion from a damaged Spanish galleon in Faial (Azores). It was policy for two or more ships to travel together, so as to give each other assistance if necessary. Total loss due to weather *(Ulisses*, lost near Cabo Verde in 1808) or from capture (*N*ª *S*ª *da Vitória e Minerva*, by the French, off Sri Lanka in 1809) was relatively infrequent. Accident and disease were by far the most important cause of loss of life.[2]

To maintain the merchant shipping lanes clear of pirates, regular missions were undertaken. Patrolling the coast, particularly the Algarve and the Straits (based on Gibraltar), discouraged the many corsairs (based on the North African coast as far afield as Tripoli) from putting out to sea. The first reaction, on encounters that occurred mostly by chance, was to flee. If, however, the ships got sufficiently close, well-trained Portuguese sailors and their guns would usually capture their prize.

Merchant men gathered in convoys, sometimes sixty or more strong, were escorted as far as the Atlantic Islands. Beyond that point, far from land, there was little danger until the Brazilian coast was reached. On their return, on a predetermined date, a squadron would be dispatched to cruise the area on the high seas, where the convoy was expected to pass; and escort it to the estuary of the Tagus. Occasionally the squadron would escort the convoy all the way to Brazil, principally to bring back gold and precious stones belonging to the crown. On 25 April 1769 the line-of-battle ship *N^a S^a dos Prazeres* set sail from Lisbon, convoying two ships going to India and several merchant men going to different ports in Brazil. In July she put into Bahia, badly damaged from the rough passage. On 29 May 1770 she anchored in the Tagus, having made the crossing from Rio de Janeiro in ninety-four days. She brought gold, credit notes and coins for the king, totalling 908,087,712 réis, and also eleven safes filled with diamonds. In addition, she brought an even greater sum for private individuals.

Another duty of the navy was to transport important dignitaries to their posts, and deportees to their place of exile. Mail and the carriage of timber, spices and other New World riches were often the cargo of these fighting ships.

During the period 1773 to 1777 a squadron, under the command of Robert MacDouall (one of the many British officers serving in the Portuguese navy), consisting of four line-of-battle ships (flagship *Santo Antônio e São José*), ten frigates and a number of smaller vessels, was active in the south of Brazil, to defend Santa Catarina from attacks from Spain.

$\sim$ **LINE-OF-BATTLE SHIPS**

Príncipe Real

Constructed under the direction of Manuel Vincente Nunes.	
Built at	Arsenal da Marinha, Lisbon
Launched	13 July 1771
Name change from	*N^a S^a da Conceição* in 1794
Left Service (sold or broken up)	1830 (from 1822 used as a prison)
Length x breadth x depth	200' x 50' x 21'
Complement	950 men
Number of guns size 36/18/9 pounder	30/32/18
Captain in November 1807	F. José do Canto de Castro e Mascarenhas

Afonso de Albuquerque

Constructed under the direction of Manuel Vincente Nunes	
Built at	Arsenal da Marinha, Lisbon
Launched	26 July 1767
Name change from	N^a S^a dos Prazeres in 1797
Left service (sold or broken up)	1825
Length x breadth x depth	182' x 44' x 19'
Complement	634 men
Number of guns size 24/18/9 pounder	26/28/8
Captain in November 1807	Inácio da Costa Quintela

Rainha de Portugal

Constructed under the direction of Torcato José Clavina	
Built at	Arsenal da Marinha, Lisbon
Launched	28 September 1791
Left service (sold or broken up)	1848
Length x breadth	181'6" x 47'6"
Complement	669 men
Number of guns size 24/18/9 pounder	28/22/16
Captain in November 1807	Francisco Manuel de Souto Maior

Conde D. Henrique

Constructed under the direction of Manuel Vincente Nunes	
Built at	Arsenal da Marinha, Lisbon
Launched	1763
Name change from	N^a S^a do Pilar (Cananea) in 1794
Left service (sold or broken up)	1820
Length x breadth x depth	191' x 47' x 21'
Complement	753 men
Number of guns size 36/18/9 pounder	28/30/16
Captain in November 1807	José Maria de Almeida

Martim de Freitas

Constructed under the direction of Antônio da Silva	
Built at	Bahia, Brazil
Launched	29 January 1763
Name change from	*S. Antônio e S. José*, then in 1794 to *Infante D. Pedro Carlos*, and yet again, in 1807, to *Martim de Freitas*
Left service (sold or broken up)	1828
Length x breadth x depth	182' x 44' x 21'
Complement	634 men
Number of guns size 24/12/9/1 pounder	26/28/12/4
Captain in November 1807	Manuel de Menezes

D. João de Castro

Constructed under the direction of Manuel Vincente Nunes	
Built at	Ribeira das Naus, Lisbon
Launched	1766
Name change from	*Nª Sª do Bom Sucesso* in 1800
Left service (sold or broken up)	1822
Length x breadth x depth	182' x 44' x 20'
Complement	633 men
Number of guns size 24/12/9 pounder	26/32/16
Captain in November 1807	Manuel João de Lócio

Medusa

Constructed under the direction of Torcato José Clavina	
Built at	Arsenal da Marinha, Lisbon
Launched	26 August 1786
Name change from	*Nª Sª do Monte do Carmo* in 1786
Left service (sold or broken up)	1825 (from 1819 used as a prison)
Length x breadth	197'3" x 45'
Complement	663 men
Number of guns size 24/18/9 pounder	28/33/9
Captain in November 1807	Henrique da Fonseca de Souza Prego

Príncipe do Brasil

Constructed under the direction of Manuel Costa	
Built at	Bahia, Brazil
Launched	12 September 1802
Name change from	N^a S^a do Pilar (Cananea) in 1794
Left service (sold or broken up)	1822
Length x breadth	186'0" x 48'6"
Complement	663 men
Captain in November 1807	Francisco de Borja Salema Garção

~ FRIGATES

Golfinho e N^a S^a do Livramento

Constructed under the direction of Torcato José Clavina	
Built at	Ribeira das Naus, Lisbon
Launched	26 June 1782
Left service (sold or broken up)	1816
Length x breadth	135' x 32'
Complement	300 men
Number of guns	36
Captain in November 1807	Luis da Cunha Moreira

N^a S^a da Vitória e Minerva

Constructed under the direction of Torcato José Clavina	
Built at	Arsenal da Marinha, Lisbon
Launched	19 July 1788
Left service (sold or broken up)	Captured in 1809 by the French frigate Bellone off the coast of Sri Lanka
Length x breadth	156'9" x 58'
Complement	349 men
Number of guns	50
Captain in November 1807	Rodrigo José Ferreira Lobo

Urânia

Constructed under the direction of Torcato José Clavina	
Built at	Arsenal da Marinha, Lisbon
Launched	15 December 1792
Name change from	*Ulisses* in 1807
Left service (sold or broken up)	Sank off Cabo Verde in 1809
Length x breadth	132'6" x 34'
Complement	391 men
Number of guns	38
Captain in November 1807	D. João Manuel de Menezes

Santa Teresa, Thetis

Constructed under the direction of Manuel Joaquim. In 1807, rigged as a transport vessel.	
Built at	Bahia, Brazil
Launched	September 1793
Left service (sold or broken up)	September 1824
Length x breadth	135' x 34'
Complement	300 men
Number of guns	40
Captain in November 1807	Paulo José Miguel de Brito

~ CORVETTE

Voador

Constructed under the direction of Torcato José Clavina.	
Built at	Arsenal da Marinha, Lisbon
Launched	1763
Left service (sold or broken up)	1820
Length x breadth x depth	191' x 47' x 21'
Complement	753 men
Number of guns size 36/18/9 pounder	28/30/16
Captain in November 1807	José Maria de Almeida

Lebre

Constructed under the direction of Torcato José Clavina.	
Built at	Arsenal da Marinha, Lisbon
Launched	16 October 1788
Name change from	*Lebre Grande*, as there was another vessel named *Lebre Pequeno*
Left service (sold or broken up)	1818
Length x breadth	97′ x 30′
Complement	135 men
Number of guns	24
Captain in November 1807	Daniel Thompson (Englishman)

Vingança

Purchased in 1800. Originally rigged as a cutter. In 1804 changed to Brigantine.	
Left service (sold or broken up)	1814
Complement	97 men
Number of guns	18
Captain in November 1807	James Nicolas Keating (Englishman)

Boa Ventura[3]

Origin unknown, first mentioned in 1799	
Left service (sold or broken up)	1819
Complement	112 men
Number of guns	6

Condessa de Resende

Purchased in Brazil	
Complement	79 men
Number of guns	20
Captain in November 1807	Basilio Ferreira de Carvalho

~ SCHOONERS

Curiosa

Purchased in Lisbon in 1807. Badly damaged during the first few days of the voyage and with water for only fifteen days, she arrived back at Lisbon on 10 December 1807 and was taken by the French.

Name change from	*Minerva*
Left service (sold or broken up)	Registration ceases on her transfer to the province of Cabo Verde in 1813
Complement	43 men
Number of guns	14
Captain in November 1807	Isidoro Francisco Guimarães

Furão

Purchased in Lisbon, 1806	
Complement	60 men
Number of guns	8
Captain in November 1807	Joaquim Marins

PROFILE OF THE BRITISH SQUADRON[4]

~ LINE-OF-BATTLE SHIPS

Achilles

Achille Class 1795, based on the design of the French ship of the line Pompee, taken in 1793.	
Built at	Cleverly, Gravesend
Launched	16 April 1795
Left service (sold or broken up)	1865
Length x breadth x depth	182′2″ x 49′0$^{1/2}$″ x 21′10$^{1/2}$″
Displacement/Complement	1,916 tons/640 men
Number of guns size 32/18 pounder	30/36
Number of carronades size 32 pounder	18
Captain in November 1807	Sir Richard King

Audacious

Arrogant Class 1758, Sir Thomas Slade design.	
Built at	Randell, Rotherhithe
Launched	23 June 1783
Left service (sold or broken up)	1815

Length x breadth x depth	168' x 46'9" x 19'9"
Displacement/Complement	1,604 tons/550 men
Number of guns size 32/18/9 pounder	28/28/28
Captain in November 1807	T Le M Grosselin

Bedford

Royal Oak Class 1765, Williams design.	
Built at	Woolwich Dockyard
Launched	27 October 1775
Left service (sold or broken up)	1817
Length x breadth x depth	168'6" x 46'9" x 20'
Displacement/Complement	1,606 tons/556-600 men
Number of guns size 32/18/9 pounder	28/28/18
Captain in November 1807	James Walker

Conqueror

Conqueror Class 1795, two decker, John Henlow design modified by Mars Class.	
Built at	Graham, Harwich
Launched	23 November 1801
Left service (sold or broken up)	1825
Length x breadth x depth	176' x 49' x 20'9"
Displacement/Complement	1,842 tons/550 men
Number of guns 32/18/9 pounder	28/30/6
Captain in November 1807	Israel Pellow

Elizabeth

Repulse Class 1800, William Rule design.	
Built at	Perry, Blackwell
Launched	23 May 1807
Left service (sold or broken up)	1820
Length x breadth x depth	174' x 47'4" x 20'
Displacement/Complements	1,706 tons/590 men

Number of guns size 32/18 pounder	28/32
Captain in November 1807	Rt Hon Henry Curzon

Foudroyant

Foudroyant Class 1788, two decker, John Henslow design. Ex-Superb.	
Built at	Plymouth Dockyard
Launched	31 August 1798
Left service (sold or broken up)	1861
Length x breadth x depth	184' x 50'6" x 22'6"
Displacement/Complement	2,054 tons/650 men
Number of guns size 32/24/12	30/32/18
Captain in November 1807	N Thompson

Hibernia

Hibernia Class 1790 (first rate), three decker. Lengthened version of the Ville de Paris. Initially class as 110-, later 120-gun ship.	
Built at	Plymouth Dockyard
Launched	17 November 1804
Left service (sold or broken up)	1855
Length x breadth x depth	201'2" x 53' x 22'4"
Displacement/Complement	2,499 tons/850 men
Number of guns size 32/24/18 pounder	32/32/36
Number of carronades size 32 pounder	16
Captain in November 1807	John Conn

London

London Class 1759 three decker, Sir Thomas Slade design, later a 98-gun ship.	
Built at	Chatham Dockyard
Launched	24 May 1766
Left service (sold or broken up)	1811
Length x breadth x depth	177'6" x 49' x 21'
Displacement/Complement	1,870 tons/750 men

Number of guns size 32/18/12/6 pounder	28/30/30/2
Captain in November 1807	Thomas Western

Marlborough

Fame/Hero Class 1799 (third rate), two decker, John Henslow design.	
Built at	Barnard, Deptford
Launched	22 June 1807
Left service (sold or broken up)	1835
Length x breadth x depth	175' x 47'6" x 20'6"
Displacement/Complement	1,792 tons/640 men
Number of guns size 32/18 pounder	14/6
Number of carronades size 32/18 pounder	14/6
Captain in November 1807	Graham Moore

Monarch

Monarch/Ramilles Class 1760, Sir Thomas Slade design.	
Built at	Deptford Dockyard
Launched	21 July 1765
Left service (sold or broken up)	1813
Length x breadth x depth	168'6" x 46'9" x 19'9"
Displacement/Complement	1,697 tons/550-600 men
Number of guns size 32/18/9 pounder	28/28/18
Captain in November 1807	R Lee

Plantagenet

Plantagenet Class 1794, William Rule design.	
Built at	Woolwich Dockyard
Launched	22 October 1801
Left service (sold or broken up)	1817
Length x breadth x depth	181' x 47' x 19'9"
Displacement/Complement	1,777 tons/590 men

Number of guns size 32/18/9 pounder	28/28/18
Captain in November 1807	William Bradley

Theseus

Culloden/Thunder Class 1769, Sir Thomas Slade design.	
Built at	Perry, Blackwall
Launched	25 September 1786
Left service (sold or broken up)	1814
Length x breadth x depth	170' x 46'6" x 19'11"
Displacement/Complement	1,652 tons/550-600 men
Number of guns size 32/18/9 pounder	28/28/28
Captain in November 1807	J P Beresford

~ FRIGATES

Amazon

Amazon Class 1796, William Rule design.	
Built at	Woolwich Dockyard
Launched	18 May 1799
Left service (sold or broken up)	1817
Length x breadth x depth	150' x 39'5" x 13'9"
Displacement/Complement	1,038 tons/284 men
Number of guns size 18/9 pounder	28/10
Number of carronades size 32 pounder	8
Captain in November 1807	William Parker

Solebay

Thetis/Amazon Class 1771, Williams design.	
Built at	Adams & Barnard, Deptford
Launched	26 March 1785
Left service (sold or broken up)	Lost July 1809 off the African coast
Length x breadth x depth	126' x 35' x 12'2"
Displacement/Complement	677 tons/220 men

Number of guns size 12/6 pounder and 12 swivels	26/6
Captain in November 1807	A Sproule

~ SLOOPS

Confiance

Sloop, ex-French privateer La Confiance, 1796 of Bordeaux; taken in 1805.	
Length x breadth x depth	117' x 31'23/4" x 14'
Displacement/Complement	491 tons/140 men
Number of guns size 6 pounder	2
Number of carronades size 32 pounder	22
Captain in November 1807	James Lucas Yeo

Redwing

Cruiser Class 1796, William Rule design.	
Built at	Warren, Brightlingsea
Launched	30 August 1806
Left service (sold or broken up)	Lost 1827 off West Africa
Length x breadth x depth	100' x 30'0" x 12'9"
Displacement/Complement	382 tons/121 men
Number of guns size 6 pounder	2
Number of carronades size 32 pounder	16
Captain in November 1807	Thomas Usher

POSITION AT NOON OF HMS *Bedford* ON HER JOURNEY TO BRAZIL

	Latitude	Longitude	Bearing & Distance
Wed. Dec. 9	33° 45' N	19° 6' W	W End of Madeira S17°W 18 Leagues
Thur. Dec. 10	32° 53' N	18° W	Madeira W End EbS½S 12 Leagues
Fri. Dec. 11	31° 49' N	18° 37' W	Ferro Island S7°E 82 Leagues
Sat. Dec. 12	29° 45' N	18° 20' W	Ferro Island S¾E 42 Leagues

Sun. Dec. 13	28° 27′ N	18° 36′ W	SW Pᵗ of Ferro Island in sight S½E 15 Lgs
Mon. Dec. 14	27° 41′ N	18° 12′ W	SW End of Ferro Island in sight NE 2 Lgs
Tue. Dec. 15	25° 59′ 15″ N	18° 24′ W	Isle of Sal S24°W 205 Leagues
Wed. Dec. 16	24° 8′ 30″ N	19° 8′ W	Isle of Sal S26°W 167 Leagues
Thur. Dec. 17	23° 14′ 45″ N	19° 25′ W	Isle of Sal S27°W 149 Leagues
Fri. Dec. 18	22° 39′ 44″ N	19° 41′ W	Isle of Sal S27°W 135 Leagues
Sat. Dec. 19	21° 12′ 55″ N	20° 19′ W	Isle of Sal S30°W 102 Leagues
Sun. Dec. 20	18° 49′ 19″ N	20° 27′ W	Isle of Sal S51°W 64 Leagues
Mon. Dec. 21	16° 46′ 48″ N	20° 29′ W	Bonavista N° Pᵗ S75°W 44 Leagues
Tue. Dec. 22	11° 11′ 15″ N	20° 54′ W	St Pauls S31°W 244 Leagues
Wed. Dec. 23	11° 11′ 15″ N	20° 54′ W	St Pauls S31°W 244 Leagues
Thur. Dec. 24	9° 15′ 40″ N	20° 6′ W	St Pauls S36°W 207 Leagues
Fri. Dec. 25	7° 25′ N	21° 20′ W	St Pauls S42°W 175 Leagues
Sat. Dec. 26	6° 2′ 58″ N	21° 26′ W	St Pauls S49°W 156 Leagues
Sun. Dec. 27	4° 23′ 29″ N	21° 29′ W	St Pauls S59°W 134 Leagues
Mon. Dec. 28	3° 45′ N	21° 32′ W	St Pauls S69°W 157 Leagues
Tue. Dec. 29	3° 33′ N	21° 39′ W	St Pauls S70°W 152 Leagues
Wed. Dec. 30	3° 36′ N	21° 36′ W	St Pauls S70°W 155 Leagues
Thur. Dec. 31	3° 20′ N	21° 18′ W	St Pauls S72°W 157 Leagues

~1808

Fri. Jan. 1	2° 58′ N	21° 48′ W	St Pauls S77°W 180 Leagues
Sat. Jan. 2	2° 39′ N	21° 52′ W	St Pauls S79°W 176 Leagues
Sun. Jan. 3	2° 19′ 29″ N	22° 9′ W	St Pauls S80°W 161 Leagues
Mon. Jan. 4	2° 7′ N	22° 9′ W	St Pauls S80°W 138 Leagues
Tue. Jan. 5	2° 31′ 15″ N	22° 15′ W	St Pauls S76°W 133 Leagues
Wed. Jan. 6	-	-	-
Thur. Jan. 7	1° 33′50″ N	23° 23′ W	Cape Frio S36°W 1780 Miles
Fri. Jan. 8	0° 46′ 52″ N	24° 12′ W	Cape Frio S35°W 1710 Miles
Sat. Jan. 9	0° 4′ 28″ S	25° W	Cape Frio S34°W 1670 Miles
Sun. Jan. 10	0° 55′ 17″ S	25° 29′ W	Cape Frio S39°W 1690 Miles

Mon. Jan. 11	2° 0' 0" S	26° 39' W	Cape Frio S34°W 1495 Miles
Tue. Jan. 12	3° 9' 35" S	27° 19' W	Cape Frio S34°W 1410 Miles
Wed. Jan. 13	4° 35' 43" S	28° 3' W	Cape Frio S33°W 1290 Miles
Thur. Jan. 14	5° 30' 45" S	28° 37' W	Cape Frio S33°W 1220 Miles
Fri. Jan. 15	6° 34' 36" S	29° 15' W	Cape Frio S32°W 1170 Miles
Sat. Jan. 16	7° 22' 40" S	30° W	St Salvador S45°W 162 Leagues
Sun. Jan. 17	8° 24' 19" S	30° 20' W	C. Augustine S88°W 185 Ms St Salvador 560 Miles
Mon. Jan. 18	9° 28' 45" S	32° 49' 15" W	St Salvador S62°W 460Miles
Tue. Jan. 19	10° 43' 31" S	34° 1'30" W	St Salvador S68°W 370 Miles
Wed. Jan. 20	11° 38' 30" S	38° 15' W	St Salvador S69°W 235 Miles
Thur. Jan. 21	12° 25' 49" S	37° 15' W	St Salvador S77°W 151 Miles
Fri. Jan. 22	13° 5' 21" S	38° 4' 15" W	St Salvador N60°W 35 Miles PM Arrival
Fri. Feb. 26	-	-	Left St Salvador
Sat. Feb. 27	14° 11' 48" S	37° 22' W	Trinadada [sic] S50°E 205 Leagues
Sun. Feb. 28	15° 50' 16" S	36° 35' W	Cape Frio S36°W 186 Leagues
Mon. Feb. 29	17° 38' 6" S	35° 55' W	Cape Frio S48°W 168 Leagues
Tue. Mar. 1	19° 47' 57" S	35° 47' W	Cape Frio S62°W 141 Leagues
Wed. Mar. 2	21° 27' 39" S	36° 4' W	Cape Frio S76°W 126 Leagues
Thur. Mar. 3	22° 30' 52" S	37° 4' W	Cape Frio S85°W 102 Leagues
Fri. Mar. 4	22° 35' 35" S	38° 9' W	Cape Frio S85°W 80 Leagues
Sat. Mar. 5	23° 45' S	39° 20' W	Cape Frio S88°W 56 Leagues
Sun. Mar. 6	22° 54' 1" S	41° 6' W	Cape Frio West 20 Leagues
Mon. Mar. 7			AM Entering Bay PM Arrival

Position At Noon Of HMS *Marlborough* On Her Journey To Brazil

1807	Latutude	Longitude	Bearing & Distance
Sun. Nov. 29	38° 36' N	9° 32' W	Madeira S46°W 165 Leagues
Mon. Nov. 30	38° 29' N	9° 42' W	Burlings N4°E 19 Leagues

Tue. Dec. 1	38° 47′ N	10° 56′ W	Porto Santo 165 Leagues
Wed. Dec. 2	38° 13′ N	12° 0′ W	Cape Roxent N75°E 43 Leagues
Thur. Dec. 3	37° 59′ N	13° 18′ W	-
Fri. Dec. 4	37° 46′ N		Porto Santo S28°W 89 Leagues
Sat. Dec. 5	37° 25′ N	14° 27′ W	Madeira S23°W 99 Leagues
Sun. Dec. 6	37° 5′ N	14° 52′ W	St Maria in the Azores West 169 Leagues
Mon. Dec. 7	35° 56′ N	15° 2′ W	Madeira S24°W 69 Leagues
Tue. Dec. 8	34° 53′ N	15° 20′ W	Madeira S30°W 47 Leagues
Wed. Dec. 9	35° 5′ N	16° 10′ W	Madeira S13°W 46 Leagues
Thur. Dec. 10	33° 12′ N	16° 40′ W	-
Fri. Dec. 11		18° 8′ W	Island of Palma S7°E 79 Leagues
Sat. Dec. 12	30° 23′ N	18° 22′ W	Palma S20°E 37 Leagues
Sun. Dec. 13	29° 16′ N	18° 10′ W	Isle Sal Cape Vert S18°W 266 Leagues
Mon. Dec. 14	28° 53′ N	18° 5′ W	Isle Sal S20°W 260 Leagues
Tue. Dec. 15	27° 41′ N	17° 50′ W	Isle Sal S23°W 241 Leagues
Wed. Dec. 16	25° 40′ N	-	-
Thur. Dec. 17	25° 5′ N	18° 55′ W	Isle Sal Cape Vert S24°W
Fri. Dec. 18	24° 48′ N	18 50′ W	Cape Blanco S23°E 90 Leagues
Sat. Dec. 19	24° 32′ N	19° W	Salt Isd. S24°..57′W 523 Miles
Sun. Dec. 20	23° N	19° 45′ W	Isle Sal S26°W 140 Leagues
Mon. Dec. 21	20° 42′ N	20° 56′ W	Isle Sal S20°W 92 Leagues
Tue. Dec. 22	18° 13′ N	21° 47′ W	Isle Sal S35°W
Wed. Dec. 23	16° 2′ N	22° 37′ W	St Iago [sic] N° Point S38°W 29 Leagues
Thur. Dec. 24	-	-	At anchor Port Praya Bay, St Iago [sic]
Fri. Dec. 25	-	-	At anchor
Sat. Dec. 26	-	-	At anchor
Sun. Dec. 27	-	23° 28′ W	Cape Frio in Brazil S25°W 823 Leagues
Mon. Dec. 28	11° 27′ N	23° 28′ W	Isle of St Paul S8°W
Tue. Dec. 29	8° 26′ N	23° 35′ W	St Pauls S22°W 164 Leagues
Wed. Dec. 30	6° 5′ N	23° 12′ W	-
Thur. Dec. 31	5° 2′ N	23° 10′ W	Cape Frio S33°..4′W 1975 Miles

1808	Latitude	Longitude	Bearing & Distance
Fri. Jan. 1	3° 21′ N	23° W	Cape Frio S34°..53′W 1899 Miles
Sat. Jan. 2	2° 34′ N	22° 57′ W	Cape Frio S35°..52′W 1853 Miles
Sun. Jan. 3	1° 43′ N	23° 44′ W	Cape Frio S35°..32′W 1799 Miles
Mon. Jan. 4	0° 55′ N	24° 50′ W	Cape Frio S34°..57′W 1721 Miles
Tue. Jan. 5	0° 38′ S	26° 4′ W	Cape Frio S33°W 1580 Miles
Wed. Jan. 6	1° 52′ S	26° 48′ W	Cape Frio S34°..59′W 1506 Miles
Thur. Jan. 7	3° 33′ S	27° 46′ W	Cape Frio S35°..19′W 1388 Miles
Fri. Jan. 8	5° 46′ S	28 40′ W	Cape Frio S36°..49′W 1265 Miles
Sat. Jan. 9	8° 22′ S	29° 7′ W	Cape Frio S39°..25′W 1073 Miles
Sun. Jan. 10	11° 18′ S	30° 4′ W	Cape Frio S40°..15′W 926 Miles
Mon. Jan. 11	13° 56′ S	30° 50′ W	Cape Frio S30°..50′W 781 Miles
Tue. Jan. 12	16° 37′ S	31° 15′ W	Cape Frio S31°..15′W 661 Miles
Wed. Jan. 13	19° 17′ S	32° 36′ W	-
Thur. Jan. 14	20° 41′ S	-	-
Fri. Jan. 15	22° 5′ S	37° 29′ W	Cape Frio S83°..48′W 203 Miles
Sat. Jan. 16	22° 49′ S	39° 39′ W	Rio de Janeiro 211 Miles
Sun. Jan. 17	23° 12′ S	-	Rio de Janeiro 4 Leagues PM Arrival

POSITION OF HMS *LONDON* WHILST SAILING ALONE

1807	Latitude	Longitude	Bearing & Distance
Mon. Dec. 7	35° 47′ N	15° 46′ W	E. End Madeira S12°W 61 Leagues
Tues. Dec. 8	35 52′ N	15° 46′ W	Porto Santo S37°W 27 Leagues
Wed. Dec. 9	33° 11′ N	16° W	Porto Santo S22°W 8 Leagues
Thur. Dec. 10	32 34′ N	-	S° End of S° Desertos W½S
Fri. Dec. 11	-	-	At anchor Funchal Roads I. of Madeira
Sat. Dec. 12	-	-	At Anchor
Sun. Dec. 13	32° 10′ N	17° 20′ W	Madeira N28°W 11 Leagues
Mon. Dec. 14	32° 11′ N	17° 39′ W	West End of Madeira NbE 3 Leagues
Tues. Dec. 15	31° 19′ N	17° 39′ W	Palma S6°W 54 Leagues

Wed. Dec. 16	29° 41′ N	17° 59′ W	Palma NW End S5°W 13 Leagues
Thur. Dec. 17	29° 21′ N	19° 53′ W	Palma in sight SE 15 Leagues
Fri. Dec. 18	27° 46′ N	-	East End of Ferro SW 11 Miles
Sat. Dec. 19	27° 31′ N	17° 21′ W	-
Sun. Dec. 20	26° 5′ N	17° 33′ W	Island of Sal 212 Miles
Mon. Dec. 21	24° 19′ N	19° 4′ W	Island Sal S24°W 162 Leagues
Tues. Dec. 22	22° 15′ N	21° 17′ W	Bona Vista S17°W 125 Leagues
Wed. Dec. 23	19° 47′ N	21° 11′ W	Bona Vista S24°W 83 Leagues
Thur. Dec. 24	17° 48′ N	21° 26′ W	Bona Vista S384°W 41 Leagues
Fri. Dec. 25	15° 15′ N	22° 23′ W	St Iago [sic] Port Praya 30 Leagues

Appendix C:

Treaties, Decrees, Proclamations and Letters.

CHAPTER I

Baron Humboldt[1]

Having received news that a certain Baron Humboldt continues his journeys into the interior of this State, it is necessary for you to be on the alert and, if this news proves to be correct, or if any other stranger should be travelling within your district, you must conduct him and all his entourage to this capital. However, treat them with all respect and attend to their needs. You should only accompany them and prevent them, on their journey, from making political and philosophic enquires. God keep you well.

Palace of St Luiz do Maranhão the 12th of October 1800.

D. Diogo de Souza – Captain Domingos Lopes Ferreira.

Treaty Of Fontainebleau[2]

Secret treaties agreed, on the 27th of October, between the Emperor of the French and His Catholic Majesty Carlos IV of Spain; signed on the following bases and articles:

Article I. The Province, between the Douro and the Minho, including the town of Oporto will be given, with all rights and sovereignty, to HM King of Etruria with the title of Northern Lusitania.

Article II. The Province of Além-Tejo and the Kingdom of Algarves will be given, with all rights and sovereignty, to the Prince of Peace so that he may usufruct it with the title of Prince of Algarves.

Article III. The Provinces of Beira, Trás-os-Montes and of Portuguese Extremadura will remain on deposit until General Peace, when the contracting parties will decide on their destiny in accordance with the circumstances.

Article IV. The Kingdom of Northern Lusitania will belong to the descendants of HM King of Etruria by inheritance and in accordance with the laws of succession which are in use by the reigning family of HM King of Spain.

Article V. The Principality of Algarves will belong to the descendants of the Prince of Peace, by inheritance and in accordance with the laws of succession which are in use by the reigning family HM King of Spain.

Article VI. In the absence of legitimate descendants of the King of Etruria and Northern Lusitania or of the Prince of Algarves, these countries will be formally transferred to HM the King of Spain, but never united under the same person, with the crown of Spain.

Article VII. The Kingdom of Northern Lusitania and the Principality of Algarves will recognise as their protector His Catholic Majesty the King of Spain and under no circumstances, can these Sovereigns make peace or war without his participation.

Article VIII. In the event that the Provinces of Beira, Trás-os-Montes and Portuguese Extremadura, now confiscated are offered in a General Peace, then the House of Bragança, in exchange for Gibraltar, Trindade and other colonies that the English have won from Spain and her allies, will be given to them with all rights and sovereignty and with the same conditions and ties with respect to His Catholic Majesty the King of Spain as exist with the King of Northern Lusitania and the Prince of Algarves.

Article IX. HM the King of Etruria cedes all rights and sovereignty to the Kingdom of Etruria to HM the Emperor of the French and King of Italy.

Article X. When the definite occupation of the Portuguese Provinces takes place, the different princes who will posses them will nominate commissioners to determine their natural boundaries.

Article XI. The Emperor of the French and King of Italy will be Guarantor, to His Catholic Majesty King of Spain, of his possession on the continent located south of the Pyrenees.

Article XII. HM Emperor of the French and King of Italy undertakes to recognise His Catholic Majesty King of Spain Emperor of the Two Americas; when everything is made ready for HM to take this title. This may occur on the occasion of the General Peace or, at the latest, within three years.

Article XIII. The two contracting parties will come to an agreement on the islands, colonies and other overseas properties of Portugal.

Article XIV. The present treaty will remain secret and will be ratified; the ratifications to be exchanged in Madrid within, at the latest, twenty days from the date of signing Fontainebleau the 27ᵗʰ of October 1807, signed: Miguel Duroc; D. Eugênio Izquierdo de Ribeira e Lezaun.

The preceding Articles of the Treaty were approved, accepted, ratified and confirmed, under a sacred promise, by the Emperor Napoleon, who signed with his hand and put his seal on 29 October 1807.

The above treaty resulted in the signing of a secret Convention between the contracting parties, by which:

Article I. A Corps of Imperial French Troops, numbering twenty five thousand infantry and five thousand cavalry, will enter Spain and march directly to Portugal. It will unite with a Corps of eight thousand infantry and three thousand cavalry from Spain with thirty artillery pieces.

Article II. At the same time a Division of Spanish troops, of ten thousand men, will take possession of the Province of Entre Minho e Douro and of the town of Oporto; another Division of six thousand men, likewise of Spanish troops, will take possession of the Provinces of Além-Tejo and of the Kingdom of Algarves.

Article III. Whilst in transit through Spain, French troops will be supplied and maintained by Spain, and their wages paid by France.

Article IV. From the moment that the combined troops enter Spain, the Provinces of Beira, Trás-os-Montes and Portuguese Extremadura that will remain confiscated, will be administered by the Commander General of the French Troops and moneys levied will revert to France. The Provinces that will form the Kingdom of Northern Lusitania and the Principality of Algarves will be administered and governed by the General Commander of the Spanish troops that takes possession of them and moneys levied will revert to the benefit of Spain.

Article V. The centre Corps will be under the orders of the (Local) Commander of the French Troops and those Spanish troops united to them will be under his command; notwithstanding, if the King of Spain or the Prince of Peace should prefer, these troops will come under the orders of the General Commander of the French Troops.

Article VI. A Corps of forty thousand French troops will gather in Bayonne, at the latest by the 20ᵗʰ of November next, so as to be ready to enter Spain and transfer to Portugal should the English send for reinforcements and threaten to attack her. This new Corps will not enter Spain until the contracting parties are in agreement on this matter.

Article VII. The present Convention will be ratified, and the exchange of ratifications will take place at the same time as the treaty of this date. Fontainebleau 27th of October 1807. Signed Duroc: E Izquierdo.

This convention was approved, accepted, ratified, signed and sealed by Napoleon on 29 October 1807.

Convention of the 22nd of October 1807[3]

D. João, by the Grace of God, Prince Regent of Portugal and of the Algarves, here and beyond the Oceans, in Africa of Guinea and of Conquests, Navigation and Commerce of Ethiopia, Arabia, Persia, India etc. Let all take note of this Letter of Confirmation, Approval and Ratification. That on the 22nd of October of this year, a Convention was concluded and signed in the city of London, between Myself and His Most Serene and All Powerful Prince George III, King of the United Kingdom of Great Britain and Ireland, My Affectionate Brother and Cousin; with the objective of maintaining untouched the Portuguese Monarchy, the Island of Madeira and the Other Overseas Possessions; and, invested with full powers, on My side Dom Domingos Antônio de Sousa Coutinho of My Council, Nobleman of My House and My Extraordinary and Plenipotentiary Minister to that Court, and on the side of His Britannic Majesty, the Right Honourable George Canning Privy Councillor of His Majesty and His Principal State Secretary for Foreign Affairs. The contents of this Convention are as follows:

In the name of the Holy and Undivided Trinity:

Following the communication by His Royal Highness the Prince Regent to His Britannic Majesty of the difficulties being faced by the unjust demands of the French government, and of his determination to transfer to Brazil the seat and fortunes of the Portuguese Monarchy before complying with all the demands… And in order to discuss these measures and reach a satisfactory conclusion, His Royal Highness the Prince Regent appointed as his Plenipotentiary, the Knight Sousa Coutinho of his Council and his Extraordinary Envoy and Minister Plenipotentiary resident in London. His Majesty, the King of the United Kingdom of Great Britain and Ireland named as his Plenipotentiary, the Rt. Hon. George Canning, of his Privy Council and his Principal Secretary of State for Foreign Affairs. After the communication of their plenary powers and finding them in good order, the following articles were agreed:

Article I. Until there is certainty of a definite hostile declaration by France against Portugal or that Portugal, in order to avoid a war with France agrees to some form of hostile act against Great Britain, closing her ports to the English flag; no expedition will be undertaken by the British government against the Island of Madeira or any other Portuguese possession; when such an expedition is judged to be necessary it shall be communicated and agreed with His Royal Highness the Prince Regent's Minister resident in London.

On his side His Royal Highness the Prince Regent undertakes, from now on, not to allow any reinforcement of troops (except for the purpose of intelligence or in agreement with His Britannic Majesty) to be sent to Brazil or to the Island of Madeira, nor to send or to allow the assistance of any French Officer either in the service of France or that of Portugal.

In addition he undertakes to send, without delay, secret orders to the Governor of Madeira not to offer any resistance to an English expedition whose commanding officer declares, under his word of honour, that the expedition was prepared with the knowledge of and in agreement with His Royal Highness the Prince Regent.

Article II. In the event that His Royal Highness the Prince Regent is forced to carry out his magnanimous decision to transfer to Brazil; or without being forced by the attitude of the French against Portugal, His Royal Highness decides to undertake the voyage to Brazil, or to send a prince of his family; His Britannic Majesty is ready to help him in this enterprise, protecting the embarkation of the Royal Family and providing an escort to America. For this purpose His Britannic Majesty undertakes to order the preparation, in the ports of England, of a squadron of six line-of-battle ships and dispatch it at once to the coast of Portugal and to have ready for embarkation, an army of five thousand men, to be sent to Portugal at the first request of the Portuguese government.

Part of this army will remain garrisoned on the Island of Madeira, but will not disembark until His Royal Highness has landed on the island or gone past it, on his way to Brazil.

Article III. But, in the unhappy circumstances that the Prince Regent in order to avoid war with France, is forced to close the ports of Portugal to English ships, the Prince Regent agrees, immediately following the ratification of this Convention, that England may land troops on the Island of Madeira. The commander of the English expedition declaring to the Portuguese government that the island will be kept in trust for His Royal Highness the Prince Regent, until the conclusion of a definite peace between Great Britain and France.

The instructions to be given to the said English commander for the administration of the island, during its occupation by the forces of His Britannic Majesty, will be agreed with His Royal Highness the Prince Regent's Minister in London.

Article IV. His Royal Highness the Prince Regent promises never, under any circumstances, to cede the whole or part of his naval or merchant fleets or to unite them with France or Spain or any other nation.

In the event of transferring to Brazil, he agrees to take his naval and merchant fleets with him, be they equipped or otherwise, or not being able to carry this out, to transfer on trust to Great Britain that part that he is unable to take with him. His Royal Highness will agree later with His Britannic Majesty a plan for sending, with all safety, these vessels to Brazil.

Article V. In the event of the closure of Portuguese ports, His Royal Highness agrees to send immediately to Brazil half his fleet; maintaining the other half, some five or six line-of-battle ships and eight or ten frigates partly (at least) armed , in the port of Lisbon. On the first sign of hostility on the part of France or Spain, that naval force should join the British squadron, designated for this purpose, and serve to transport His Royal Highness and the Royal Family to Brazil. In order to better ensure the successful carrying out of this agreement, the Prince Regent assumes the obligation to place in command of his squadron in the port of Lisbon, as well as those [ships] that are sent to Brazil, officers whose political opinions are approved by Great Britain. The two contracting parties agree to authorise the Portuguese and English commanders in Lisbon on the one hand, and on the coasts of Portugal on the other, to carry out secret communications with the purpose of eventually joining together the Portuguese and English squadrons. As to that half of the military navy that can be sent to Brazil, on arrival there it will be disarmed, unless the two governments agree otherwise.

Article VI. Once the seat of the Portuguese Monarchy has been established in Brazil, His Britannic Majesty assumes the obligation, in his name and that of his successors, never to recognise as King of Portugal anyone who is not the heir and legitimate representative of the Royal Family of Bragança; and to renew and maintain with the Regency, that His Royal Highness may have set up in Portugal before leaving for Brazil, the friendly relations that have for so long bound the two crowns – Portugal and Great Britain.

Article VII. When the Portuguese government is established in Brazil, a treaty of commerce and support will be negotiated between the governments of Portugal and Great Britain.

Article VIII. This Convention will be maintained secret for the present and shall not be disclosed without the consent of the two contracting parties.

Article IX. It will be ratified, by one side and by the other, and the ratifications will be exchanged in London within six weeks or sooner from the date of signature.

In faith we, the undersigned, Plenipotentiary of His Royal Highness the Prince Regent of Portugal and His Britannic Majesty, by virtue of our powers, sign and seal with our arms, this Convention.

London, 22ⁿᵈ of October 1807

The Chevalier (Knight) de Sousa Coutinho: George Canning declare that the carrying out of that part of the said Article, which agrees to send a squadron and troops of His Majesty to the Tagus, in order to protect the embarkation of the Royal Family of Portugal, depended on the security that would be given; that is the handing over to the commander of the British troops the forts of St. Julião and Bugio, as well as the fort of Cascais, if the embarkation is effected in that place. In the Peniche, if the Royal Family has transferred to that Peninsula. They will remain under the commander until the objective for which the troops were sent has been achieved.

The undersigned, His Britannic Majesty's Principal Secretary of State for Foreign Affairs, in agreeing to Article II of this Convention received orders from the King to Royal Highness determines to whom they should be restored.

The Chevalier de Sousa Coutinho, Plenipotentiary of His Royal Highness the Prince Regent of Portugal, finding himself not authorised by the instructions that he had been given to agree to this obligation, the undersigned received orders to add this explanatory note to the Treaty and to ask that the above protection should be submitted to the Prince Regent for ratification.

London, 22ⁿᵈ of October 1807

GEORGE CANNING

Additional Article. In the event of the closure of Portuguese ports to the English flag, a port on the Island of Santa Catarina or any other place on the coast of Brazil will be established where all English goods which at present are imported without restriction into Portugal, will be freely brought in by English ships; paying the same duties as are presently paid on these same articles brought into Portugal; this arrangement to last until a new agreement has been drawn up. This additional Article will have the same force and value as if it had been included, word for word, in the Convention signed today. It will be ratified at the same time.

In good faith we, the undersigned, Plenipotentiaries of His Royal Highness the Prince Regent of Portugal and of His Britannic Majesty, by virtue of our respective power, sign and place our seal on this additional Article.

London, 22ⁿᵈ of October 1807.

The Chevalier de Sousa Coutinho:

GEORGE CANNING

I sign *sub spe rati*, declaring that I do not possess instructions on this matter assuming that His Royal Highness, on reopening the ports of Portugal, can reconsider or alter this Article.

Article II Additional. It is clearly understood and agreed that, from the moment that the ports of Portugal are closed to the English flag and whilst this situation continues, the treaties existing between Great Britain and Portugal should be considered to be suspended as they concede the Portuguese flag privileges and exemptions not enjoyed by other neutral nations and, in accordance with the law of nations, not compatible with mere neutrality. This additional Article will have the same force and value as if it had been included, word for word, in the Convention signed today. It will be ratified at the same time. In good faith we the undersigned, Plenipotentiaries of His Royal Highness the Prince Regent of Portugal and of His Britannic Majesty by virtue of our respective powers sign and place our seal on this Additional Article.

London, 22nd of October 1807.
The Chevalier de Sousa Coutinho:
GEORGE CANNING

I sign *sub spe rati*, declaring that I do not possess instructions on this matter assuming that His Royal Highness, on reopening the ports of Portugal, can reconsider or alter this Article.

The present Convention was submitted to me and, having examined and fully considered all that it contains, I approve, ratify and confirm all that it contains and each of the clauses and conditions except: some phrases of the introduction; the first paragraph of Article IV; the first paragraph of Article V; for the reasons to be attached to this Convention, by My Minister and State Secretary for Foreign Affairs and War; promising in faith and with the Royal Word to observe and execute it and to have it observed and executed, not allowing that anything whatsoever be done to the contrary. In witness and in confirmation of the above I have signed and sealed, with My Great Seal, and have the Convention ratified and countersigned below by the said Minister and State Secretary for Foreign Affairs and War. Palace of Nª Sª da Ajuda, 8th of November 1807.

The Prince JB Antônio de Araújo de Azevedo.

Observations on the above Ratification:
The preamble of the Convention of the 22nd of October, 1807, begins with the supposition, contained in the following words: '*ayant fait communiquer... totalité de ces damandes*', His Royal Highness has always promised His Britannic Majesty, directly and through the respective ministers, not to carry out the imprisonment of individuals or the confiscation of goods; but never said that he would rather transfer the cornerstone of the Portuguese Monarchy, than to accede to the propositions.

The following documents make and repeat these statements:

Note sent to HRH's minister in London, dated 12 August 1808:

> HRH orders me to inform you of his firm resolution, never to agree to the confiscation of goods belonging to British citizens: you should assure this fact to the British ministry – HRH expects, in reciprocity to this just and dignified action – that the government does not order the commanders of its Navy to take hostile action against Portuguese ships. Any action of this nature would make, both France and Spain, clamour loudly against our not accepting their proposition.

Another note, dated 20 August, to the same minister:

> The goods belonging to the English are not in any danger and, if the need arises to escort them, a squadron or part of one to carry out this objective, is unnecessary; one or two vessels of war, in or outside the Tagus, should be sufficient: I again assure you that HRH is determined that he would first lose total control of his country, rather than sacrifice British citizens and their goods.

This same note continues:

> For this same reason I will write to you, on another occasion, for you to discuss with this court as to how it can contribute to the safety of the royal family protecting, with her naval forces, their withdrawal. In the event that circumstances force this action, I will have the orders from HRH on this sad and important business that is so dear to us, as this is the only way to save part of the Portuguese monarchy, and so pass on to their descendants.

CHAPTER II

Decree
The Prince Regent, Our Lord, has requested
That the following decree be sent to the dispatch office of the palace:

It has always been my most earnest desire during the current war to conserve total neutrality, in view of the well known benefits that this would bring to the subjects of this crown; but, not being able to maintain it any longer and, considering that a general peace is beneficial to all, I have decided to join the Continental System uniting myself with the

Emperor of the French and King of Italy and His Catholic Majesty, with the object of contributing, as far as I am able, to maritime peace. I therefore order that the ports of this Kingdom be closed to war and merchant ships belonging to Great Britain. The dispatch office of the palace will carry out this order by decree and send it to the necessary locations so that it comes to the notice of everyone. Palace of Mafra 20th of October 1807.

With the initial of the Prince Regent Our Lord.

Gibraltar Chronicle (Saturday, 5 December)
From the *Madrid Gazette*, Irun, 8 November
Detailed account of the French troops of all descriptions which have entered Spain, through Irun.

Oct 19	70th Regiment, Infantry of the Line: Officers 63, Privates 2,299; General of Brigade Ladril. 47th Regiment: Officers 32, Privates 1,247; General of Division Laborde. Regiment No. 4 (Swiss): Officers 41, Privates 1,260.
20	2 Battalions of the 86th: Officers 63, Privates 2,382; General of Brigade Brenier.
21	1 Battalion No. 15: Officers 25, Privates 937. Corps of Artillery: Officers 12, Privates 306. Pieces of ordnance of various nature 36, ammunition boxes 82, wagons 7, travelling forges 4. Drivers: Officers 4, Privates 280.
22	1 Battalion of the 2nd Regiment Light Infantry: Officers 16, Privates 1,004. I Battalion of the 4th Regiment: Officers 11, Privates 750.
23	1 Battalion of the 12th Regiment Light Infantry: Officers 16, Privates 900. 1 Battalion of the 15th Regiment: 24 Officers, 1,020 Privates.
24	1 Battalion of the 58th Regiment of the Line: Officers 22, Privates 1,030.
	1 Battalion of the 32nd Regiment: Officers 20, Privates 1,019
25	No. 2 Swiss Infantry: Officers 35, Privates 1,100: General of Brigade Carlot. 21 wagons of the travelling Hospital, 1 travelling forge of ditto, with 12 Officers of Health, Officers 5, Privates 44.
26	1 Battalion of the 21st Regiment – Light Infantry: Officers 20, Privates 496. 1 Battalion of the 32nd Regiment: Officers 30, Privates 106: General of Division Travot. Two Divisions of Artillery, with 81 wagons belonging to the Park, 64 Ammunition wagons, 7 carriages, 3 forges: Officers 6, Privates 131. Drivers: Officers 5, Privates 200. Ditto 21 wagons, 1 forge, 11 Officers of Health, 5 Privates and 44 Drivers.

27	1 Battalion 26th Regiment Infantry of the Line: Officers 29, Privates 412. 2 Battalions of Legions of the South and No. 1 Light Infantry: Officers 31, Privates 859. 21 wagons of the same, 1 forge of the travelling hospital, 12 Officers of Health. Drivers: Officers 12, Privates 52.
28	2 Battalions 66th Regiment of the Line: Officers 51, Privates 848. Hanoverian Legion Light Infantry: Officers 20, Privates 740.
29	Detachment of Light Infantry No 32: Officers 1, Privates 32. Detachment of the Legion of the South: Officers 1, Privates 28. 2 Battalions 82nd Regiment Infantry of the Line: Officers 30, Privates 572, General of Brigade Fuzier. Drivers' detachment consisting of Drivers 10 and Privates 182
30	Flank company of the 82nd: Officers 3, Privates 120. Commander in Chief with his Staff. Regiment of Chasseurs No. 26 with the Commander in Chief: 6 Officers, 160 Privates. Horses: In the C in C's suite 62 and in the Imperial Gendarmerie, with several Imperial Officers, 40.
31	Provisional Regiment of the 1st and 3rd Dragoons: Officers 13, Privates 498.
	Horses 522, General of Brigade Margaron. Military equipages: 53 wagons, 1 forge. Officers 3, Privates 166.
Nov 1	3rd Provisional Regiment consisting of the 4th & 5th Dragoons: Officers 9, Privates 502. Civil Branch of the Artillery: Officers 1, Artificers 25. Wagons 5; Drivers: Officers 3, Privates 16. General of Division Kellerman. 1 Aide de Camp, 1 Chef de 1'Etat Major, 20 horses, 10 Servants. Soldiers of different corps: Officers 1, Privates 87.
2	9th and 15th Provisional Regiment of Dragoons: Officers 11, Horses 521. Major General Tiebault with 2 Aides de Camp and 5 Commissaries. Part of a Regiment of Horse, 11 baggage wagons: Officers 20, Drivers 28.
3	14 wagons with the Military Chest of the Army: Officers 3, Drivers 54.

Gibraltar Chronicle (Saturday, 26 December)
Extract from *Le Moniteur* Paris, 12 November 1807:

England has within two years sent forth four expeditions.

The first was against Constantinople…

The second expedition from England was against Egypt…

The third English expedition was against Monte Video and Buenos Ayres…

Their 4th expedition has been the most notorious. It was that of Copenhagen…

After these four expeditions, which so clearly show the moral and military decline of England, let us look at the situation that it has brought to Portugal. The Prince Regent of Portugal loses his throne: he loses it, influenced by the intrigues made by merchants in Lisbon. How does England, that powerful Ally, behave? She sees with indifference, what passes in Portugal. What will she do when Portugal is conquered? Will she go and seize upon Brazil? No; if the English make that attempt the Catholics will drive them out. The fall of the House of Bragança will remain as further proof that the destruction of whosoever attaches himself to England, is inevitable.

Minutes of the Meeting of the State Council, Convened by His Royal Highness The Prince Regent Our Lord, on the night of 24th of November 1807[4]

The State Council, convened by His Royal Highness, took place in his presence. He ordered that the news received from the interior, that French troops had invaded this Monarchy having arrived in Abrantes, should be communicated to the undersigned Counsellors. He ordered to be disclosed to the State Counsellors: the note received from Lord Strangford, addressed to the Council and to the State Secretary D. Antônio de Araújo, in which he asked for an appointment with His Royal Highness: in order to make proposals that would lead permanently deciding the relations that would exist between the two Monarchies; also a note, received at the same time, from Sir Sidney Smith, the commander of the English squadron that was blockading the port of this capital, addressed to the same minister and State Secretary in which he announces the hostile action he would take should Portugal's attitude not be friendly: threatening with a strict blockade and with the seizure of the naval and Brazil merchant ships.

It appeared to the undersigned State Counsellors that as all avenues of negotiation had been closed and as there was nothing that could be done to remove the threat to the continued existence of the Monarchy, sovereign and with independence for His Royal Highness, as his Kingdom was now invaded by French troops, no time should be lost in accelerating the embarkation of His Royal Highness the Prince Regent Our Lord and the Royal Family to Brazil.

In these circumstances a reply should be sent to Lord Strangford, that His Royal Highness conceded the requested appointment.

The note from Sir Sidney Smith should be answered to the effect that His Royal Highness was disposed to receive the English squadron in his ports and, that it was his desire, that this should take place as soon as possible.

That the troops that were at that very moment occupying the margins, fortresses and batteries of the Tagus should be transferred from these locations and occupy the positions to be determined by HRH, and that orders should be sent to the governors of the towers and fortresses to allow all English ships, whether of war or merchant, to enter the port.

That as HRH had decided to transfer to Brazil, a Regency Council should be established in the same manner that had occurred in the past, on those occasions when this Reign had found itself without a legitimate Sovereign. This Regency, with the royal powers to be given by HRH, should be constituted of outstanding and high ranking military persons, to be appointed by his Royal Highness.

Palace of Nª Sª da Ajuda, 24th of November 1807.
MARQUIS OF POMBAL – MARQUIS ADMINISTRATOR (MARQUIS OF BELAS) – VISCOUNT OF ANADIA – D. JOÃO DE ALMEIDA DE MELO DE CASTRO – D. FERNANDO JOSÉ DE PORTUGAL – D. ANTÔNIO DE AZEVEDO.

Decree [5]

Having sought with all my powers to preserve the neutrality which, up to now, my loyal and beloved subjects have enjoyed and, in spite of having exhausted my Royal Treasury and subjected myself to many sacrifices, even going to the extreme of closing the ports of my Kingdom to the citizens of my historic and loyal ally, the King of Great Britain; having exposed the commerce of my vassals to total ruin and, consequently, serious losses to the income of my Crown; in spite of this I learn that in the interior of my Kingdom troops belonging to the Emperor of the French and King of Italy, to whom I had united in the Continental System in the hope of avoiding further troubles, are marching towards this capital. I have tried to avoid the fatal consequences that would arise from putting up a defence, more damaging than advantageous, only serving to shed blood and human loss, possibly arousing the troops that cross this reign, even though they announce that they will not commit any hostility. Knowing at the same time, that they [troops] are specially directed at my Royal Person and that, therefore, my loyal subjects would be less interfered with if I were to leave this Kingdom; I have decided, in benefit of my subjects, together with the Queen my mother, and all the Royal Family to depart for America and settle in the town of Rio de Janeiro until the return of a general peace. Considering further, that it is my duty to leave the government of these Kingdoms properly taken care of, for their sake as well as that of my people, I have decided to appoint, to govern in my absence, my beloved and esteemed cousin the Marquis of Abrantes; Francisco da Cunha de Menezes, Lieutenant General of my Armies; D. Francisco Rafael de Castro, Head of the Patriarchal Church; Pedro de Mello Breyner, of my Council, who will act as President of my Royal Treasury in the absence of Luiz de Vasconcellos e Souza who, because of illness, is unable to act; Francisco de Noronha, Lieutenant General of my Armies and President of the Board of Justice; and, in the absence of any of these, Count Monteiro Mor, whom I have appointed President of the Senate, with assistance of two Secretaries: Count Sampaio or in his place Miguel Pereira Forjaz, Chief Justice of the Peace and Procurator of the Crown and João Antônio Salter de Mendonça, because of the trust I have in all of them and because of the considerable experience they accumulate of government matters. I have a clear conscious of the way that my Kingdoms and People will be ruled; Governors will discharge their obligations and, whilst God permits that I remain absent from this capital, administer justice with impartiality, distributing rewards and punishments as deserved. The same Governors should have this understood and should carry out the above, together with the instructions that will be signed with this decree; the respective secretariats should be informed accordingly.

Palace of N^a S^a da Ajuda 26th of November 1807 with the initial of the Prince Regent

Our Lord.

Instructions that are part of the decree

The Governors that I have appointed by Royal Decree, on this date, to rule in my absence these Kingdoms should swear the usual oath in the presence of the Patriarch Cardinal; they should, with all diligence, care and energy, administer justice impartially and observe rigorously the laws of this Kingdom. Nations will continue to enjoy all the privileges given, either by myself or by the Kings, my ancestors. All the consultations presented by the respective courts will be decided by a majority of votes, always observing the laws and customs of the Kingdom. All posts in the magistrature, justice and treasury will be filled following the procedures practised by myself. Military appointments, so as to defend citizens and the property of my loyal subjects, will be based on merit. As far as possible, peace should be maintained in the Kingdom. The troops of the Emperor of the French and King of Italy, whilst in this Kingdom, should be adequately billeted and their requirements furnished avoiding any offence, punishing were it to occur; maintaining harmony with the armies of those nations with which we are united to on the Continent. In the absence of any Governor, his successor will be elected by a majority of votes. I trust to your honour and to your virtue, and that My People will not suffer in my absence and, God permitting me to return quickly, that I may find everyone happy and satisfied, good order and tranquility reigning as it should amongst subjects that have received my paternal care.

Palace of N^a S^a da Ajuda 26th of November 1807

PRINCE.

CHAPTER VI

Court Orders Of 25-11-07
Gibraltar Chronicle (2 January 1808)

His Majesty, taking into consideration the circumstances under which Portugal had been compelled to shut her ports against the ships and goods of His Majesty's subjects, is pleased by and with the advice of his Privy Council to order, and is hereby ordered, that all ships and goods belonging to Portugal, which have been and are now detained in the ports of this Kingdom, or elsewhere, shall be restored, upon being pronounced, by the High Court of Admiralty, or by the Court of Vice-Admiralty, in which proceedings may have been, or shall be commenced, to belong to subjects and inhabitants of Portugal and not otherwise liable to confiscation; and that the said ships and goods be permitted to proceed to any neutral port, or to Portugal.

At the Court of the Queen's Palace, 25th of November 1807 – present, the King's Most Excellent Majesty in Council.

CHAPTER V

Order to Captain Moore to hoist
A broad pennant after passing Madeira[6]

Whereas the very extraordinary circumstances of the translation of the Portuguese government and Navy from Europe to the Brazils [sic], and also that of the Fleet of Portugal conveying His Royal Highness the Prince Regent and the whole of the Royal family requiring the protection of a Squadron of His Majesty's Ships, make it necessary that an officer of higher rank than a Captain should command such Squadron destined likewise to remain on that station for the protection of the Government and territory from all attempts of the enemy. I have therefore thought fit that you should hoist a broad pennant on board HMS *Marlborough* of which you are Captain so soon as you shall have passed the Island of Madeira and you are in consequence hereby authorised and directed to hoist a broad pennant on board accordingly and to wear the same in the absence of a Senior Captain until you shall receive further orders. Given under my hand on board HMS *Hibernia* 3rd of December 1807.

(signed) W SIDNEY SMITH
To Captain Moore HMS *Marlborough*
By order of the Rear Admiral (signed) Richard Speare

Instructions to Commodore Moore
HMS **Marlborough**[7]

Whereas by a Convention between his Britannic Majesty and HRH the Prince Regent of Portugal signed in London the twenty second of October 1807, it is stipulated in case the Prince Regent should find himself forced to give entire and full effect to his Magnanimous resolution to convey himself to the Brazils [sic] or, if without being forced HRH should decide to undertake that voyage; His Britannic Majesty will be ready to aid in this enterprise, to protect the Embarkation of the Royal family, and to escort them to America. And His Majesty having agreed to furnish a squadron for that service and you having received my order to hoist a broad pennant after you shall have passed the Island of Madeira on board HMS *Marlborough* of which you are and to remain Captain, and to take the Captains of the other ships destined to form that squadron under your orders. You are therefore and in pursuance of the Convention aforesaid, hereby required and directed to proceed with the aforesaid squadron in conjunction with the Portuguese Fleet, but particularly and in preference those ships on board which the Prince and the Royal family of Portugal maybe and escort them to such Port or Place in the Brazils [sic] as His Royal Highness may decide to go to affording them every aid and assistance in your power. HRH having promised in the convention never to cede in any case either the whole or part of his Military or Commercial Navy or to unite with that of France or Spain or any other Power, but having engaged to conduct (with himself) his Military and Commercial navy you are to facilitate the same all in your power; but should any ships be so disabled as to be unable to proceed, you are in execution of the 4th Article of the Convention to indicate Plymouth as the Port to which they may proceed for repairs and supplies preparations having been made for such contingency; and with the consent of the Prince you may put a Pilot or two on board to direct their course thither. On your arrival at the Brazils [sic] you are to dispose of the force under your orders as shall be most conductive to the object of protecting the territory from invasion by the enemy, and supporting the Prince Regent's government, concerting measures with HRH for that purpose. You are to protect the trade of His Majesty's subjects and annoy that of the enemy, without detaching any ship to such a distance from the vulnerable points of the territory of Brazil as to leave them exposed to any sudden attack of the enemy from the French or Spanish establishments in South America, or from Europe. It is my intention to reinforce you with Frigates and Small Vessels as soon as I have any disposable.

If considering the state of the means of defence in the Brazils [sic] you find that three Line of Battle ships in addition to those means is sufficient force to meet any attack you may have reason to apprehend, you may in the confidence that any enemy's force from Europe will be followed by a British one, reduce the Squadron to three sail of the line, and should you decide that the *Marlborough* shall be one of the Ships to return to Europe, you are to leave the command with the unexecuted part of these instructions, and any other you may judge necessary, to the senior officer you may leave behind you. Calling (and directing all ships returning to Europe to call) in Madeira and off Lisbon, to report the state of things in the southern station and to receive orders from me and for so doing this shall be your order.

Given under my hand on board HMS *Hibernia* at Sea this 5th day of December 1807.

(signed) W SIDNEY SMITH
To Commodore Moore HMS *Marlborough*
By order of Rear Admiral (signed) Richard Speare

Chapter VI

Letter from the Count of Ponte to the Count of Arcos,
Dated 7 January 1808[8]

Your Excellency.

The merchant ship from this port, the *Príncipe*, anchored here after a journey of 36 days, coming directly from the city of Lisbon. From the news of the 33 passengers, from the master of this vessel and from all the crew, it would appear that the said vessel left Lisbon on the 29th of November, in company with all the fleet under the command of Vice-Admiral Manoel da Cunha Souto. It is bringing to this city the Prince Regent our Lord and Our August Queen, as well as all the Royal Family and nobility that could be accommodated in the ships of the convoy. This news becomes more plausible, not only from the news that our squadron – on crossing the bar – joined the English squadron that was blockading the port, which then made the greatest demonstrations of respect and courtesy, the English admiral going on board the flagship the *Príncipe Real* for nearly three hours; but also from the enclosed copy of the decree, brought by all, and which was presented to me. I trust that this confidential communication is in accordance with our sovereign's wishes, since this letter is being sent to Your Excellency in conformity with the orders that I gave the above commander, whom I have complete trust in carrying them out.

God keep Your Excellency many years.

Bahia 7th of January 1808.

His Excellency Count of Arcos

Count of Ponte

Royal Warrant

Count of Ponte, of my Council, Governor and Captain-General of the Territory of Bahia, friend. I, the Prince Regent, that much loves you, sends you greetings. Considering the request that you sent to my Royal presence, on the commerce of this territory – interrupted and in suspense – with substantial losses to my subjects and to my Royal Treasury, by reason of the critical and well-known conditions existing in Europe and, wishing to give to this important matter some measure capable of quickly and effectively reducing these losses, I order the following measures, that are to remain temporary, until a system to regulate such matters, can be consolidated. Firstly: to allow into the customs house in Brazil any kind of articles, textiles or goods, carried, or by foreign ships from nations that are in peace and harmony with my royal crown, or by ships belonging to my subjects paying, on arrival, twenty four per cent, as follows: twenty per cent gross duty and four relative to the previously established contributions; regulating the charge of this duty by register rather by individual customhouse, as is currently in use. Wines, spirits and olive-oil, known as liquids, to pay double this rate of duty, presently due. Secondly: that not only my subjects, but also foreigners may export to whatever port they wish – the produce of commerce or agriculture, that I dearly wish to promote – any type of goods or colonial produce, except for Brazil wood, or others that are known to be in short supply, paying on export, the duties already established in the Territories. I declare that laws, royal warrants and other orders that heretofore prohibited the reciprocal commerce and shipping between my subjects and foreigners, are hereby suspended and without effect. To be executed with the zeal and effectiveness that I expect from you. Written in Bahia, on the 28th of January 1808 – Prince – To the Count of Ponte.

Letter from the Count of Ponte to the Viscount of Anadia, *8 March 1808*[9]

Your Excellency.

On the 6th of the current month, by the master of the smack *Nossa Senhora da Conceição*, I received from Your Excellency your letter dated February 5th and, with great joy and pleasure, had for the first time confirmed that the Serene Princess D. Maria Benedita and the Serene Infantas D. Marianna, D. Maria Francisca and D. Izabel Maria had arrived at that port; also to find Your Excellency free from the dangers and discomforts of your lamentable journey. Obeying Your Excellency's orders, I inform you that on the 22nd of January at 2.00 a.m. I was given the news that large vessels had been seen on the north coast, on the 21st at 4.00 p.m. I doubled the watches and, next, a report was received of a sighting of three line-of-battle ships, a full-rigged ship and two brigs: almost certainly British vessels. Until midday this was the belief but, when their flags became visible, the royal standard could be seen. I immediately gave orders to remove the shot from the guns, so as to be able to fire the merited salutes, and went myself on board the ship *Príncipe Real*, to receive orders from the Prince Our Lord, whom, filled with enthusiasm and relief I found, with all the Royal Family, in a perfect state of health. The line-of-battle ships *Príncipe Real*, *Afonso de Albuquerque*, the English ship *Bedford*, the frigate *Urânia*, the brig *Trez-Corações*, and an American schooner anchored, at 4.00 p.m.

His Royal Highness told me that he would disembark, if this could take place without removing from the ships beds or other objects, not only for himself and members of the Royal Family, but also for servants and for the families that had accompanied him. I did everything that I could to prepare, in the shortest possible time, the necessary accommodations. I was successful in that Her Majesty the Queen Our Lady, Their Royal Highnesses with their servants and families disembarked on the 24th at 5.00 p.m. The Prince Regent deciding on the time, so as not to suffer from the torrid sun.

On the 10th of February the line-of-battle ship *D. João de Castro* anchored here; on board were the Duke and Duchess of Cadaval with their children, the Counts of Belmonte and some other families. On the 30th of November they lost their masts, arriving at Paraíba making water, and thence came to this port. On orders from His Royal Highness, she disarmed and remained behind to repair the extensive damage she had suffered, dividing her passengers, officers and baggage amongst the other ships. For this reason the *Activo* and the Imperator *Adriano* were made ready to continue the journey with the squadron.

On the 16th of the said month the line-of-battle ship *Medusa*, that was without masts, was forced to put into Pernambuco and there, making those repairs that were possible, followed on to this port. She carried D. Antônio de Araújo, Counsellor José Egídio, Chief Justice Thomaz Antônio Corte-Real and other families.

Her Majesty and Highness remained until the 24th of February, when they then decided to continue their journey. However, embarking at midday, certain inconveniences appeared that prevented their departure that afternoon. On the 25th, as the horizon was rather cloudy and the wind unfavourable, the Prince Regent Our Lord decided to postpone the departure for the following day, the 26th. He departed (26th) at 4.00 p.m. with an excellent wind and tide, leaving us with the expectation that he would arrive, at this capital, in six or seven days of a happy journey.

On this assumption, I will refrain from narrating all that happened during this time; as Your Excellency will have good and faithful witnesses who were present. His Royal Highness distributed favours to military officers, promoting them to the next level and filling vacancies, decorating them with the insignia of the Orders of Christ and Aviz. As for the Church, he conferred benefits and sinecures; to the ministers, the insignia of Christ, to those who did not already have it; to individuals, he attended with infallible justice to their demands.

This resumes that which I can tell you about the royal persons of our august sovereigns and, if I did not immediately communicate with Your Excellency, it was because we daily expected the rest of the squadron at this port, as there was no indication that they had passed this latitude; there was considerable uncertainty of them enjoying a satisfactory journey, in view of the damaged ships that arrived here every day.

God Bless Your Excellency Bahia 8th of March 1808.

His Excellency Viscount of Anadia

COUNT OF PONTE

Letter from the Count of Ponte to the Count of Arcos, on 8 March 1808 [10]

Your Excellency

On the 5th of the current month, I received the letter from Your Excellency of the 5th of February last and I can, in reply to your important request, assure Your Excellency that on the 22nd of January there anchored in this port, the line-of-battle ships *Príncipe Real*, *Afonso de Albuquerque*, *Bedford* and the frigate *Urânia*. They brought Her Majesty the Queen Our Lady, His Royal Highness the Prince Regent, his August Wife, and the remainder of the Royal Family and those in their service that accompanied them from the port of Lisbon. Disembarking in this city they stayed until the 26th of February, date on which they left with a favourable wind, for that capital. I am infinitely grateful to Your Excellency for the good news of the safe journey of the princesses and infantas, that are at this port; by the brig *Santo Antônio Rei* I await anxiously for news – as promised by Your Excellency – in your letter of the 29th of January, to which I refer.

God Bless Your Excellency Bahia 8th of March 1808.

His Excellency Count of Arcos

COUNT OF PONTE

Decree of 3 May 1808 [11]
Institutes the new order of the sword

It being of the greatest importance for August Sovereigns, Kings and Emperors to institute new Orders of Knighthood, so as to be able to recompense the most significant services, both of their subjects and of illustrious strangers, that have not received any equivalent remuneration or compensation, other than honour.

This practice has been the habit of the greatest Princes – nearly always at the most significant times – including, amongst them, my fortunate journey to these States of Brazil, which I hope will result not only, in restoring the losses suffered by my people in the Kingdom of Portugal, but also many benefits and achievements of honour and glory, due to their loyalty. Also, abundance for my treasures in America and commercial freedom which I have conceded to my people.

Considering that the three Military Orders, that exist in my Kingdoms, are of a religious nature: and so can only be bestowed on those that are fortunate to enjoy our Holy Religion. To those in the armed services that merit the highest honours, or other occupations or services whose merit requires me to frequently have (the order) available for use; also in the demands made by important enterprises; for these and other motives, as noble and prestigious, I have resolved to renew and augment the only Order of Knighthood which was instituted exclusively for civil purposes, by one of the Portuguese Kings – the Order of the Sword – instituted by King D. Afonso V of enlightened memory. I have already made use of it in the city of Bahia, ordering the issue of a medal with the inscription 'Courage and Loyalty', with which I have rewarded two well-deserving subjects of my faithful and ancient ally, the King of Great Britain. Only time will indicate the number of Knights, Grand Crosses and Commanders, with their respective land or pensions, and other considerations in favour of those persons, who with so much loyalty accompanied and assisted me, sacrificing their own interests to the greater honour and obedience due to me. On the other hand, it is not convenient to delay its renewal, as it is more worthy of esteem the closer it is to its origin. I am therefore confirming the said Order of Knighthood, known as the Sword, which was instituted by my ancestor of glorious memory – D. Afonso V known as the African – in 1459. To have the same results as if it had been newly created by myself, and renewed after my safe arrival at the port of the city of Bahia. I wish this Decree to be the basis of its institution; I hereby order D. Fernando José de Portugal of My State Council, Minister Assistant to the Dispatch of My Office and President of the Royal Treasury, to present the new statutes, resulting from the meetings which I have ordered and from my instructions. Palace of Rio de Janeiro, 13th of May 1808. With the initial of the Prince Regent Our Lord.

Chapter VIII

Proclamation [12]
Governor of Paris, first aide-de-camp of HM the Emperor of the French and King of Italy, General in Chief, Grand Cross of the Order of Christ in these Reigns, Residents of Lisbon
My army is going to enter your town. I have come to save your port and your Prince from the harmful influence of England. This Prince, of upright virtues, has been led astray by the treacherous Counsellors that surround him, to be delivered up by them to my enemies; they dare to expose his personal security; his subjects are not be sacrificed because of the cowardice of a few noblemen.

Residents of Lisbon, remain calm in your homes; do not fear anything from the army or myself. Only our enemies and the wicked need fear us.

The Great Napoleon, my Master, sends me to protect you; I will protect you. Junot.

Proclamation [13]
Lucas De Seabra Da Silva, Counsellor Of The Prince Regent Our Lord, Nobleman Knight Of His Royal House, Justice Of The Royal Household, Chancellor Of The Court And Of The Court Of Appeal, Superintendent General Of The Police Of The Court And Kingdom
May all Residents of this Capital and its limits take notice. No one should refuse the French and Spanish Money, that the troops of His Majesty Emperor and King offer to pay for the victuals which they need; carry out what is needed, anyone who does not do so will be severely punished at the direction of the police. Until the Government takes other measures this should be strictly observed; this proclamation to be prepared and exhibited. Lisbon, 30th of November 1807. Lucas de Seabra da Silva.

Proclamation [14]
Governor of Paris, First Aide-de-Camp of HM the Emperor of the French and King of Italy, General in Chief, Grand Cross of the Order of Christ in These Reigns, Residents of the Kingdom of Portugal.

A French Army is about to enter your Territory. It comes to free you from English rule; it makes forced marches to free your beautiful City of Lisbon from the fate of Copenhagen. This time, the hopes of the treacherous English government will be frustrated. Napoleon, who turned his attention to the destiny of the Continent, has taken care that the prey, of the Tyrant of the seas, will not fall into his power. Your Prince declared war against England, we fight a common cause. Residents of the land, fear nothing. My Army is as well disciplined as it is brave. I will answer on my honour for their good behaviour. Shelter it everywhere, as is its due as Soldiers of Napoleon the Great. Let him have, as is his right, the food that he needs; but above all, residents of the land, remain tranquil in your homes. Any Soldier of the French Army found stealing will be disciplined with the most rigorous punishment.

Any individual, of whatever class, who has received a donation unjustly, will be taken before a Council of War to be tried in accordance with all the strictness of the law.

Any individual of the Kingdom of Portugal, not being a front line soldier found taking part in an armed group, will be shot.

Any individual found to be head of an assembly or a conspiracy, aimed at arming the inhabitants against the French Army, will be shot.

Every town or village in which a member of the French Army is assassinated will pay a tax of not less than three times its annual income. The four principal inhabitants will be held as hostage for the payment of the sum; so that justice may be exemplary. The first city, town or village where a Frenchman is assassinated, will be burned and entirely razed to the ground.

But I want to persuade myself that the Portuguese know where their true interests lie; that, following the peaceful vision of their Prince, will receive us as friends and, particularly, that the beautiful City of Lisbon will see with pleasure my entering its walls – leading an Army to save her from being an eternal prey to her enemies on the Continent.

General Headquarters of Alcântara 17th of November 1807.

Proclamation[15]

Governor of Paris, First Aide-de-camp of HM The Emperor of the French and King of Italy, General in Chief, Grand Cross of The Order of Christ In These Reigns, Residents of the Kingdom of Portugal

HM the Emperor, Our August Master has turned his attention to your interests; all doubts should disappear: the fate of Portugal has been decided. Future prosperity is assured, as Napoleon the Great has taken you under his almighty protection.

The Prince of Brazil, abandoning Portugal, renounced all his Rights to the Sovereignty of this Reign. The House of Bragança has ceased to rule in Portugal.

The Emperor Napoleon desires that the whole of this beautiful Country be well administered and governed in his Name, by the General in Chief of His Army.

The task, imposed on me by the benevolence and confidence of my Master, is difficult to accomplish, but I hope to do so with dignity: helped by the most learned citizens of the Reign and by the good will of the people.

I have established a Council of Government to guide me in the worthy causes that I should undertake: administrators will be sent to the Provinces to develop the means of improving and putting order and economy into the Administration.

I order that roads be built and canals cut, so as to improve communications and allow agriculture and the national industry to develop; both causes essential in the development of a country. Together with a vigorous, suffering and self-reliant people, these objectives will not be difficult to realise.

The Portuguese Troops, led by their most able commanders, will very quickly form one family with the Soldiers of Marengo, Austerlitz, Jena and Friedland; between them there will be no rivalry other than for honour and discipline.

Taxes well administered will ensure that each worker receives compensation for his work; public education, that mother of civilisation of the people, will spill over the Provinces, the Algarve and Beira Alta; one day they also will have their Camões.

The religion of your Country, the same we all share, will be protected and helped by that same desire that was able to restore it, in the vast French Empire; but free of the superstitions that dishonour it and the interferences that hamper it.

Public peace will no longer be disturbed by dangerous brigands, the result of idleness; and, in case there should exist incorrigible evil persons, an active police will free society from them. Deformed beggars will no longer drag their filth through the proud Capital, nor in the interior of the Reign; work houses will be established, and the unfortunate poor will there find refuge; the lazy will be employed in their own upkeep.

Citizens of the Kingdom of Portugal remain assured and peaceful; I have taken of those who may want to lead you to revolution and who do not mind if blood is spilled, as long as it is the blood of the Continent. Dedicate yourselves, with confidence to your work, you will collect the rewards; should it become necessary, in the beginning, to make some sacrifices, it is to enable government to better your destiny. They are, however, necessary for the maintenance of a great Army and to carry out the ambitious projects of the Great Napoleon: his watchful eyes are on you, and your future happiness is assured; he will love you as much as he loves his French subjects; be careful though to merit the benefits, it is up to you.

Palace of the General Headquarters in Lisbon, 1ˢᵗ of February 1808.

JUNOT

Proclamation[16]

Royal Palace, Milan 23rd of December 1807 Napoleon, Emperor of the French, King of Italy and Protector of the Rhine Confederation, we have decreed the following:

Note I

Article I. An Extraordinary War Contribution of one hundred million francs will be imposed on the kingdom of Portugal, to serve as ransom for all the properties, of any type, belonging to private individuals.

Article II. This contribution will be divided amongst the Provinces and Cities, in accordance with the wealth of each one, under the General in Chief of Our Army; the necessary steps will be taken for its prompt collection.

Article III.

All property belonging to the Queen of Portugal, to the Prince Regent and those princes that receive endowments will be confiscated. All property belonging to those Noblemen who accompanied the Prince, when he abandoned the Country, and who have not returned to the Kingdom by February 15th 1808 will likewise be confiscated.

Napoleon

Chapter IX

Decree of the 17th of September[17]

Desirous of demonstrating how much I honour and respect the person of Sir Sidney Smith, Rear Admiral Commander in Chief of His Britannic Majesty's squadron anchored in this port: I give him as benefit the lands located beyond the shore, near to St. Domingos, which were rented by my Royal Treasury to Manoel Martins Ferreira, Agostinho Vicente and to Joaquim Pereira and which now belong to Jacinto de Mello Menezes Palhares; as well, the rural residence that belonged to João de Deos, with a dwelling place, six slaves and a canoe for the use of the same dwelling place, with the land as shown by the title deeds of the last proprietor. So that Sir Sydney Smith and his successors will own them as their own, without any rent or taxes, to freely dispose of as he wishes. The Treasury Council to take note and issue the necessary letter of donation.

Palace of Rio de Janeiro, 17th of September 1808 – With the Initial of the Prince Regent Our Lord – Folio 88v. of the 1st Book, Secretariat of the Empire.

Glossary of Nautical Terms

Anchor – A ship carried anchors of various weights for different purposes and occasions; a 74-gun ship would carry four anchors, each weighing some three and a half tons (one on either side of the bows, known as the 'best bower' and the 'little bower', and two spares), other anchors in use included a stream weighing just under one ton and the smaller kedge.

Articles of war – made up of thirty-six articles, stating offences and their punishment. It was usual to gather together the crew at regular intervals and read out the articles.

Barge – see launch.

Beat to quarters – order given, by beating on a drum, to take up station at the guns.

Bends – knots.

Bent – to attach a sail to the yard.

Best bower – see anchor.

Blue at the mizzen – blue flag flown at the mizzen mast to indicate that a rear admiral of the blue is on board.

Blue light – night signal of position.

Bonnet – a small additional sail attached to the foot of a jib or staysail.

Bore up – move closer to.

Box up – to veer around.

Braces – ropes used to move the yards to different positions.

Brail – haul sail up (bundle) for furling.

Brig – a fully square-rigged vessel with two masts.

Brigantine – two-masted vessel with square-rigged foremast and fore- and aft-rigged mainmast with square sail on the topmast (later these sails disappeared).

Brigatt – see brigantine.

Broached – 1. opened; 2. cause ship to present side to wind and waves.

Brought to – to bring to a halt, usually a ship being chased.

Catharpin legs – a device fitted on either side of the point where the lower shrouds meet the upper (furtock shrouds), which when tightened, allows greater freedom of movement of the yards.

Caulk – fill seams to make them waterproof.

Chase (chace) – unidentified ship which, it has been decided, should be intercepted.

Clue – lower corner of a sail.

Commodore – a temporary position, not a promotion; commander of a small squadron of ships, usually a senior post captain.

Courses – see sail.

Cutter – see launch.

Deadman – Dodman Pt. (Cornwall).

Deck – Above the hold, a typical 74-gun line-of-battle ship would have the orlop deck, then a lower and a higher gun deck; the top deck was covered at the bow (forecastle), and at the stern (poop), leaving an uncovered part at the centre (quarter).

Deep – When death occurred on board the body would be sewn into a canvas bag, weighted and thrown overboard, usually with a short religious ceremony.

Detain – Once boarded, after the transfer of an officer and men the ship would, until further notice, keep station with the squadron.

d – ditto, same.

Driver – see sail.

Exchanged numbers – see signal.

F – fathom, length or depth equivalent to six feet.

Fidded – fit upper mast in place with supports.

Filled – sails with wind so as to move ship forward.

Fishing – mending.

Flying jib – see sail.

Fore royal – see sail.

Foresail – see sail.

Fore topgallant – see sail.

Fore topsail – see sail.

Frigate – a three-masted square-rigged ship, smaller than a line-of-battle ship, but faster and with significant fire power. The unarmed lower deck meant that she could heel and thus carry sail in strong winds or a heavy sea.

Furkin, Firkin – cask holding about nine gallons.

Furled – sail gathered on the yard.

Gallant – see sail.

Galliot – small single-decked vessel, usually with both sails and oars.

Gig – see launch.

Head – the fore part of the ship.

Hogshead – cask holding fifty gallons.

Hoisted a broad pennant – signal flag indicating that a commodore is on board.

Hove to – to stop. A square-rigged ship would accomplish this by filling some sails and backing others so as to balance the force of the wind.

Jib – see sail.

Jolly boat – see launch.

K – knot, measurement of speed equivalent to nautical mile; a line with knots at regular intervals attached to a piece of wood (log) allowed to run out for a fixed number of seconds. The number of knots indicated the speed.

Kedge – see anchor.

Launch – one of the various boats carried on board a ship. Others included gig, cutters, yawls, pinnaces, jolly boats and barges.

Lead – a line with a lead weight at its extreme, containing a substance that could pick up particles from the bottom. Coloured markers at regular intervals helped to quickly measure the depth, expressed in fathoms.

League – about three miles.

Lee – see leeward.

Leeward – towards the side sheltered from the wind.

Lighter – a small transport vessel.

Log – wooden device attached to a line, see K.

Loosed – unfurled, allow sail to be set.

Lugger – vessel with its fore and aft sails set on a yard.

Main royal – see sail.

Mainsail – see sail.

Main topgallant – see sail.

Main topsail – see sail.

Mast – The three masts (fore, main and mizzen) of a ship were made up of sections, attached one above the other. Thus, for instance, the mainmast was made up of the lower mast firmly attached to the ship, the topmast, topgallant mast and royal mast. Yards were set at 90° and used to attach the various sails.

Messenger – Because the thickness of the anchor cable was too great for it to be used on the capstan, an endless cable of smaller diameter, known as a messenger, was used instead, the anchor cable being attached to it by 'nippers' and, as brought in, the anchor cable would be attached at a higher position and released at the last point so that the cable could be stored below in the orlop deck.

Mid. – midshipman.

Mizzen or Mizon – see mast.

Mizzen royal – see sail.

Mizzen topgallant – see sail.

Mizzen topsail – see sail.

Mustered by divisions – the formal gathering together of the crew, usually for inspection.

Oakum – loose fibres from old ropes used for caulking.

Occly. – occasionally.

Orlop – see deck.

Pinnace – see launch.

Pipe – cask for liquids, about 105 gallons.

Puncheon – cask for liquids holding between 72 and 120 gallons.

Reef – reducing sail area by tying part of the sail, with the reef lines existing on either side, to the yard with a reef knot; various parallel reef lines gave several options as to area reduced, thus first, second.

Royal Masts – see masts.

Sail – A three-masted ship would carry sail on her fore, main and mizzen masts. In order of masts and starting from below, the quadrilateral sails were named foresail (or course), fore topsail, fore topgallant and fore royal, then mainsail (or course), main topsail, main topgallant and main royal, mizzen topsail, mizzen topgallant and mizzen royal. The mizzen mast did not carry a course. Instead a boom projecting back carried a spanker or driver. Studding sails were carried on additional yards that could be extended out from the fore and mainmast yards and took the name from the position from which they were hung. Sky sails were carried above the royals. Staysails were triangular or quadrilateral, hung between masts, also forward of the foremast, attached to the bowsprit. They were named after the mast where their heads were tied. A boom extending from the bowsprit carried the triangular flying (outer) and inner jibs. Sprit sails were carried from yards hung underneath the bowsprit.

Sail of the line – a three-masted fully square-rigged ship of sufficient size and fire power so as to take her place in the line of battle.

Schooner – two- or more masted vessels having fore and aft rigging on all masts. Variations included topsail schooner (with square sails on the fore topmast), staysail and Bermuda schooners.

Schr. – schooner.

Sheet anchor – see anchor.

Shifted – taken down and changed.

Shortened – reduced (area of sail).

Signal (private) – commands, information and identification (of a particular ship) were given by signals, usually shown as flags representing numbers corresponding to a previously agreed code.

Sloop – vessels that varied considerably in size, number of masts and rigging. Within the navy it reflected the rank of officer in command, rather than actual specifications.

Slops – clothes for sailors, which could be bought from the purser, and discounted from pay at the end of a voyage.

Sound – measure depth.

Spanker – see sail.

Split – to tear a sail.

Spring – crack or break in a boom, spar or section of a mast.

Standing in – heading for.

Stays – ropes used to support a mast in position, part of the standing rigging.

Staysail – see sail.

Stream anchor – see anchor.

Struck – to lower, usually 'struck her colours': that is, surrendered.

Studding – see sail.

Sway up – raising a yard or sail.

Sweepers – oarsmen.

Tacked – see wore.

Taken aback – sails pressed against mast, not in the position desired, caused by change of wind direction.

Tierce – one third of a pipe.

Topgallant – see sail.

Unbent – see bent.

Weighed – take up anchor, ready to move position.

Windward – towards the side exposed to the wind.

Wore – the act of bringing the ship into the wind; similar to tacking but with her stern rather than her head brought round. As a result the move took 225° rather than 125° (tacking).

Wr. – weather.

Yard – see masts.

Yawl – see launch.

Notes

PREFACE

1. D. João, 1767–1826, later 27th King of Portugal. See Appendix A.
2. D. José Francisco Xavier, 1761–1788.
3. D. Maria I, 1734–1816, 26th Queen of Portugal. See Appendix A.
4. Martins, Joaquim Pedro de Oliveira, *História de Portugal,* 9th edn, Lisboa, Parceria Antonio Maria Pereira, 1991, p. 395. [1st edn, 1879].
5. Boiteaux, Lucas Alexandre, *A marinha de Guerra brazileira nos reinados de D. João VI e D. Pedro I*, Rio de Janeiro, Imprensa Nacional, 1913, p. 9.
6. Monteiro, Tobias, *História do Império: a elaboração da independência*, Rio de Janeiro, F Briguet, 1927, vol. 1, pp. 45–6.
7. LIMA, Manuel de Oliveira, *Dom João VI no Brazil 1808–1821*, Rio de Janeiro, Typ. do Jornal do Comércio, 1908, vol. 1, p. 37.
8. ZUQUETE, Afonso Eduardo Martins, *Nobreza de Portugal e do Brasil*, Lisboa, Editorial Enciclopédia, 1960, vol. 1, p. 658.
9. Copies of the logbooks and reports from the captains have been lodged by the author in the Historic Archive of the Imperial Museum, Petrópolis, Brazil.
10. Light, Kenneth H, *The Migration of the Royal Family of Portugal to Brazil 1807–08, Logbooks of HM Ships before the Tagus in November 1807 and of those that took part in the Voyage to Brazil, together with Reports and Letters from Captain James Walter of HMS Bedford, who Escorted the Queen and the Prince Regent to Bahia, and Commodore Graham Moore of HMS Marlborough, who Escorted the Portuguese Fleet to Rio de Janeiro*, Rio de Janeiro, Private printing by Kenneth H Light, 1995.

CHAPTER I

1. D. Sebastião José de Carvalho e Melo, 1699–1782, 1st Marquis of Pombal (1769) and 1st Count of Oeiras (1759).
2. CHEKE, Marcus, *Carlota Joaquina: Queen of Portugal*, New York, Sidgwick & Jackson, 1947, pp. 11–12.
3. D. Pedro Clemente Francisco José Antônio, 1717–1787. He was the fifth child of D. João V, 1689–1750, 24th King of Portugal and his wife D. Maria Ana of Austria.
4. D. Antônio de Araújo de Azevedo, 1754–1817, 1st Count of Barca (1815). See Appendix A.

5. Napoleon Bonaparte, 1769–1821, consul 1799–1804 and then Napoleon I, Emperor of the French 1804–1814 and 1815.

6. Charles-Maurice de Talleyrand-Perigord, 1754–1838, served in several ministerial posts, until becoming Prince of Benevento in 1807. As a prince it was considered to be below his dignity to be a minister – a diplomatic way of reducing his power.

7. GRAHAM, Maria, *Journal of a Voyage to Brazil and Residence There During Part of the Years 1821, 1822, 1823*, London, Longman Hurst, 1824, pp. 40–1.

8. Ibid. P. 38; PEREIRA, Ângelo, *D. João VI: príncipe e rei*: *A retirada da família real para o Brasil*, Lisbon, Empresa Nacional de Publicidade, 1953, vol. 1, p. 107.

9. PEREIRA, *D. João VI príncipe e rei*, vol. 1, p. 102.

10. Percy Clinton Sidney Smythe, 1780–1855, 6th Viscount Strangford and Baron Panhurst (1825). See Appendix A.

11. D. Domingos Antônio de Sousa Coutinho, 1760–1833, Plenipotentiary Minister to the Court of St James, 1st Count (1812) and 1st Marquis of Funchal (1833). See Appendix A.

12. Jean Lannes, 1769–1809, Duke of Montebello in 1807, when he was created one of Bonaparte's marshals.

13. D. João de Almeida de Melo e Castro, 1756–1814, 5th Count of Galvêas. See Appendix A.

14. D. Diogo Inácio de Pina Manique, 1733–1805. See Appendix A.

15. NORONHA, Eduardo de, *Pina Manique*: *o intendente de antes quebrar...*, Oporto, Livraria Civilização Editora, 1940, p. 150.

16. NORONHA, *Pina Manique...*, pp. 192–3.

17. PEREIRA, *D. João VI príncipe e rei...*, vol. 1, pp. 97–100.

18. PEREIRA, *D. João VI príncipe e rei...*, vol. 1, pp. 113–126.

19. D. Rodrigo de Souza Coutinho, 1745–1812, president of the Royal Treasury (1801), 1st Count of Linhares (1808). See Appendix A.

20. PEREIRA, *D. João VI Príncipe e Rei...*, vol. 1, pp. 123–4.

21. MORAIS, A. J. de Melo, *História da transladação da corte portuguesa para o Brasil em 1807–1808*, Rio de Janeiro, Livraria da Casa Imperial de E Dupont Editora, 1872, p. 74.

22. See Appendix C.

23. GRAHAM, *Journal of a Voyage to Brazil...*, pp. 37–8.

24. Jean Andoche Junot, 1771–1813, Duke of Abrantès. See Appendix A.

25. M. François Maximilien Gérard, 1755–1827, Count of Rayneval.

26. SCHOM, Alan, *Trafalgar: Countdown to Battle*, London, Penguin, 1990, p. 69.

27. Charles James Fox, 1749–1806, Foreign Minister in 1806.

28. GRAHAM, *Journal of a Voyage to Brazil...*, p. 40.

29. LIMA, *Dom João VI no Brazil...*, p. 20.
30. GRAHAM, *Journal of a Voyage to Brazil...*, pp. 39–40.
31. MONTEIRO, *História do Império...*, p. 6.
32. D. Lourenço de Lima, 1767–1839, 1st Count of Mafra (1836). See Appendix A.
33. PEREIRA, *D. João VI: Príncipe e Rei...*, vol. 1, pp. 149–151.
34. D. Carlota Joaquina, 1777–1830. See Appendix A.
35. SOUSA, Octávio Tarquino de, *A vida de D. Pedro I*, Rio de Janeiro, J Olympo, 1952, vol. 1, p. 28.
36. D. Pedro de Almeida Portugal, 1754–1813, 3rd Marquis of Alorna (1795) and 6th Count of Assumar (1802). See Appendix A.
37. D. Tomas José Xavier de Lima Vasconcelos Brito Nogueira Teles da Silva, 1779–1822, 2nd Marquis of Ponte do Lima and 15th Viscount of Vila Nova de Cerveira.
38. D. Bernardo José Maria da Silbeira e Lorena, 1756–1818, 5th Count of Sarzedas.
39. Sabugal – As from 1678 this title belonged to the Counts of Óbitos and Palma. From about 1770 until 1839 this title was not renewed.
40. D. Carlos IV, 1748–1819, married his cousin D. Maria Luiza de Bourbon, 1751–1819. Their eldest surviving child was D. Carlota Joaquina.
41. Cheke, *Carlota Joaquina...*, p. 7.
42. DURANT, Will; DURANT, Ariel, *The Story of Civilization: the Age of Napoleon*, New York, Simon & Schuster, 1975, vol. 9, pp. 212–3.
43. D. Manuel Alvarez de Faria Rios Sánchez Zarzosa Godoy, 1767–1851, Prince of Peace and of Basano, Duke of Alcudia and Sueca.
44. Fontainebleau, 27 October 1807. For complete text see Appendix C.
45. LIMA, *D. João VI no Brazil...*, p. 30.
46. Lucien Bonaparte, 1775–1840.
47. DURANT, *The Story of Civilization...*, vol. 9, p. 665.
48. LIMA, *D. João VI no Brazil...*, p. 38.
49. LIMA, *D. João VI no Brazil...*, p. 40.
50. POB (01).
51. LIMA, *D.João VI no Brazil: 1808-1821*, p. 38.
52. PRO FO 63/55(01).
53. MARTINS, Enéas Filho, O *Conselho de Estado português e a transmigração da família real em 1807*, Rio de Janeiro, Arquivo Nacional, 1968, p. 5.
54. D. Ayres José Maria de Saldanha Albuquerque Coutinho Mattos e Noronha, 1784–1864, 2nd Count of Ega (1771). See Appendix A.
55. D. Manuel José Antônio Hilário, 2nd Count of Campo-Alange.
56. PRO FO 63/55 (02).
57. MARTINS, *Conselho de Estado português...*, p. 5.
58. MANCHESTER, Alan K, A *transferência da corte portuguêsa para o Rio de Janeiro*. Journal of the Instituto Histórico e Geográfico Brasileiro, 1968, vol. 277,

p. 5.

59. D. José Egídio Álvares de Almeida, 1767–1832, Baron (Portuguese title, 1818) and Marquis (Brazilian title, 1826) of Santo Amaro.

60. POB (02).

61. PRO FO 63/55 (03).

62. PRO FO 63/65 (04).

63 D. José Xavier de Noronha Camões de Albuquerque de Sousa Moniz, 1741–1811, 4th Marquis of Angeja and 6th Count of Vila Verde. See Appendix A.

64. D. Henrique José de Carvalho e Melo, 1748–1812, 2nd Marquis of Pombal (1786). See Appendix A.

65. D. José Luis de Vasconcelos e Sousa, 1740–1812, 1st Marquis of Belas (1801) and 6th Count of Pombeiro (1783). See Appendix A.

66. D. João Rodrigues de Sá e Melo, 1755–1809, 1st Count of Anadia (1808). See Appendix A.

67. D. Fernando José de Portugal e Castro, 1752–1817, 1st Count (1808) and 2nd Marquis of Aguiar (1813). See Appendix A.

68. MARTINS, *O Conselho de Estado português...*, pp. 23–9.

69. Ibid. p. 25.

70. See Appendix C.

71. BOITEAUX, *A Marinha de Guerra brasileira...*, wrote that the proposition was summarily rejected by Britain.

72. MARTINS, *O Conselho de Estado português...*, p. 26.

73. CHEKE, *Carlota Joaquina...*, pp. 14–15.

74. LIMA, D. *João VI no Brazil...*, p. 50.

75. PRO FO 63/55 (01).

76. PRO FO 63/55 (03).

77. PRO FO 63/55 (05).

78. PEREIRA, Ângelo, *Os filhos D'El Rei D. João VI*, Lisbon, Empresa Nacional de Publicidade, 1946, p. 102.

79. ESPARTEIRO, Antônio Marques, *Subsídio para a história da Marinha de Guerra; Nau Rainha de Portugal*. Anais do Clube Naval, Lisbon, Nov/Dec 1943, pp. 677–701.

80. POB (03).

81. D. Pedro, 1798–1834, Prince of Beira, 1st Emperor of Brazil, 28th King (Pedro IV) of Portugal. See Appendix A.

82. D. Maria Francisca Benedita, 1746–1829.

83. PRO FO 63/56 (03).

84. Manuscript that belonged to Francisco Gomes da Silva apud PEREIRA, *Os filhos D'El Rei D. João VI*, p. 103.

85. MARTINS, *O Conselho de Estado Português...*, p. 7.

86. D. Miguel, 1802–1866, 29th King of Portugal. See Appendix A.

87. PRO FO 63/55 (08).

88. ESPARTEIRO, Antônio Marques, *História naval brasileira: a viagem*, Rio de Janeiro, Serviço de Documentação Geral da Marinha, 1979, vol. 2, p. 325.

89. MORAIS, *História da transladação...*, p. 31.

90. PEREIRA, *Os Filhos D'El Rei...*, p. 104.

91. MARTINS, *O Conselho de Estado Português...*, p. 36.

92. PRO FO 63/55 (07).

93. PEREIRA, *Os Filhos D'El Rei...*, pp.104–6; MARTINS, *O Conselho de Estado Português...*, p. 7.

94. MARTINS, *O Conselho de Estado Português...*, pp. 38–9.

95. PRO FO 63/55 (09).

96. Ibid.

97. Ibid.

98. PEREIRA, *Os Filhos D'El Rei...*, pp. 129–32. These letters are kept at the National Historic Archives, Madrid.

99. PRO FO 63/55 (08).

100. PRO FO 63/55 (10).

Chapter II

1. PRO FO 63/58 (01).

2. LIMA, *D. João VI no Brazil: 1808-1821*, p. 44.

3. PEREIRA, *Os Filhos D'El Rei...*, p. 106.

4. MONTEIRO, *História do Império...*, p. 16.

5. PRO FO 63/58 (01).

6. D. Vasco Manuel de Figueired Cabral da Câmara, 1767–1830, 1st Count of Belmonte (1805). See Appendix A.

7. PEREIRA, *Os Filhos D'El Rei...*, p. 107.

8. D. Thomé Xavier de Souza Coutinho de Castello Branco e Menezes, 1753–1813, 13th Count of Redondo (1791) and 1st Marquis of Borba (1811). See Appendix A.

9. PEREIRA, *Os Filhos D'El Rei...*, p. 108.

10. PRO FO 63/58 (01).

11. PEREIRA, *Os Filhos D'El Rei...*, pp. 103–7.

12. MARTINS, *O Conselho de Estado português...*, p. 48. For full text see Appendix C.

13. PRO FO 63/58 (02).

14. PRO FO 63/58 (03).

15. PRO FO 63/58 (04).

16. Ibid.

17. Ibid.

18. POB (04). Admiral Lord Cuthbert Collingwood, 1750–1810.

19. PRO FO 63/55 (11).

20. POB (05).

21. POB (06).

22. MONTEIRO, *História do Império...*, p. 27; MORAIS, *História da transla-dação...*, pp. 49–50 quotes the text in full.

23. MARTINS, *O Conselho de Estado português...*, p. 50. Quotes MADELIN, Louis, *Histoire du Consolat et de L'Empire: L'Affaire d'Espagne*, Paris, Hachette, 1958 vol. 7; "...Si le Portugal ne fait pas ce que je veux, la maison de Bragance ne regenera plus dans deux mois ..."

24. MARTINS, *O Conselho de Estado português...*, p. 59.

25. PEREIRA, *D. João VI, príncipe e rei...*, vol. 1, pp. 162–3.

26. Jean-Baptiste Nompère, 1756–1834, Count of Champagny, later Duke of Cadore.

27. PEREIRA, *D. João VI, príncipe e rei...*, vol. 1, p. 162.

28. MORAIS, *História da Tansladação...*, p. 52.

29. POB (07).

30. D. Pedro José Joaquin Vito de Menezes Coutinho, 1777–1823, 6th Marquis of Marialva (1795), 8th Count of Castanhede. See Appendix A.

31. POB (08).

32. MORAIS, *História da trasladação...*, p. 52.

33. MONTEIRO, *História do Império...*, p. 32.

34. Ibid, p. 32.

35. BECKFORD, William, *A corte da Rainha D. Maria I: Correspondence of W Beckford (1787)*, Lisbon, Tavares Cardoso & Irmão, 1901.

36. Russian Minister accredited to the Madrid court.

37. PEREIRA, *D. João príncipe e rei...*, vol. 1, pp. 172–3.

38. POB (09).

39. POB (10).

40. HORWARD, Donald D, *Portugal and the Anglo-Russian Naval Crisis (1808)*. Naval War College Review, Newport RI, Naval War College, 1981, vol.34, no. 4, pp. 49–50; MORAIS, *História da trasladação...*, p. 52.

41. CASTRO, José Ferreira Borges de, *Collecção de tratados, convenções, contratos e actos públicos celebrados entre a coroa de Portugal e as mais potências desde 1640 até o presente*, Lisbon, Imprensa Nacional, 1856–1858, vol.4, pp. 236–54. See Appendix C.

42. POB (11).

43. MARTINS, *O Conselho de Estado português...*, pp. 63–4.

44. PRO FO 63/55 (06).

45. MORAIS, *História da transladação...*, p. 50.
46. D. Ferdinando VII, 1784–1833, 42nd King of Spain 1808, 1814–33.
47. MARTINS, *O Conselho de Estado português...*, pp. 54–67. Most of the documents are dated 2 November.
48. POB (12).
49. MONTEIRO, *História do Império...*, p. 27.
50. POB (13).
51. MARTINS, *Conselho de Estado português...*, p. 68. D. Lourenço claimed illness and, in fact, did not return.
52. Ibid. pp. 68–9.
53. For explanation see Chapter IV, p. 40.
54. PRO ADM 1/19 (03).
55. PEREIRA, *D. João príncipe e rei...*, vol. 1, pp. 160–172.
56. *Gibraltar Chronicle*, 5 December 1807, Garrison Library, Gibraltar. See Appendix C.
57. PEREIRA, *D. João príncipe e rei...*, vol. 1, pp. 192–203.
58. Ibid. p. 161.
59. Ibid. p. 177. Oliveira Barreto must have been a businessman, friendly to Junot when he served as Ambassador.
60. PEREIRA, *D. João príncipe e rei...*, vol. 1, pp. 177–9.
61. NEVES, José Acursio das, *História geral da invasão dos francezes em Portugal e da restauração deste reino*, Porto, Edições Afrontamento, 1884, vol. I, pp. 201–2.
62. PEREIRA, *D. João príncipe e rei...*, vol. 1, p. 181.
63. MONTEIRO, *História do Império...*, pp. 49–50.
64. MONTEIRO, *História do Império...*, pp. 43–4. Also *Gibraltar Chronicle*, 26 December. See Appendix C.
65. See Appendix C for minutes of this historic State Council meeting.
66. D. Joaquim José de Azevedo, 1761–1835, 1st Baron of Rio Seco (1813) and 1st Viscount with honours (1819); in Brazil, Marquis of Jundiaí (1826). See Appendix A.
67. Francisco Bartollozi, 1725–1815 and Henri L'Evêque, 1769–1832.
68. POB (14).
69. D. Francisco da Silva Telo e Meneses, 1723–1808, 1st Marquis of Vagos (1802) and 6th Count of Aveiras (1779). See Appendix A.
70. Sousa, *A vida de D. Pedro* I..., p. 55.
71. Lima, *D. João VI no Brasil...*, p. 47.
72. Ibid. p. 49.
73. For the complete proclamation, see Appendix C.
74. Monsenhor Lourenço Caleppi, 1741–1817. See Appendix A.
75. ROSSI, Camilo Luis de, *Memória sobre a evasão do nuncio apostólico Monsenhor*

Caleppi, da corte de Lisboa para o Rio de Janeiro, ed. by. Dr. Jerônimo de Avelar Figueira de Melo, In ANAIS da Biblioteca Nacional, Rio de Janeiro, Anais da Biblioteca Nacional, 1939. vol. 61, pp. 19-20. [Document originally translated from the Secret Archive of the Vatican no.143.]

76. D. José Caetano da Silva Coutinho.
77. D. Pedro de Sousa Holstein, 1781–1859, 1st Count, Marquis and Duke of Palmela (1833). After embarking was, for lack of space on board, forced to return ashore, and would only arrive in Brazil twelve years later, in 1820. See Appendix A.
78. MORAIS, *História da transladação...*, p. 58.
79. POB (15).
80. BRANDÃO, Raul, *El-Rei Junot*, Lisbon, Monteiro & Cia, 1912, p. 107.
81. CHEKE, *Carlota Joaquina...*, p. 21.
82. O'NEIL, Lieutenant Count Thomas, A *Concise and Accurate Account of the Proceedings of the Squadron under the Command of Rear Admiral Sir Sydney Smith KS&c in Effecting the Escape of the Royal Family of Portugal to the Brazils, on November 29, 1807; and also the Sufferings of the Royal Fugitives etc. during their Voyage from Lisbon to Rio de Janeiro: with a Variety of other Interesting and Authentic Facts,* London, J Barfield, 1810, pp. 17–20.
83. NEVES, *História geral da invasão...*, pp. 177 and 204.
84. Desembargador Lucas Seabra da Silva, who succeeded Pina Manique.
85. ROSSI, *Memória sobre a evasão do núncio apostólico...*, pp. 21–2.
86. SORIANO, Simão José da Luz, *História da guerra civil*, Lisbon, Imprensa Nacional, 1866–1893. vol. 2, p. 676.
87. PEREIRA, *D. João VI príncipe e rei...*, vol. 1, p. 182.

Chapter III

1. PRO FO 94/163 (01).
2. PRO ADM 1/19 (18).
3. ESPARTEIRO, Antônio Marques, *Três séculos no mar, (1640–1910)*, Lisbon, Ministério da Marinha, 1974–1987.
4. JACKSON, Sir William G F, *The Rock of the Gibraltarians*, 2nd edn, London, Ashford, Buchan & Enright, 1990, p. 203.
5. CALMON, Pedro, *História naval brasileira: a abertura dos portos*, Rio de Janeiro, Serviço de Documentação Geral da Marinha, 1979, vol. 2, p. 337.
6. Arthur Wellesley, 1768–1852, Duke of Wellington (England), Duke of Talavera (Spain), Duke of Vitória, Marquis of Torres Vedras and Count of Vimeira (Portugal), Prince of Waterloo (Low Countries), and Knight of the Order of the Garter (England) and of the Golden Fleece (Spain).
7. William Carr Beresford, 1768–1854, Viscount and Baron Beresford of Abuera and Cappoquin (England), Duke of Elvas (Spain), Count of Trancoso (Portugal),

Knight Grand Cross of the Order of the Bath (England), Knight of the Tower and Sword (Portugal) and of San Fernando (Spain).

8. LONGFORD, Elizabeth. *Wellington: the Years of the Sword*, London, Weidenfeld & Nicholson, 1969, pp. 232– 4.

9. George Canning, 1770–1827.

10. PRO FO 94/163 (01).

11. Ibid.

12. PRO FO 94/163 (02).

13. Sir William Sidney Smith, 1764–1840, Rear Admiral of the Blue. See Appendix A.

14. PRO ADM 1/19 (02).

15. PRO ADM 1/19 (02). Sir John Moore, 1761–1809. He was Captain Graham Moore's (HMS *Marlborough*) elder brother.

16. Captain Thomas Western, PRO ADM 1/19 (01).

17. She was broken up in 1811.

18. Captain John Conn, 1764–1810. At Trafalgar he captured the *Nepomuceno* by ramming her.

19. PRO ADM 1/19 (02).

20 KING, Dean, *A Sea of Words*, New York, Henry Holt & Co, 1995, p. 15.

21. O'BRIAN, Patrick, *Men-of-War: Life in Nelson's Navy*, New York, W W Norton & Company, 1974, p. 18.

22. Admiral Sir William Yong, 1751–1821.

23. *Gibraltar Chronicle*, 28 November 1807.

24. In the distance.

25. PRO ADM 1/19 (01).

26. William Wellesley-Pole, 1763–1845, Baron Maryborough (1821) and 3rd Earl of Mornington (1842).

27. DAVA, Sobel, *Longitude*: *The True Story of a Lone Genius who Solved the Greatest Scientific Problem of his Time,* New York, Walker & Company, 1995.

28. Sir Richard King 2nd Bart., 1774–1834. He became Rear Admiral (1812) and Vice-Admiral (1821).

29. SCHOM, *Trafalgar...*, p. 348.

30. PRO ADM 1/19 (03).

31. Cascais.

32. Cape Raso.

33. PRO ADM 1/19 (03).

34. PRO ADM 1/19 (03).

35. PRO ADM 1/19 (03).

36. MORAIS, *História da transladação...*, p. 7.

37. PRO ADM 1/19 (03).

38. PRO FO 63/56 (02).

Chapter IV

1. Captain Israel Pellow, 1758–1832. At Trafalgar Captain Pellow, commanding the *Conqueror*, sent a junior officer and five marines on board the French flagship, the *Buocentaure*, to accept the surrender of the combined French and Spanish fleets from Admiral Villeneuve – an unusual happening, to say the least.
2. PRO FO 63/56 (01).
3. PRO ADM 1/19 (03).
4. PRO ADM 1/19 (15).
5. PRO ADM 1/19 (03).
6. PRO ADM 4206 (01).
7. PRO ADM 1/19 (06).
8. PRO ADM 1/19 (06) and (14).
9. PRO ADM 1/19 (06). Distance.
10. PRO ADM 1/19 (06).
11. Lee or sheltered. A lee shore is, therefore, the dangerous shore downwind from a ship.
12. PRO ADM 1/19 (08).
13. PRO ADM 1/19 (06).
14. PRO ADM 1/19 (08).
15. PRO FO 63/56 (01).
16. PRO ADM 1/19 (04) and (09).
17. PRO ADM 1/19 (06).
18. PRO ADM 1/19 (06).
19. PRO FO 63/56 (01).
20. PRO ADM 1/19 (06).
21. PRO ADM 1/19 (10).
22. PRO FO 63/56 (01).
23. PRO FO 63/56 (01).
24. PRO FO 63/56 (01).
25. PRO FO 63/56 (01).
26. PRO ADM 1/19 (11).
27. PRO ADM 1/19 (12).
28. Sir James Lucas Yeo, 1782–1818.
29. O'NEIL, *A Concise and Accurate Account...*, p. 9.
30. PRO FO 63/56 (01).
31. PRO ADM 1/19 (13).
32. *Gibraltar Chronicle*, 2 January 1800. See Appendix C.
33. PRO ADM 1/19 (25). Captain Yeo might have become another of Britain's naval

heroes had he not died, in 1818, at the age of 36, from illness on a passage home from Jamaica.

34. BARROW, John, *The Life and Correspondence of Admiral Sir William Sidney Smith GCB*, London, Richard Bentley, 1848, vol. 2, p. 270.

35. The Russian squadron in the event was trapped in the Tagus through 1808. Eventually the ships were taken to England in custody and their crews sent back to Russia. At the end of the war the ships were returned.

36. PRO ADM 1/19 (07).

37. Certainly a challenge, but not of a belligerent nature.

38. The comradeship existing between seamen when their needs were paramount was absolute. However in battle, no holds were barred.

39. ROSSI, *Memória sobre a evasão do Núncio Apostólico...*, p. 21.

40. PEREIRA, *D. João VI príncipe e rei...*, vol. 1, p. 182.

41. PEREIRA, *D. João VI príncipe e rei...*, vol. 1, p. 112.

42. PEREIRA, *Os filhos D'El Rei D. João VI*, p. 112.

43. MONTEIRO, *História do Império...*, p. 39.

44. PRO ADM 1/19 (17).

45. ESPARTEIRO, *História naval brasileira...*, p. 331.

46. PEREIRA, *D. João VI príncipe e rei...*, vol. 1, p. 190.

47. MOORE, Sir Graham, Diary Manuscript: ADD 9303/17 to 21, Cambridge, University Library Cambridge, 1807.

CHAPTER V

1. O'NEIL, *A Concise and Accurate Account...*, p. 25.

2. PRO ADM 1/19 (19).

3. D. Pedro Carlos, 1787–1812, Infante of Spain. See Appendix A.

4. D. Carlota Joaquina's six daughters were: D. Maria Teresa, 1793–1874, married her first cousin, Infante D. Pedro Carlos and subsequently her uncle and brother-in-law, D. Carlos V, 1788–1855 'Carlist King of Spain'; D. Maria Isabel Francisca, 1797–1818, married D. Fernando VII, 1784–1833, King of Spain; D. Maria Francisca de Assis, 1800–1834, 1st wife of D. Carlos V, 'Carlist King of Spain'; D. Isabel Maria, 1801–1876, Regent of Portugal, 1826–1828; D. Maria da Assunção, 1805–1834; D. Ana de Jesus, 1806–1857, married the Duke of Loulé.

5. D. Maria Ana, 1736–1813, daughter of D. José I and D. Maria Ana Vitória de Bourbon.

6. ESPARTEIRO, *História naval brasileira...*, p. 325.

7. PRO ADM 1/19 (19).

8. PRO FO 63/56 (01).

9. O'NEIL, *A Concise and Accurate Account...*, p. 34.

10. MACAULAY, Neill, *Dom Pedro: a luta pela liberdade no Brasil e em Portugal*

1798–1834, Rio de Janeiro, Record, 1993, p. 344.

11. PRO FO 63/56 (01).

12. NAPIER, W E, *History of the War in the Peninsular*, London, Constable, 1828. Macaulay, in *Dom Pedro I: a luta pela liberdade*, p. 345, writes that considerable public discussion on the matter took place in London, following the publication of the pamphlet, *A Sketch of the Causes and Consequences of the Late Emigration to the Brazils*, by Ralph Rylance's and the August 1808 issue of Hipolito da Costa's, *Correio Braziliense*. Angelo Pereira, in *Os filhos D'El Rei D. João VI*, p. 104, publishes an anonymous letter written by a Portuguese, previously in the private archives of D. João VI. The letter denies that the initiative for the voyage lay with the British government; it was written following a discussion in the press, in October 1814, principally in the *Morning Chronicle*. Tobias Monteiro, in *História do Império*, pp. 44–7, argues that Lord Strangford's merit is not in persuading the Prince Regent to leave, but in convincing him, once on board, to proceed with the journey. As already mentioned, Lord Strangford did not meet the Prince Regent on the night of the 28th.

13. Vice-Admiral Manuel Da Cunha Souto Maior.

14. PRO ADM 1/19 (19).

15. PRO ADM 1/19 (19).

16. PRO ADM 1/19 (19).

17. PRO ADM 1/19 (19).

18. PRO ADM 1/19 (19).

19. O'NEIL, *A Concise and Accurate Account...*, p. 24.

20. PRO ADM 1/19 (19).

21. ANONYMO, *Observador portuguez histórico, e político de Lisboa desde o dia 27 de novembro do anno de 1807 em que embarcacou para o Brazil o Príncipe Regente Nosso Senhor e toda a real família, por motivo da invasão dos francezes neste Reino etc. Contém todos os editaes ,ordens públicas e particulares, decretos, sucessos fataes e desconhecidos nas histórias do mundo; todas as batalhas, roubos e usurpações até o dia 15 de setembro de 1808, em que foram expulsos, depois de batidos, os francezes – Offerecido Ao Illustrissimo e Excellentissimo Senhor D. Rodrigo de Souza Coutinho, conde de Linhares, Grão Cruz das Ordens de Aviz e da Torre e Espada etc.*, Lisbon, Impressão Régia, 1809, p. 19.

22. PEREIRA, *D. João VI príncipe e rei...*, vol. 1, p. 186.

23. National Archive, Code 730, Rio de Janeiro.

24. Letter from Count of Limires dated 26 March 1808, Imperial Museum Historic Archive, Petrópolis, R J.

25. PORTELA, Joaquin Pires Machado, *Chegada da família real portugueza à província da Bahia em janeiro de 1808*. Comunication dated 7 January 1808 from the Count of Ponte to the Count of Arcos. Journal of the Instituto Histórico e

Geográfico Brasileiro, Rio de Janeiro, 1882.

26. National Archive, Code 730, Rio de Janeiro.
27. NEVES, *História geral da invasão...*, p. 181.
28. PEREIRA, *D. João VI príncipe e rei...*, vol. 1, p. 184. Letter from D. Araújo to D. João VI dated 25 January 1808 informing him that this ship was at Recife and that several ships of the squadron had been seen at St Tiago.
29. BOITEAUX, *A Marinha de guerra brasileira...*, p. 13.
30. ANONYMO, *Observador portuguez...*, p. 7.
31. BARROW, *The life and correspondence...*, p. 269.
32. GRAHAM, *Journal of the Voyage to Brazil...*, p. 45.
33. PRO ADM 1/19 (19).
34. ESPARTEIRO, *História naval brasileira...*, p. 331.
35. ANONYMO, *Observador portuguez...*, p. 22.
36. BRANDÃO, *El-Rei Junot*, p. 144.
37. PRO ADM 1/19 (19).
38. In fact the decision had been made, but they would only reach their station on 8 December.
39. PRO ADM 1/19 (19).
40. PEREIRA, *D. João VI príncipe e rei...*, vol. 1, p. 183.
41. Captain the Hon Henry Curzon of HMS *Elizabeth*.
42. PRO ADM 1/19 (25).
43. PRO ADM 1/19 (25).
44. See Appendix C.
45. See APRO ADM 1/824 (02).Appendix C.
46. PRO ADM 1/824 (02).
47. National Archive, Code 730, Rio de Janeiro.
48. PRO ADM 1/824 (01).
49. Cape Verde Isles.
50. PEREIRA, *Os filhos D'El Rei...*, p. 115.
51. POB (16).
52. SOARES, Joaquim Pedro Celestino, *Quadros Navaes,* 2nd edn, Lisbon, Imprensa Nacional, 1961, pp. 123–4; ESPARTEIRO, *História naval brasileira...*, pp. 332–3.
53. PRO ADM 1/2159 (01).
54. MOORE, Sir Graham, Diaries, ADD 9303/17–21, Cambridge University Library, Cambridge, mn.
55. PRO ADM 1/2159 (01).
56. RANGEL, Alberto, *Os dois ingleses, Strangford e Stuart*, Rio de Janeiro, Conselho Federal de Cultura, Arquivo Nacional, 1972, p. 7.
57. PRO FO 63/58 (05).

Chapter VI

1. D. João Manuel de Meneses, 1783–1831, 1st Count (1810) and 1st Marquis of Viana (1821). See Appendix A.
2. PRO ADM 1/2704 (01).
3. PRO ADM 1/2704 (01).
4. PRO ADM 1/2704 (01).
5. PRO ADM 1/2704 (01).
6. PRO ADM 1/2704 (01).
7. From the logbook of the frigate *Urânia*.
8. PRO ADM 1/2704 (01).
9. Ibid.
10. MORAIS, *História da transladação...*, p. 65.
11. BOITEAUX, *A Marinha de Guerra brasileira...*, p. 14.
12. The logbook of the *Urânia* records that the salutes started the night before.
13. PRO ADM 1/2704 (01).
14. Ibid.
15. PRO ADM 1/2704 (01).
16. PRO ADM 1/2704 (01).
17. PEREIRA, *D. João VI príncipe e rei...*, vol. 1, p. 184.
18. Old and useless rope, cut up for oakum; the material used, with melted pitch, to stop up seams (caulk).
19. PRO ADM 1/2704 (02).
20. MONTEIRO, *História do Império...*, p. 59.
21. A degree is equivalent to 60 miles.
22. PORTELLA, *Chegada da família real...*, p. 7. See Appendix C.
23. D. João de Saldanha da Gama Mello Torres Guedes de Brito, 1773–1809, 6th Count of Ponte (1802). See Appendix A.
24. D. Marcos Noronha de Brito, 1771–1828, 8th Count of Arcos of Val-de-Vez. See Appendix A.
25. PRO ADM 1/2704 (01).
26. PRO ADM 1/2704 (02).
27. Caetano Pinto de Miranda Montenegro, Governor of Pernambuco, 1804–1817.
28. Queen Charlotte, 1744–1818, wife of HM George III.
29. PRO ADM 1/2704 (02).
30. See Appendix C for complete dispatches.
31. ESPARTEIRO, *História naval brasileira...*, p. 333.
32. PRO ADM 1/2159 (01).
33. PEREIRA, *D. João VI príncipe e rei...*, vol. 1, p. 184. Letter dated 25 January from D. Araújo to the Prince Regent.
34. ESPARTEIRO, *História naval brasileira...*, p. 333.

35. Commanded by Captain Henrique da Fonseca de Sousa Prego.

36. PEREIRA, *D. João VI príncipe e rei...*, vol. 1, p. 184.

37. Ibid.

38. PRO ADM 1/2704 (02).

39. Ibid.

40. National Archive, Code 730, Rio de Janeiro.

41. FAZENDA, José Vieira, *Antiqualhas e memórias: transladação da família real*, Journal of the Instituto Histórico e Geográfico Brasileiro, Rio de Janeiro, 1923 vol. 147, p. 531.

42. PRO ADM 1/2704 (02).

43. See Appendix C.

44. *Journal of the Imperial Senate of Brazil*, Rio de Janeiro, National Press, 1826. vol. 3, p. 99.

45. PRO ADM 1/2704 (02).

46. O'NEIL, *A Concise and Accurate Account...*, p. 33.

47. *COLLECÇÃO das Leis do Brazil de 1808*. Decree of 13 May 1808, Rio de Janeiro, Imprensa Nacional, 1891, p. 28. On 29 November 1808 the detailed regulations of the Order were published in *Collecção das Leis...*, p. 167–70. See Appendix C.

48. PRO ADM 1/2704 (02).

49. The letters have written in the margin, in a different handwriting, '10 May Own Rec. and approve of this proceedings'; PRO ADM 1/2704 (01).

50. PRO ADM 1/2159 (01).

51. D. Miguel Caetano Alvares Pereira de Melo, 1765–1808, 5th Duke of Cadaval, 7th Marquis of Ferreira and 8th Count of Tentúgal. See Appendix A.

52. Pereira, *D. João VI príncipe e rei...*, vol. 1, p. 185.

Chapter VII

1. PRO ADM 1/2159 (01).

2. Ibid.

3. PRO ADM 1/2159 (01).

4. Captain Francisco Manuel de Souto Maior.

5. Captain José Maria de Almeida.

6. PRO ADM 1/2159 (01).

7. National Archive, Code 730, Rio de Janeiro.

8. PRO ADM 1/2159 (01).

9. MOORE, *Diaries mn*, ADD 9303/1–21.

10. ESPARTEIRO, *História naval brasileira...*, p. 330.

11. O'NEIL, *A Concise and Accurate Account...*, pp. 26–30.

12. In fact this was more than sufficient information to identity her. Also her log will

have recorded the encounter taking place.

13. PRO ADM 1/19 (24).
14. National Archive, Code 730, Rio de Janeiro.
15. PRO ADM 1/2159 (01).
16. ESPARTEIRO, *História naval brasileira...*, p. 329.
17. PRO ADM 1/2159 (01).
18. Ibid.
19. PRO ADM 1/2159 (01).
20. National Archive, Code 730, Rio de Janeiro.
21. ESPARTEIRO, *História naval brasileira...*, p. 334.
22. PRO ADM 1/19 (26).
23. National Archive, Code 730, Rio de Janeiro.
24. According to Commodore Moore's report to the Admiralty dated 9 March, news of the safe arrival in St Salvador reached Rio de Janeiro on 12 February. As no ship is recorded coming in on that date, presumably the news came in with a brig of war on the 11th.
25. SANTOS, Luiz Gonçalves dos, *Memórias para servir à história do Reino do Brasil*, ed Edusp, São Paulo, Itatiaia, 1981, pp. 13–14.
26. A 68-foot long boat, usually carrying a crew of 40.
27. PRO ADM 1/2159 (01).
28. O'NEIL, *A Concise and Accurate Account...*, pp. 35–6.
29. SANTOS, *Memórias para servir à história...*, p. 20.
30. PRO ADM 1/2159 (01).
31. SANTOS, *Memórias para servir à história...*, p.32.

CHAPTER VIII

1. MONTEIRO, *História do Império...*, pp. 50 –1.
2. Ibid. p. 51.
3. ANONYMO, *Observador português...*, pp. 19–22. This diary of an anonymous observer, published in 1809, gives us a first-hand account of what life was like under the yoke of Junot. Unless otherwise stated, all references are to this diary.
4. NEVES, *História geral da invasão dos franceses...*, p. 205.
5. See Appendix C.
6. Ibid.
7. ROSSI, *Memória sobre a evasão do Nuncio Apostólico...*, p. 24–41.
8. CHAMBERS, J W, *Lisbon in Wartime, 1807*, Journal of the British Historical Society of Portugal, Lisbon, 1984.
9. See Appendix C.
10. This event may have been the one referred to by Boiteaux, *A Marinha de Guerra brasileira...*, p. 13.

11. See Appendix C.
12. See Appendix C.
13. CHAMBERS, *Lisbon in Wartime...*, p. 27.

CHAPTER IX

1. Sir Charles Cotton, 1753–1812; entered the navy (1772), succeeded to the baronetcy (1795), promoted to Rear Admiral (1797) and Vice-Admiral (1802). Commander-in-Chief in the Tagus (1808) and of the Channel fleet (1811).
2. BARROW, *The life and correspondence...*, p. 281. The writer is mistaken, as Sir Sidney sailed on the *Foudroyant*.
3. PRO ADM 1/2519 (02).
4. Under the command of Captain Jonas Rose.
5. In honour of the Spanish Infante D. Pedro Carlos.
6. O'NEIL, *A Concise and Accurate Account...*, p. 41–7.
7. NAVAL CHRONICLE, London, 1808, vol. 20, p. 438.
8. ARAÚJO, José Paulo de Figueirôa Nabuco, *Legislação brazileira ou colecção chronológica das leis, decretos, resoluçoes de consulta, procisões etc.*, Rio de Janeiro, [s.n.], 1836, p. 75.
9. BARROW, *The life and correspondence...*, p. 277. Letter from the Rt Hon W W Pole to Sir Sidney Smith, Admiralty Office, 28 December 1807.
10. MORAIS, *História da transladação...*, p. 88.
11. RANGEL, *Os dois inglezes Strangford e Stuart*, pp. 44–113.

APPENDIX A

1. Unless otherwise stated the sources used were: PINTO, Albano da Silveira, *Resenha das familias titulares e grandes de Portugal*, Lisbon, Arthur da Silva, 1883, 2 vols.; and FREIRE, Anselmo Braacamp, *Brasões de sala de Cintra*, Coimbra, Imprensa da Universidade, 1921.
2. Portugal never introduced the 'salic' law. Consequently females were not excluded from dynastic succession.
3. RANGEL, *Os dois inglezes. Strangford e Stuart*, p. 5–7.
4. NORONHA, *Pina Manique...*, p. 230; TAVARES, Adérito; and PINTO, José dos Santos, *Pina Manique: um homem entre duas épocas*, Lisbon, Casa Pia de Lisboa, 1990.
5. PEREIRA, *D. João VI príncipe e rei...*, vol. 1, p. 142.
6. Ibid. Publishes a letter on p. 147, from D. Lourenço de Lima (dated 2 September 1806) to his cousin, Count of Villa Verde, subsequent to a meeting with M. de Talleyrand on 15 August, and with the Emperor on the 26th.
7. Ibid. pp. 143–145, op. cit. Letters from D. Lourenço de Lima to the Count of Palmela, asking for help (dated 13 October 1818), and from the Count of Palmela

to D. João, dated 17 November 1818, explaining the measures taken, and asking for his approval.

8. CHAGAS, Manuel Pinheiro, *Diccionario Popular*, Lisbon, Typ. Lallement Frères, 1883.

9. BECKFORD, William, *Recollections of an Excursion to Alcobaça and Batalha*, Paris, Societé des Éditions Lês Belles Lettres, 1956, p. 228. Probably not true; Beckford may have felt jealous, as at that time he was, supposedly, having an amorous affair with the young marquis. In any case D. Miguel was born in 1802!

10. ROSSI, *Memória sobre a evasão do nuncio apostólico...*, p. 6–11.

11. George Brydges, Lord Rodney, Admiral of the White, 1718–1792.

12. Today Akko, in Israel.

13. Admiral Sir H W Richmond, 2nd Earl Spencer, First Lord of the Admiralty, 1794–1801.

14. Sir John Knox Laughton, Lord Barham, 1758–1813.

15. GRAHAM, Gerald S, HUMPHREYS, R A, *The Navy and South America 1807–1823*, London, Navy Records Society, 1962, p. 3.

16. NAVAL CHRONICLE, London, 1808, vol. 20, p. 438. For a romantic description of the investiture, see O'NEIL, *A Concise and Accurate Account...*, pp. 4–7.

17. ARAÚJO, *Legislação Brazileira...*, p. 75.

18. GRAHAM, *The Navy and South America...*, p. 3.

19. Ibid.

20. *THE NATIONAL DICTIONARY OF BIOGRAPHY*, London, 1903, p. 800.

Appendix B

1. ESPARTEIRO, *Três séculos no mar: 1640-1910* and *História naval brasileira: A viagem*, pp. 326–330.

2. LAVERY, Brian, *Nelson's Navy: the Ships, Men and Organisation*, London, Conway Maritime Press, 1993, p. 187. Lavery gives, for the British navy during the period 1793–1815, these incredible figures: losses due to disease and individual accidents 70,000 to 80,000; losses due to shipwreck and fire 13,000; losses due to enemy action 6,500.

3. Not included in list given by Squadron Major-General and Chief of Division Joaquin José Monteiro Torres to Sir Sydney Smith; also the *Boa Ventura, Condessa de Resende, Furão and Ninfa,* but recorded by Esparteiro, Historia naval brasileira ..., p.330

4. LYONS, David, *Sailing Navy List*, Navy List, London, 1993 and 1807.

Appendix C

1. MORAIS, *História da transladação...*, p. 74.
2. ANONYMO, *Observador portuguez...*, p. 9.
3. CASTRO, *Colecção de tratados...*, pp. 236–62; PRO FO 94/163 (01).
4. MARTINS, *Conselho de Estado português...*, pp. 70–1.
5. ANONYMO, *Observador portuguez...*, p. 15.
6. PRO London ADM 1/19 (20).
7. PRO London ADM 1/19 (21).
8. PORTELA, *Chegada da família real...*, pp. 7–8.
9. PORTELA, *Chegada da família real...*, pp. 8–10.
10. PORTELLA, *Chegada da família real...*, pp. 10–11.
11. *COLLEÇÃO das leis do Brazil...*, pp. 28–9.
12. ANONYMO, *Obeservador portuguez...*, p. 20.
13. Ibid. p. 20.
14. ANONYMO, *Obeservador portuguez,...* p. 25.
15. ANONYMO, *Obeservador portuguez...*, pp. 151–5.
16. Ibid. p. 161.
17. ARAÚJO, *Legislação brazileira...*, p. 75.

Bibliography

AlmeidA, João Ricardo Pires de, *D. João rei de Portugal e dos Algarves e imperador titular do Brasil: elogio histórico*, Edição comemorativa, Rio de Janeiro, 1885.

Anonymo, *Observador portuguez histórico, e político de Lisboa desde o dia 27 de Novembro do anno de 1807 em que embarcou para o Brazil O Príncipe Regente Nosso Senhor e toda a real família, por motivo da Invasão dos francezes neste Reino etc. – Contém Todos os editaes, ordens publicas e particulares, decretos, successos fataes e desconhecidos nas histórias do mundo; todas as batalhas, roubos e usurpações até o dia 15 de setembro de 1808, em que foram expulsos, depois de batidos, os francezes –offerecido Ao Ilustríssimo e Execellentíssimo Senhor D. Rodrigo de Souza Coutinho, Conde de Linhares, Grã Cruz das Ordens de Aviz e da Torre e Espada etc.*, Lisbon, Impressa Regia, 1809.

Araújo, José Paulo de Figueirôa Nabuco, *Legislação brazileira ou collecção chronologica das leis, decretos, resoluções de consulta, procisões etc.*, Rio de Janeiro, [s.n.], 1836.

Azevedo, Manoel Duarte Moreira de, *No tempo do rei: conto histórico*, Rio de Janeiro, Azevedo, 1899.

Barrow, John, *The life and Correspondence of Admiral Sir William Sidney Smith GCB*, London, Richard Bentley, 1848, 2 vols.

Beckford, William, *A corte da rainha D. Maria I: correspondência de W. Beckford (1787)*, Lisbon, Tavares Cardoso & Irmão, 1901.

_____ *Recollections of an Excursion to Alcobaça and Batalha*, Paris, Société des Éditions Les Belles Letres, 1956, [1st edn], 1840.

_____ *The journal of William Beckford in Portugal and Spain 1787–1788*. ed. with introduction and notes by Alexander Boyd, London, Rupert-Hart Davis, 1954.

Beirão, Caetano, *História breve de Portugal*, Lisbon, Editorial Verbo, 1941.

Bellegarde, Henrique Luiz de Niemeyer, *Resumo da história do Brasil*, Rio de Janeiro, Typografia de J E S Cabral, 1845.

Boiteaux, Lucas Alexandre, *A Marinha de Guerra brasileira nos reinados de D. João VI e D. Pedro I*, Rio de Janeiro, Imprensa Nacional, 1913.

Brandão, Raul, *El-Rei Junot*, Lisbon, Monteiro & Cia, 1912.

Calmon, Pedro, *História naval brasileira: a abertura dos portos*, Rio de Janeiro, Serviço de Documentação Geral da Marinha, 1979, vol 2.

Calmon, Pedro, *O rei do Brasil: vida de D. João VI*, Rio de Janeiro, J Olympio, 1935.

Cancio, Henrique, *D. João VI*, Bahia, Diário da Bahia, 1909.

Castro, José Ferreira Borges de, *Collecção de tratados, convenções, contratos e actos públicos celebrados entre a coroa de Portugal e as mais potências desde 1640 até ao presente*, Lisbon, Imprensa Nacional, 1856–1858.

Chagas, Manoel Pinheiro, *Dicionário popular*, Lisbon, Typ. Lallement Frères, 1883, 14 vols.

Chambers, J W, *Lisbon in Wartime 1807*, Journal of The British Historical Society of Portugal, Lisbon, 1984.

Cheke, Marcus, *Carlota Joaquina: Queen of Portugal*, New York, Sidwick & Jackson, 1947.

Cintra, Assis, *Rei Fujão*, Rio de Janeiro, [s.n.], 1935.

Collecção das Leis do Brazil de 1808, Rio de Janeiro, Imprensa Nacional, 1891.

Constancio, Francisco Solano, *História do Brasil desde o seu Descobrimento por Pedro Alvares Cabral até a abdicação do Imperador D. Pedro I*, Paris, Livraria Portuguesa, 1839.

Denis, Ferdinand, *Résumé de l'histoire du Brésil*, 2nd edn, Paris, Lecointe et Durey, 1825.

Durant, Will; Durant, Ariel, *The Story of Civilization: the Age of Napoleon*, New York, Simon & Schuster, 1975, 11 vols.

Esparteiro, Antônio Marques, *História naval brasileira: a viagem*, Rio de Janeiro, Serviço de Documentação Geral da Marinha, 1979, vol. 2

_____ *Subsídios para a história da Marinha de Guerra: nau Rainha de Portugal*. Anais do Clube Naval, Lisbon, 1943.

_____ *Três séculos no mar, 1640–1910*, Lisbon, Ministério da Marinha, 1974–1987, 30 vols.

Fazenda, José Vieira, *Antiqualhas e memórias: chegada da família real*, Revista do Instituto Histórico e Geográfico Brasileiro vol. 142, Rio de Janeiro, 1920.

Fazenda, José Vieira, *Antiqualhas e memórias: trasladação da família real*, Revista do Instituto Histórico e Geográfico Brasileiro vol. 147, Rio de Janeiro, 1923.

Freire, Anselmo Braacamp, *Brasões de sala de Cintra*, Coimbra, Imprensa da Universidade, 1921, 3 vols.

Graham, Maria, *Journal of Voyage to Brazil and Residence There During Part of the Years 1821, 1822, 1823*, London, Longman Hurst, 1824.

Graham, Gerald S; Humphries, R A, *The Navy and South America 1807–1823*, London, Navy Records Society, 1962.

Horward, Donald D, *Portugal and the Anglo-Russian Naval Crisis (1808)*. Naval War College Review, Newport RI, Naval War College, 1981.

Imprensa Nacional, *Collecção das Leis do Brazil de 1808*, Rio de Janeiro, 1891.

Jackson, Sir William G F, *The Rock of*

the Gibraltarians. 2nd edn, London, Ashford, Buchan & Enright, 1990.

Journal of the Imperial Senate of Brazil, Rio de Janeiro, National Press, 1826.

Junot, Laure Saint-Martin [Duchesse d'Abrantès], At the Court of Napoleon: Memoirs of the Duchesse d'Abrantès, London, Windrush Press, 1991.

_____ Souvenirs d'une Ambassade, Paris, [s.n.], 1834, 18 vols.

King, Dean, A Sea of Words, New York, Henry Holt & Co, 1995.

Lavery, Brian, Nelson's Navy: the Ships, Men and Organisation, London, Conway Maritime Press, 1989.

Light, Kenneth H, The Migration of the Royal Family of Portugal to Brazil 1807–1808, Logbooks of HM Ships before the Tagus in November 1807 and of those that took part in the Voyage to Brazil, together with Reports and Letters from Captain James Walker of HMS Bedford, who Escorted the Queen and the Prince Regent to Bahia, and Commodore Graham Moore of HMS Marlborough, who Escorted the Portuguese Fleet to Rio de Janeiro, Rio de Janeiro, Private printing by Kenneth H Light, 1995.

Lima, Alexandre de Azevedo, Termos náuticos em português e em inglês, Rio de Janeiro, Imprensa Naval, 1935, vol. 1.

_____ Termos náuticos em português e em inglês, 2nd edn, Rio de Janeiro, Imprensa Naval, 1939, vol. 2.

_____ Compêndio da história do Brasil, Rio de Janeiro, Laemmert, 1843.

_____ Synopsis ou deducção chronologica dos fatos mais notáveis da história do Brasil, Recife, Typ. De M F De Faria, 1845.

LIMA, Manuel de Oliveira, Dom João VI no Brazil, 1808–1821, Rio de Janeiro, Typ. do Jornal do Commercio, 1908.

Longford, Elizabeth, Wellington: The Years of the Sword, London, Weidenfeld & Nicholson, 1969.

Lyons, David, Sailing Navy List, London, National Maritime Museum, 1993. [Navy List of 1807].

Macaulay, Neill, Dom Pedro I: a luta pela liberdade no Brasil e em Portugal (1798–1834), Rio de Janeiro, Record, 1993.

Macedo, Joaquim Manoel de, Lições de história do Brasil para uso dos alunos do Imperial Colégio Pedro Segundo, Rio de Janeiro, Domingos José Gomes Brandão, 1863.

Madelin, Louis, Histoire du Consolat et de l'Empire: L'Affaire D'Espagne, Paris, Hachette, 1958, vol. 7.

Manchester, Alan K, A transferência da corte portuguesa para o Rio de Janeiro. Journal of the Instituto Histórico e Geográfico Brasileiro, Rio de Janeiro, 1968, vol. 277.

Martins, Enéas Filho, O Conselho de Estado português e a transmigração da família real em 1807, Rio de Janeiro, Arquivo Nacional, 1968.

Martins, Joaquim Pedro de Oliveira, História de Portugal, 9th edn, Lisbon, Parceria Antonio Maria Pereira, 1991, [1st edn 1879].

Monteiro, Tobias, História do Império: a elaboração da independência, Rio de Janeiro, F Briguet, 1927. 2 vols.

Moore, Sir Graham, *Diaries, ADD 9303/17–21*, Cambridge University Library, Cambridge, mn.

Morais, A J de Melo, *A Independência e o Império do Brasil*, Rio de Janeiro, Typ. O Globo, 1877.

_____ *Chorographia Histórica*, Rio de Janeiro, Typ. De Pinheiro & Co, 1863, 2 vols.

_____ *História da trasladação da corte portuguesa para o Brasil em 1807–1808*, Rio de Janeiro, E Dupont, 1872.

Napier, W E, *History of the War in the Peninsula*, London, Constable, 1828, 4 vols.

Naval Chronicle, London, 1808, vol. 20, p. 438.

Neves, José Acursio das, *História geral da invasão dos francezes em Portugal e da restauração deste reino*, Oporto, Edições Afrontamento, 1984. 5 vols.

Noronha, Eduardo de, *Pina Manique: o intendente de antes quebrar…*, Oporto, Livraria Civilização Editora, 1940.

O'Brian, Patrick, *Men-of-War: Life in Nelson's Navy*, New York. W W Norton & Company, 1995.

O'Neil, Lieutenant Count Thomas, *A Concise and Accurate Account of the Proceedings of the Squadron under the Command of Rear Admiral Sir Sidney Smith KS&c in effecting the Escape of the Royal Family of Portugal to the Brazils on 29 November 1807; and also the Sufferings of the Royal Fugitives etc. during their Voyage from Lisbon to Rio Janeiro: with a Variety of other Interesting and Authentic Facts*, London, J Barfield, 1810.

Pereira, Angelo, *As senhoras infantas filhas de El Rei D. João VI*, Lisbon, Editorial Labor, 1938.

_____ *D. João VI príncipe e rei: A retirada da família real para o Brasil*, Lisbon, Empresa Nacional de Publicidade, 1953, vol. 1.

_____ *D. João VI príncipe e rei: A bastarda*, Lisbon, Empresa Nacional de Publicidade, 1955, vol. 2.

Pereira, Angelo, *D. João VI príncipe e rei: A Independência do Brasil*. Lisbon, Empresa Nacional de Publicidade, 1956, vol. 3.

_____ *João VI príncipe e rei: Últimos anos dum reinado tormentoso*, Lisbon, Empresa Nacional de Publicidade, 1958, vol. 4.

_____ *Os filhos D'El Rei D. João VI*, Lisbon, Empresa Nacional de Publicidade, 1946.

Pinheiro, José Pedro Xavier, *Epítome da história do Brasil desde o seu descobrimento*, Rio de Janeiro, Typ. Universal de Laemmert, 1870. 2 vols.

Pinto, Albano da Silveira, *Resenha das famílias titulares e grandes de Portugal*, Lisbon, Arthur da Silva, 1883. 2 vols.

Portella, Joaquim Pires Machado, *Chegada da família real portugueza à província da Bahia em Janeiro de 1808*. Revista do Instituto Histórico e Geográfico Brasileiro vol. 65, Rio de Janeiro, 1882.

Rangel, Alberto, *Inventário dos documentos do arquivo da Casa Imperial do Brasil existentes no Castelo d'Eu* [lodged in the Imperial Museum, Petrópolis], Rio de Janeiro, Serviço Gráfico do Ministério da Educação e Saúde, 1939, 2 vols.

_____, *Os dois ingleses: Strangford e Stuart*, Rio de Janeiro, Conselho Federal de Cultura, Arquivo Nacional, 1972.

Rio Seco, Visconde de, *Exposição analytica e justificativa da conducta, e vida publica do Visconde do Rio Seco desde o dia 25 de Novembro de 1807*, MM Museu Imperial, Petrópolis, 1821.

Rodrigues, J C, *Catalogo annotado dos livros sobre o Brasil e de alguns autographos e manuscriptos pertencentes a J C Rodrigues*, Part. 1: *descobrimento da América, Brasil colonial, 1492–1822*, Rio de Janeiro, Typ. do Jornal do Commercio, 1907.

Rossi, Camilo Luís de, *Memória sobre a evasão do núncio apostólico Monsenhor Caleppi, da corte de Lisboa para o Rio de Janeiro*. ed. by Dr. Jerônimo de Avelar Figueira de Melo,, Rio de Janeiro, Anais da Biblioteca Nacional, 1939, v. 61. [Document originally translated from the Secret Archive of the Vatican no.143].

Russell, E F L, *Knight of the sword*: *Sir W S Smith*, London, Victor Gallancz, 1964.

Sá, José D'Almeida Corrêa de, *D. João João VI e a independência do Brasil*, Lisbon, Artes Gráficas, 1937.

Santos, Luiz Gonçalves dos, *Memórias para servir à história do Reino do Brasil*, ed. Edusp, São Paulo Itatiaia, 1981. 2 vols.

Schom, Alan, *Trafalgar: Countdown to Battle*, London, Penguin, 1990.

Silva, J M Pereira da, *História da fundação do Império brasileiro*, Rio de

Janeiro, Garnier, 1864. 7 vols.

Soares, Joaquim Pedro Celestino, *Quadros navaes*, 2nd edn, Lisbon, Imprensa Nacional, 1961.

Sobel, Dava, *Longitude: the True Story of a Lone Genius who solved the Greatest Scientific Problem of his Time*, New York, Walker & Company, 1995.

Soriano, Simão José da Luz, *História da guerra civil*, Lisbon, Imprensa Nacional, 1866–1893, vol. 2, 15 vols.

Sousa, Octávio Tarquíno de, *A vida de D.Pedro I*, Rio de Janeiro, J Olympio, 1952, 3 vols.

Souza, Antonio Caetano de, *Memórias dos grandes de Portugal*, Lisbon, Sylviana, 1754.

Tavares, Adérito; Pinto, José dos Santos, *Pina Manique*: *um homem entre duas épocas*, Lisboa, Casa Pia de Lisboa, 1990.

The National Dictionary Of Biography, London, 1903

Thiers, Louis-Adollphe, *Histoire du Consulat et de l'Empire*, Paris, [s. n.], 1845–1862, 19 vols.

Varnhagen, Francisco Adolpho de, *História geral do Brasil*, 3rd edn, São Paulo, Melhoramentos, 1927–1936, 5 vols.

Vidal, Frederick Gavazzo Perry, *Genealogias Reaes Portuguesas: descendência de S. M. El-Rei o Senhor Dom João VI*, Lisbon, Guimarães & Cia, 1923.

Züquete, Afonso Eduardo Martins, *Nobreza de Portugal e do Brasil*, Lisbon, Editorial Enciclopédia, 1960, 3 vols.

Principal Sources

Maritime Records, Lisbon
Log Book of the Frigate *Urânia*.

Imperial Museum, Petrópolis
Archives of the Imperial House of
Brazil - POB

1 Correspondence dated 27 October 1807, I. POB 7.10.1807 Barb/m1.
2 Correspondence dated Belém, 15 August 1807, D. Araújo/José Egidio, I. POB 7.10.1807 Aze C2.
3 Correspondence dated 24 August 1807, D. Araújo/José Egidio, I. POB 7.8.1807 Aze C6.
4 Correspondence dated 24 October 1807 D. Araújo/José Egidio, II. POB 20.1.1807 Aze C2.
5 Correspondence dated 27 October 1807, D. Araújo/José Egidio, II. POB 20.1.1807 Aze C5.
6 Correspondence undated, D. Araújo/José Egidio, II. POB 20.10.1807 Aze C1.
7 Correspondence dated Belém, 31 October 1807, D. Araújo/José Egidio, II. POB 20.1.1807 Aze C7.
8 Correspondence dated S. João dos Bemcarados, 30 October 1807, D. Araújo/José Egidio, II. POB 20.1.1807 Aze C6.
9 Correspondence dated S. João dos Bemcarados, 30 October 1807, D. Araújo/José Egidio, II. POB 20.1.1807 Aze C6.
10 Correspondence dated Belém, 31 October 1807, D. Araújo/José Egidio, II. POB 20.1.1807 Aze C7.
11 Correspondence dated Belém, 5 November 1807, II. POB 20.1.1807 Aze C8.
12 Correspondence dated S. João dos Bemcarados, 30 October 1807, D. Araújo/José Egidio, II. POB 20.1.1807 Aze C6.
13 Correspondence undated, D. Araújo/José Egidio, II. POB 20.1.1807 Aze C1.
14 MS Original II. POB 5.10.1821 Aze m.
15 Report dated 5 October 1821 published by Viscount Rio Seco, II. POB 5.10.1821 Aze m.
16 Document I POB (1807), J. VI P.c.

National Records Office, Rio de Janeiro
Code 730

Public Records Office, London
Foreign Office FO 63/55

1 Lord Strangford to the Rt Hon George Canning, Lisbon, 25 July 1807, Nº 42, by the *Auckland* Packet.

2 Lord Strangford to the Rt Hon George Canning, Lisbon, 2 August 1807, Nº 43, by the *Elizabeth* Packet.

3 Lord Strangford to the Rt Hon George Canning, Lisbon, 13 August 1807, Nº 46, by the *Walsingham* Packet.

4 Lord Strangord to the Rt Hon George Canning, Lisbon, 20 August 1807, Nº 47, by the Cutter *Cheerful*.

5 Lord Strangford to the Rt Hon George Canning, Lisbon, 21 August 1807, Nº 48, by the Cutter *Cheerful*.

6 Lord Strangford to the Rt Hon George Canning, Lisbon, 29 August 1807, Nº 51, by the *Townsend* Packet.

7 Lord Strangford to the Rt Hon George Canning, Lisbon, 8 September 1807, Nº 54, by the *Auckland* Packet, secret and confidential.

8 Lord Strangford to the Rt Hon George Canning, Lisbon, 9 September 1807, Nº 55, by the *Auckland* Packet, secret and confidential.

9 Lord Strangford to the Rt Hon George Canning, Lisbon, 26 September 1807, Nº 63, by HM Cutter *Alban*.

10 Lord Strangford to the Rt Hon George Canning, Lisbon, 3 October 1807, Nº 70, by the *Walsingham* Packet.

11 Lord Strangford to the Rt Hon George Canning, Lisbon, 30 October 1807, Nº 75, by the *Townsend* Packet.

Foreign Office FO 63/56

1 Lord Strangford to the Rt Hon George Canning, HMS *Hibernia*, 24 November 1807, Nº 102, by the hired Schooner *Trafalgar*

2 Lord Strangford to the Rt Hon George Canning, HMS *Hibernia*, 29 November 1807, by the *Townsend* Packet.

3 D. Araújo to Lord Strangford, Mafra, 3 October 1807.

Foreign Office FO 63/58

1 H Chamberlain to A Stanhope, Lisbon, 20 October 1807.

2 Viscount Anadia to Sr Pedro Fagundes Bacelar Bantos e Menezes, Governor of Madeira, Palace of Nª. Sª. da Ajuda, 8 October 1807.

3 Hartford Jones to the Rt Hon Robert Dundas, Funchal, 7 November 1807.

4 The Rt Hon Robert Dundas to the Rt Hon George Canning, London, 23 December 1807.

5 Lord Strangford to the Rt Hon George Canning, London, 24 December 1807.

Foreign Office FO 94/163

1 Convention between Portugal and Britain dated 22 October 1807.

2 The Rt Hon Robert Dundas to the Chevalier de Sousa Coutinho, London, 4 January 1808.

Admiralty ADM 4206

1 Secretary of State the Rt Hon George Canning to the Lords Commissioners of the Admiralty.

Admiralty ADM 1/19

1 Sir Sidney Smith to the Rt Hon W W Pole, HMS *London*, Cawsand Bay, 9 November 1807.

2 Sir Sidney Smith to the Rt Hon W W Pole, HMS *London*, Cawsand Bay, 9 November 1807, most secret.

3 Sir Sidney Smith to the Rt Hon W W Pole, HMS *London*, off the Tagus, 18 November 1807.

4 Lord Strangford to Sir Sidney Smith, HMS *Hibernia*, 20 November 1807.

5 Sir Sidney Smith to the Rt Hon W W Pole, HMS *Hibernia*, off the Tagus, 22 November 1807.

6 Sir Sidney Smith to the Rt Hon W W Pole, HMS *Hibernia*, off the Tagus, 22 November 1807, most secret.

7 Sir Sidney Smith to the Commander-in-Chief Admiral Young, HMS *Hibernia* off the Tagus, 22 November 1807.

8 Portuguese military force, 29 October 1807, communicated to Sir Sidney Smith by Mr Gambier, HM Consul at Lisbon, and a copy sent to Lt Gen Sir John Moore, secret.

9 Lord Strangford to Sir Sidney Smith, HMS *Hibernia*, 22 November 1807.

10 Sir Sidney Smith to Minister D. Araújo, HMS *Hibernia*, off the Tagus, 22 November 1807.

11 Notice of the strict blockade of the Tagus by His Britannic Majesty's squadron stationed before the mouth thereof.

12 Sir Sidney Smith to John Bell Esq, HMS *Hibernia*, off the Tagus, 22 November 1807.

13 Lord Strangford to Sir Sidney Smith, HMS *Hibernia*, 24 November 1807, secret.

14 Lord Strangford to Sir Sidney Smith, HMS *Hibernia*, 24 November 1807.

15 Sir Sidney Smith to the Rt Hon W W Pole, HMS *Hibernia*, off the Tagus, 25 November 1807.

16 John Bell to Sir Sidney Smith, Lisbon, 25 November 1807.

17 Lord Strangford to Sir Sidney Smith, Lisbon at night, 28 November 1807.

18 List of the Portuguese fleet that left on 29 November 1807, signed by Joaq^m José Monteiro Torres (Major General).

19 Sir Sidney Smith to the Rt Hon W W Pole, HMS *Hibernia*, 22 leagues west of the Tagus, 1 December 1807, secret.

20 Sir Sidney Smith to Captain Moore, HMS *Hibernia*, 3 December 1807.

21 Sir Sidney Smith to Commodore Moore, 5 December 1807.

22 Account of the provisions supplied to the Portuguese squadron from HMS *Hibernia* and *Conqueror*, 5 December 1807.

23 List of clothing supplied by HMS *Hibernia* to the *Príncipe Real*, the flagship carrying the Prince Regent.

24 Sir Sidney Smith to the Rt Hon W W Pole, HMS *Hibernia*, off the Tagus, 5 January 1808.

25 Sir Sidney Smith to the Rt Hon W W Pole, HMS *Hibernia*, at sea, Lat. 37º 47′ Long. 14º 17′, 6 December 1807.

26 Sir Sidney Smith to the Rt Hon W W Pole, HMS *Hibernia*, off the Tagus, 5 January 1808.

Admiralty ADM 1/824

1 Sir Sidney Smith to Admiral Young (Plymouth), 3 December 1807, HMS *Hibernia*, at sea.

2 Sir Sidney Smith to Admiral Young (Plymouth), 6 December 1807, HMS *Hibernia*, at sea, secret.

Admiralty ADM 1/2159

1 Commodore Moore to Rear Admiral Sir Sidney Smith, Rio de Janeiro, 9 March 1808: account of the journey and safe arrival at Rio de Janeiro of both the Portuguese fleet and the British squadron.

2 Commodore Moore to Vice Admiral Sir Cotton Bart., Rio de Janeiro, 14 March 1808, concerning the sailing of the enemy squadron from Rochefort and the preparations to cruise the coast as far as Salvador as a precaution.

Admiralty ADM 1/2704

1 Captain Walker to the Rt Hon W W Pole, 6 January 1808, explaining the reasons for the separation of the fleet and his role in accompanying the Queen and the Prince Regent, written at sea and posted after arrival at Bahia.

2 Captain Walker to the Rt Hon W W Pole, 31 January 1808, with the account of the journey and safe arrival at the Bay of All Saints (Bahia), Brazil, of the royal family of Portugal.

Signals

National Maritime Museum SIG/B/38

Logs of HM Ships

HM Ship *Achille*	**ADM 51/1700**	HM Ship *Hibernia*	**ADM 51/1730**
HM Frigate *Amazon*	**ADM 51/1659**	HM Ship *London*	**ADM 51/1857**
HM Ship *Audacious*	**ADM 51/1758**	HM Ship *Marlborough*	**ADM 51/1854**
HM Ship *Bedford*	**ADM 51/1882**	HM Ship *Monarch*	**ADM 51/1879**
HM Sloop *Confiance*	**ADM 51/1966**	HM Ship *Plantagenet*	**ADM 51/1790**
HM Ship *Conqueror*	**ADM 51/1734**	HM Brig Sloop *Redwing*	**ADM 51/1715**
HM Ship *Elizabeth*	**ADM 51/1765**	HM Frigate *Solebay*	**ADM 51/1763**
HM Ship *Foudroyant*	**ADM 51/1780**	HM Ship *Theseus*	**ADM 51/1738**